Oregon & Washington

A Guide to the State & National Parks

Barbara Sinotte
&
Peggy deLay

HUNTER
PUBLISHING

Hunter Publishing, Inc.
300 Raritan Center Parkway
Edison NJ 08818, USA
Tel (908) 225 1900
Fax (908) 417 0482

ISBN 1-555650-736-4
© 1996 Barbara Sinotte & Peggy deLay

Maps by Lissa Dailey & Kim André

Cover Photo: *Field of Flowers, Cascades in Background
Mt. Rainier National Park, WA*
Aaron Goldenberg/Global Pictures

Other titles in the Parks Series include:

ARIZONA, UTAH & NEW MEXICO;
CALIFORNIA; COLORADO; NEW ENGLAND;
NEW YORK & NEW JERSEY

Contents

Maps

A Word About Hiking . . .

Hiking is by far the most popular activity in state and national parks. Most of the hiking involves following clearly marked trails. Off-trail travel (commonly referred to as bushwhacking) is practiced by the more adventurous hikers - especially in the clearer, less populated areas of the parks.

Trails in many state parks have been rated for a combination of distance and degree of difficulty. If you are not sure which trails are appropriate for you and your family, talk to a park ranger. If you do not exercise regularly, start on beginner trails and increase your distances gradually. Trail maps are usually available either at the trail or at the ranger station.

While trail markings vary widely, there are a few common markings that everyone should be familiar with. Periodic paint blazes on trees or rocks are clearly the most popular form of trail markings. Plastic markers are often nailed to trees or metal signs are posted on wooden posts. Where there are no trees, trails may be marked with piles of rocks.

Watch for trail markers and make a habit of looking for them - for your own safety and the safety of those hiking with you. It does not take away from the enjoyment of hiking and will soon become just another "natural" thing to do.

Be careful if you attempt bushwhacking. Make your first attempts in open areas with limited undergrowth, such as a desert area where the terrain is a little easier to tackle. Bushwhacking through areas of dense vegetation is for more experienced hikers and should only be attempted with map, water and compass in hand.

Whether you are bushwhacking or carefully following trails, set a pace that will make the experience enjoyable for you. You are not in a race and can better take in the surroundings if you are walking at a comfortable pace. Remember that attempting to go too far can ruin all the fun and tire you out before you are halfway through with your hike. Stumbling or tripping is a clear sign that you may indeed need to slow down.

Remember to take frequent rest stops. Don't wait for fatigue to force you to slow down. A good rule of thumb is to take a 10- to

15-minute stop every hour or so. After awhile you will know what is best for you.

Don't try to speed over the rough areas of a trail. Watch out for tree roots and old logs that may be damp. Alternate footings should be sought. When you are uncertain as to your footing it is wise to crouch just a bit, lowering your "center of gravity" to reduce the likelihood of falling. Steep trails have caused many hikers to lose their balance and take a tumble. Descending tends to be more hazardous than ascending and requires a little more attention. Hold on to small trees or rocks. When in doubt, sit and ease your way down on your rear.

When hiking with a family, it is important to choose a trail that is comfortable for everyone. Younger children should be introduced to hiking with short walks. It is more fun and educational if they can be involved in planning the hike.

Checklist For A Day Hike

2 pairs of hiking socks	Hiking boots
Liner socks	Day pack
Long pants	Water bottle
Long-sleeved shirt	Waterproof poncho
Shell parka or windbreaker	Extra sweater
Toilet paper	Snack foods
Plastic litter bag	Map
Trail guidebook	Compass
First-aid kit	Flashlight
Pocket knife	Matches

In summer weather add:
T-shirt
Shorts
Extra water
Bug repellent
Sunscreen or lotion
Sun hat

In cold weather add:
Additional layers
Cap or hat
Thermal underwear

Hiking Safety

- Hike with a friend.
- Take plenty of drinking water.
- Let someone at the camp or at home know where you are going and when you plan on returning.
- Don't take shortcuts on switchback trails.

Oregon

Introduction

Within Oregon are a multitude of special places Oregonians have set aside to preserve outstanding examples of both history and natural beauty. An uncommon variety of outdoor experiences are available here, with parks organized into eight different areas of the state: North Coast, Central Coast, South Coast, Willamette Valley, Columbia Gorge, Eastern Oregon, Central Oregon, and Southern Oregon. Throughout the state, visitors can experience a wide range of activities, such as beaches, educational exhibits, and scenic vistas ideal for whale watching, wildlife observation, and storm watching.

Nearly 80 of Oregon's state parks offer access to the ocean shore, a 360-mile state recreation area. Many operate year-round campgrounds, and several have campsites designed for hikers and bicyclists. The North Coast is a scenic shoreline of dense forests and broad beaches, with spots once frequented by the Lewis and Clark expedition. The least populated stretch is the South Coast, which features some of the US mainland's most ruggedly beautiful seascapes, as well as some of its best fishing. The Central Coast contains the greatest concentration of resort communities; here, charter fishing trips and sightseeing cruises are available.

Within a short distance of the state's major cities are lakes, rivers, waterfalls, wooded refuges and historic sites. The Columbia River Gorge National Scenic Area – located just minutes from Portland –

preserves a wonderland of water and vegetation. State parks along the cliffs and on the river help visitors enjoy the area's recreational and scenic wealth. Several parks provide the area's best river access for windsurfers. The Willamette Valley contains most of the state's largest and oldest communities. Covered bridges and wineries are popular tourist attractions, with historic buildings and museums also open in almost every city. Farther south is the great Rogue River; there's also Crater Lake, the nation's deepest such body of water. State parks offer boaters and anglers access to the upper and central sections of the Rogue River.

High deserts, deep canyons and wild rivers define the vast open land of central and eastern Oregon. Central Oregon is a year-round recreation area characterized by alpine lakes, whitewater rivers, canyon reservoirs and geological wonders. Eastern Oregon's wide open spaces are filled with pine-forested mountains, deep canyons and spectacular rock formations. The natural beauty is breathtaking and, with Oregon's vast and varied resources, there is something for everyone to enjoy!

General Information

Campsite Information and Reservations

A new central facility, **Reservations Northwest,** handles reservations for many campgrounds in both Washington and Oregon. They have a nationwide toll-free number. Thirteen of Oregon's parks are currently on this reservation system. Contact:

Reservations Northwest
PO Box 500
Portland, OR 97207
☎ (800) 452-5687

The following parks may also be contacted directly for reservations:

Fort Stevens
Hammond, OR 97121
☎ (503) 861-1671

Cape Lookout
13000 Whiskey Creek Road W.
Tillamook, OR 97141
☎ (503) 842-4981

Devil's Lake
1452 NE 6th Street
Lincoln City, OR 97367
☎ (503) 994-2002

Beverly Beach
198 NE 123rd Street
Newport, OR 97365
☎ (503) 265-9278

South Beach
5580 South Coast Highway
South Beach, OR 97366
☎ (503) 867-4715

Beachside
PO Box 693
Waldport, OR 97394
☎ (503) 563-3220

Harris Beach
1655 Highway 101
Brookings, OR 97415
☎ (503) 469-2021

Jessie M. Honeyman State Park
84505 Highway 101 South
Florence, OR 97439
☎ (503) 997-3641

Detroit Lake
PO Box 549
Detroit, OR 97342
☎ (503) 854-3346

Prineville Reservoir
916777 Parkland Drive
Prineville, OR 97754
☎ (503) 447-4363

The Cove Palisades
Route 1, Box 60 CP
Culver, OR 97734
☎ (503) 546-3412

Wallowa Lake
72214 Marina Lane
Joseph, OR 97846
☎ (503) 432-4185

Sunset Bay
10965 Cape Arago Highway
Coos Bay, OR 97420
☎ (503) 888-4902

In addition to the 3,100 campsites at the 13 state parks listed above, there are 2,600 campsites at 37 other state parks that are available on a first-come, first-served basis.

For additional information on Oregon's parks, contact:

Oregon Parks & Recreation Department (OPRD)
1115 Commercial Street, NE
Salem, OR 97310-1001
☎ (503) 378-6305

Camping Fees

Camping fees are based on services, with basic rates between $9 and $13. The highest daily fee is $17-$20 for a full hookup (electric, water and sewer); $15-$16 is the range for a tent. A two-tiered system is now used, with higher daily fees at busier parks.

Hiker/Biker Camps

Special campsites designed for hikers and bicyclists are available at many campgrounds. Most sites include a picnic table and fire ring, with water nearby. Many are in a common area shared by other hikers and bikers. Although hiker/biker areas are normally separated from the main campground, all park facilities – such as restrooms and showers – are available.

These types of campsites are available at Beverly Beach, Bullards Beach, Cape Blanco, Cape Lookout, Carl G. Washburne, Clyde Holliday, Devil's Lake, Ecola, Fort Stevens, Harris Beach, Humbug Mountain, Jessie Honeyman, Loeb, Nehalem, Ochoco Lake, Oswald West, Saddle Mountain, Smith Rock, South Beach, Tumalo, Unity Lake and William M. Tugman state parks.

Horse Camps

Campsites accommodating horseback riders are provided at Bullards Beach State Park, Cape Blanco State Park, Nehalem Bay State Park, Silver Falls in the Willamette Valley and Emigrant Springs, east of Pendleton. These less-developed sites enable users to camp adjacent to corrals and/or hitching rails. Detailed information and reservation forms are available from park staff.

Group Camping

Special tent camping areas designed to accommodate 25 people are available at many state parks and campgrounds. These areas are popular for church outings, school groups and family reunions.

Groups may also reserve individual campsites in the same area at one of the 13 parks mentioned above between Memorial Day and Labor Day weekends. Group use at other locations may also be possible through a special request to the park manager.

Group camping is available at the following parks: Beverly Beach, Cape Lookout, Champoeg, Emigrant Springs, Farewell Bend, Fort Stevens, Jessie M. Honeyman, Joseph P. Stewart, Milo McIver, Silver Falls, Cove Palisades, Tumalo, Valley of the Rogue, and Wallowa Lake.

Year-Round Camping

The fun of camping here never ends. Sixteen parks on Oregon's all-weather coast and four on its major inland rivers contain campgrounds that remain open every day of the year. In addition, the day-use areas in almost all state parks are open year-round.

Outdoor recreational features include both freshwater and saltwater fishing, as well as hiking, wildlife viewing and sightseeing. On the coast, November through March is considered prime whale watching time.

The state parks with year-round campgrounds are: Beachside, Beverly Beach, Bullards Beach, Cape Lookout, Carl Washburne, Champoeg, Cove Palisades, Deschutes, Devil's Lake, Farewell Bend, Fort Stevens, Harris Beach, Humbug Mountain, Jessie Honeyman, Loeb, Nehalem Bay, Ochoco Lake, South Beach, Sunset Bay and Valley of the Rogue.

Yurt Camping

Beginning in 1994, a new, alternative form of camping became available at eight Oregon state coastal parks. It's based upon the use of a YURT, or Year-round Universal Recreational Tent. This is a circular, domed tent with a plywood floor, structural wall support, electricity and a clear, plexiglass skylight. It is designed to both withstand high winds and retain heat efficiently in the winter.

YURTs cost $25 per night for five people, with up to three additional people allowed at $5 each per night. Pets, cooking and smoking are not allowed inside YURTs.

This new form of camping is available at Fort Stevens, Nehalem Bay, Cape Lookout, Beverly Beach, South Beach, Jessie Honeyman, Beach and Harris Beach.

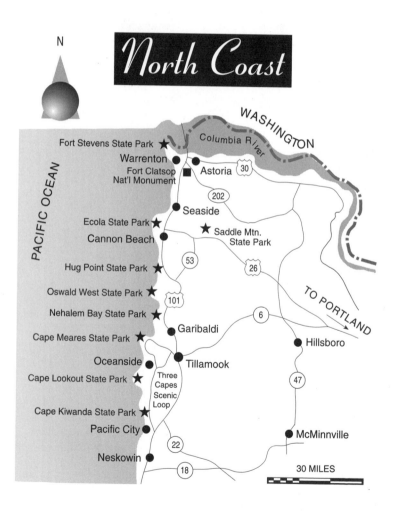

Oregon Parks

North Coast

*V*isitors to North Coast state parks will find plenty of history, hiking trails, and diverse natural areas. The north coast features the longest continuous section of the Oregon Coast Trail, a 64-mile route from the Columbia River to Tillamook Bay.

Cape Kiwanda State Park

Location: Off US 101 and Three Capes Scenic Loop, 1 mile north of Pacific City.

The beach on the southern side of Cape Kiwanda is where local fishermen and women launch their dories into the ocean. To avoid capsizing, they often push each other and quickly jump into the boat, maneuvering it out to sea. This has been a tradition since the 1920s, when commercial fishermen took them out to sea because gill-netting was banned on the Nestucca River. The fleet's late afternoon return is met by people waiting to purchase salmon and tuna "direct." The fish here are indeed plentiful; the river is a famous spawning site for salmon. Charter boats are available for ocean fishing excursions. And though there have been fewer fish and more restrictions lately, many people still fish at Cape Kiwanda.

The Pacific City Dory Derby is held here every July. It is very exciting to watch these craft circle Haystack Rock and return with their catch.

Photographers flock to Cape Kiwanda to capture the beauty of its wave-sculptured cliffs, accessed at the north end of the beach. Opportunities also abound to shoot Haystack Rock, the dory boats and the cape itself. In addition, the area is a known resting spot for indigenous birds like the brown pelican.

Not surprisingly, this is a popular location for hang-gliding – even if you're a beginner (many lessons are given here). Winds are deflected up the cliff, and the coast often provides good lifts.

The park extends north along a strip of beach to Sand Lake; between there and Cape Kiwanda lies the Oregon Coast Trail. From there, it heads over the dune and returns to the road for awhile.

Facilities: This day-use facility covers 185 acres and is open year-round; restrooms are available. Other attractions here include hiking, wildlife viewing, and scouting for tidepools.

For further information, contact: Tillamook Oregon Parks and Recreation Department, 2505 Highway 101 North, Suite A, Tillamook, OR 97141, ☎ (503) 842-5501.

Cape Lookout State Park

Location: Off US 101, 12 miles southwest of Tillamook.

Cape Lookout is a fine example of coastal headlands preserved by the state parks system. It also contains ancient forest. To appreciate this landmark, simply glance out your car window on the way up to the cape. For a closer look, take a two-mile walk out to its tip. Cape Lookout was named by sea captain John Meares, who originally intended the name for what is now Cape Meares (charts put it in the wrong place, and the name stuck.)

This vast, 2,014-acre park extends to the tip of the Netarts sand spit, which encloses Netarts Bay. Beach grass was planted over several years to stabilize the dunes.

The park's campground facilities are located along the ocean, with oceanfront sites. During stormy weather, the latter are closed off, and campers encouraged to head for more protected spots in the woods. There are picnic tables with good views of the ocean at the point where Jackson creek flows out to the sea. (Additional picnic tables may be found north of the campground.) Wildlife is plentiful here; it is easy to spot raccoons, deer and squirrels.

For an in-depth examination of this park's coastal rain forest, try hiking on the nature trail between the campground and hiker/biker camp. Cape Lookout averages over 100 inches of rain per year, and native plants flourish. These include ferns, spruce trees and western red cedar trees – all of which can be spotted while hiking. (It is worth noting that the North Coast Indians once used these same local trees to build canoes and homes.)

The Oregon Coast Trail also passes through this park. Entering from the north along the road, it borders the coast south of the campground and climbs 2½ miles through the forest to the top of the 800-foot cape summit. It emerges at the parking area, for those who hike to the tip of the cape. The trails are confusing here, with the south trail going to the tip of Cape Lookout and the north trail coming from the campground. Also perplexing is a trail branching off to the south, just a short distance away. This is actually a continuation of the Oregon Coast Trail, which descends to the beach two miles later, before proceeding to Sand Lake.

The most popular hiking trail is the Cape Lookout trail, marked only by a sign that says Wildlife Viewing Area. Though a year-round trail, caution must be taken while negotiating it in the winter – sections can become muddy and the drop-off is vertical.

To the south, you can view the huge sand dune of Cape Kiwanda. This is an excellent area for wildlife viewing. With 154 species of birds identified here, it's a birdwatcher's paradise. It's also an official whale watch site; on a clear day in April, multitudes of whale watchers gather with their binoculars.

Facilities: Special facilities at this park include a meeting hall and rustic camper cabins.

For further information, contact: Park Manager, Cape Lookout State Park, 13000 Whiskey Creek Road, West Tillamook, OR 97141, ☎ (503) 842-4981.

Cape Meares State Park

Location: Off US 101, 10 miles west of Tillamook.

Cape Meares State Park boasts a spectacular view of the ocean, as well as picnic tables, a lighthouse and an oddly contorted tree just a short distance away from the parking lot. All of these elements combine to make it the most user-friendly site on the Three Capes Loop. One of the park's boundaries is the 138-acre mainland Cape Meares National Wildlife Refuge, which is jointly managed by the US Fish and Wildlife Service. Wildlife viewing is a popular diversion here, with many people also coming to hike the trails.

The lighthouse, built in 1890, shone a beacon of alternating red and white lights until its restoration in 1963, when it was replaced by an automatic light. The gift shop and lighthouse (replete with spiral staircase) are open from May through September, and during Christmas.

Named after John Meares, an 18th-century English naval officer and explorer, this cape was originally called Cape Lookout. After being misplaced on various maps, it needed another name; hence, Cape Meares.

There are varied hiking options here, with a loop trail descending to the lighthouse via a paved path at the tip of the headland. A spur going a few steps north affords a view of a steep-walled, rocky cove with waterfalls. The trail that returns to the parking area runs along the southern edge of the headland. Benches en route allow one to rest while enjoying a seascape that includes the town of Oceanside and the Three Arch Rocks National Wildlife Refuge. This is one of Oregon's largest sea bird colonies, home to common murres, tufted puffins, cormorants and gulls.

The eastern end of Tillamook Bay offers good paddling and wildlife viewing. You'll see hang-gliders over the Cape, as nearby Maxwell Mountain affords great opportunities to lift off from 500 feet.

Facilities: Comprised of 233 acres, this day-use park is open year-round. Unique features include the Octopus Tree, an unusual ancient Sitka Spruce, and a two-mile segment of the Oregon Coast Trail.

For further information, contact: Oregon Parks and Recreation Department, 1115 Commercial Street NE, Salem, OR 97310-1001, ☎ (503) 378-6305.

Ecola State Park

Location: US 101, 2 miles north of Cannon Beach.

Ecola State Park is just north of the town of Cannon Beach. Its southern viewpoint is a breathtaking seascape of Haystack Rock and the peaks of the Coast Range, extending to Neahkahnie Mountain. The main attractions on its 1,304 acres are the offshore lighthouse, hiking, photography, wildlife viewing, ancient forest land, geology, fishing and surfing. Located not far from Fort Stevens, Ecola marks the southernmost point of the Lewis and Clark explorations on the Oregon coast. The name "Ecola" was taken from the Indian word for whale (*ekoli*) and was first used by William Clark in reference to a nearby creek. Today, visitors enjoy the trails leading over Tillamook Head to a view of rugged offshore rocks and miles of sandy beach. Designated a National Recreation Trail in 1972, it contains a path that follows roughly the same route that Lewis and Clark took over Tillamook Head. Hikers may also enjoy a great ocean view on the 1.4-mile trek to Indian Beach.

The historic Tillamook Rock Lighthouse is a mile northwest from Ecola Point. The beacon operated for nearly 100 years, despite hurricane-force gales that sometimes pushed waves over the 130-foot light. It is now used as a columbarium to entomb cremated human remains.

Facilities: Picnic tables and shelter, restrooms and a hike-in camp from the Indian Creek area. There is a summer day-use fee for vehicles. Open year-round for day use.

For further information, contact: Tillamook OPRD Office, 2505 Highway 101 North, Suite A, Tillamook, OR 97141, ☎ (503) 842-5501.

Fort Clatsop National Memorial

Location: 5 miles southwest of Astoria, off US 101.

In 1805-6, Meriwether Lewis and William Clark wintered at Fort Clatsop after their trail-blazing journey from the Mississippi River to the Pacific Ocean. Their expedition across the North American continent (between the Spanish possessions on the south and British Canada to the north) provided the first detailed knowledge of the American Northwest. It also brought a procession of trappers and settlers into the region, all of which helped to make Oregon a US territory.

President Thomas Jefferson had instructed Lewis and Clark to explore the Missouri River to its source, establish the most direct land route to the Pacific, and make scientific and geographic observations. In the interests of both trade and peace, they also were to learn what they could of the Indian tribes they encountered, and impress them with the strength and authority of the United States.

On May 14, 1804, their 45-man expedition started from the mouth of the Missouri in one 55-foot keel-boat and two smaller boats, called "pirogues." After a tedious five-month journey, they spent their first winter at Fort Mandan, which they built among the Mandan Indian villages 1,600 miles up the Missouri. Here they acquired the services of Toussaint Charbonneau, a half-breed interpreter who joined the expedition with his young Shoshone wife, Sacagawea, and infant son.

On April 7, 1805, the entire party left Fort Mandan in two pirogues and six canoes. They followed the Missouri and its upper branches into an unknown world. Near the Missouri's source the party cached the canoes.

Sacagawea's people provided horses and a guide named "Old Toby" for the grueling trip over the Continental Divide. Once on Idaho's Clearwater River, the expedition members built more canoes. After some 600 miles of travel down the Snake and Columbia Rivers, they sighted the ocean in November, 1805 – near present-day McGowan, Washington.

Within 10 days, Lewis and Clark decided to leave their storm-bound camp on the north shore and cross the river where elk were reported to be plentiful. Accompanied by a small party, Lewis scouted ahead and found a suitable site for winter quarters, evidence of enough game for the winter, and a salt supply. On December 8, 1805, the expedition members started building a fort about three miles up Netul River (now Lewis and Clark River). By Christmas Eve, they were under shelter. They named the new fort for the friendly local Indian tribe, the Clatsops. It would be their home for the next three months.

The members of the Lewis and Clark expedition remained at Fort Clatsop from December 7, 1805, until March 23, 1806. Perhaps the most important activity during their winters here was the reworking of their journals, and the preparation and organization of their scientific data. It was here, too, that Clark prepared many of the maps that were among the expedition's most significant contributions. Some of these were based purely on information supplied by Indians. Through use of the maps, Lewis and Clark determined that the way they had come was not the easiest; as a result, they decided to change part of their return route.

Indians – whom Clark described as close bargainers – came to Fort Clatsop almost daily, both to visit and trade. Lewis and Clark often wrote about the tribes in their journals, detailing their appearance, habits, living conditions, lodges, and abilities as fishermen and hunters. Much of our current information on these tribes comes from their observations.

All the men of this expedition hunted and trapped, but George Drouillard was especially adept, earning high praise from his commanders for his skills. The group killed and ate 131 elk and 20 deer. A few small animals – including otters, beavers and one raccoon – were also killed. As spring approached, the elk took to the hills; it became increasingly difficult to keep the camp supplied with meat and hides for food and clothing.

Life at the fort was far from pleasant. It rained every day but 12 of the 106 days at Fort Clatsop. Clothing rotted and fleas infested the bedding, which consisted largely of furs and hides. So pervasive was this pest that Lewis and Clark wrote they often lacked a full night's sleep. The dampness gave nearly everyone rheumatism or colds, and many suffered from other diseases, which Lewis treated vigorously. Some suffered from dislocated shoulders, injured legs, and back pains. With all this adversity, the members of the expedition continued to prepare for the return trip that would take some home to family and friends, some to wealth and fame. Others would remain in the "wilderness." But all gained a place in history, among the greatest of explorers. To the end of their days, this team of Native Americans, blacks, whites, males, and females shared vivid memories of their epic trip across the continent. They were truly the "Corps of Discovery."

A visitor center contains exhibits, audio-visual programs, and a bookstore operated by the non-profit Fort Clatsop Historical Association. Restrooms, a picnic area, and hiking trails are nearby. There is no camping in this park. The following is a partial list of exhibits and activities offered here:

Muzzle-loading demonstrations: Buckskin-clad park rangers are on hand to explain and demonstrate flintlock firearms similar to those used by the Corps of Discovery. These are offered daily; check at visitor center for times.

Ranger talks: Learn about the Lewis and Clark Expedition and its importance in our national history through various ranger talks. Topics vary, and are posted daily in the visitor center.

Cultural activities: Rangers give daily demonstrations of the tasks performed by Lewis and Clark's party. These include canoe building, woodworking, candle-making, tanning, and sewing buckskins. For times, inquire at the visitor center.

Audio-visual presentations: A 17-minute slide presentation entitled "The Farthest Reach" – as well as a 32-minute movie called "We Proceeded On" – are shown regularly at the visitor center.

For further information, contact the Park Office at ☎ (503) 861-2471 or the Oregon Parks and Recreation Department, 1115 Commercial Street NE, Salem, OR 97310-1001, ☎ (503) 378-6305.

Fort Stevens State Park

Location: Follow signs from US 101; the park is located 10 miles west of Astoria.

Fort Stevens occupies the grounds of a military outpost that guarded the mouth of the Columbia River from the Civil War through World War II. The third largest of Oregon's state parks, it has the most campsites of any of them. Throughout the campground are detailed exhibits outlining the park's many habitats and their occupants.

Summer tours of old buildings and fortifications are given in a vintage US Army truck. There is also a summer walking tour through Battery Mishler, constructed in 1897. The fee for both tours is nominal; otherwise, admission is free.

Near the wreck of the *Peter Iredale* – a four-masted, 278-foot British schooner that went aground in 1906 – is a one-mile trail from the campground to the beach. Eight miles of bike trails link the historic area to the rest of the park, providing access to Battery Russell and the shipwreck.

A viewing tower is located in parking lot "C," at the north end of the park. This is the official whale watch site. There are also bird and wildlife viewing platforms near the wetland areas. Fishing spots are situated along the Columbia River; casting for salmon is popular here.

The park's main attractions are its hiking and biking trails; its beachcombing, wildlife viewing, and fishing opportunities; the wreck of the *Peter Iredale;* and the guided tours of the fort and batteries.

Facilities: Large campground, picnic tables, group camping, hiker/biker camp, exhibit information, historic museum, restrooms with showers, and a boat dock and ramp. Open overnight, year-round.

For further information, contact: Park Manager, Fort Stevens Historic Area, Hammond, OR 97121, ☎ (503) 861-2000.

Hug Point State Park

Location: Off US 101, 5 miles south of Cannon Beach.

The name of this park was derived from the fact that 19th-century pioneers used the beach as a highway. As such, they had to "hug" this particular point at low tide to get around it. (This was only possible after an 800-foot road was blasted out of the rock and used as an early precursor to Highway 101.) The cliffs at Hug Point are loaded with caves, an open invitation to extensive exploring.

A particularly scenic trail runs 6.8 miles between Third Street in Cannon Beach to the inland route over Arch Cape. Day hikers can head in either direction from Hug Point State Park – north to Third Street, or south to Arch Cape. It is 4.1 miles north to Haystack Rock, but this hike must be done at low tide for access around several of the points. The latter trek is part of the 64-mile Oregon Coast Trail, which stretches between the Columbia River to the north and Tillamook Bay to the south. The park is comprised of 43.3 acres. In addition to hiking, other popular attractions include beachcombing, photography, fishing, a waterfall and the historic road around the point.

Facilities: Picnic tables and restrooms. Open year-round for day use.

For further information, contact: Tillamook OPRD Office, 2505 Highway 101 North, Suite A, Tillamook, OR 97141, ☎ (503) 842-5501.

Nehalem Bay State Park

*Location: From US 101, follow signs for 2½ miles;
the park is located 3 miles south of Manzanita Junction.*

Located between Nehalem Bay and the ocean shore, Nehalem Bay State Park includes the long sand spit that travels the edge of the estuary to the south. The spit was formed by the continuous dumping of sand where incoming waves meet the outward flow of the Nehalem River.

This 890-acre park includes a 2,400-foot airstrip and, thus, a fly-in camp. There is a 7½-mile equestrian trail; riders can even take their mounts on the beach. Bicyclists can enjoy the park's 1½ miles of bike paths. The beach area at the foot of Neahkahnie Mountain is a popular windsurfing spot (there is additional surfing to the north.) The main attractions are the airport, biking and horseback riding trails, crabbing, clamming, fishing, boating, hiking and windsurfing.

Facilities: Picnic tables, electrical campground sites, a horse camp (featuring 17 sites with corrals), a hiker/biker camp, wheelchair-accessible restrooms with showers, a dumping station, firewood, a meeting hall, playground, and boat ramp. (There is a day-use fee for vehicles during the summer.) Open year-round.

For further information, contact: Park Manager, 8300 Third Street, Nehalem, OR 97130, ☎ (503) 368-5943.

Oswald West State Park

Location: Off US 101, 10 miles south of Cannon Beach.

Oswald West State Park preserves a section of the Coast Range that includes Arch Cape, Neahkanie Mountain, Cape Falcon and Smuggler's Cove. It covers four miles of exquisite shoreline. It also contains 13 miles of the Oregon Coast Trail, as well as other hiking opportunities. If you wish to trek through the old-growth forest to Cape Falcon, the trail begins just west of the picnic grounds by the cove. There is a split in the trail near the beginning; one fork leads to a memorial to Matt Kramer, an Associated Press journalist who wrote articles that were crucial to the passage of the 1967 Beach Bill. Wildflower enthusiasts should venture to the summit of Neahkahnie

Mountain. A 2½-mile climb with a moderate grade of 7½%, this hike affords sea views for 50 miles.

It is a half-mile walk (foot access only) from a parking lot to 36 primitive campsites, situated in a grove of old-growth conifer trees. Wheelbarrows supplied by the State Parks Division are available to haul your equipment.

This 2,474-acre park was named after Governor Oswald West, who was in office from 1911-1915. It was under his leadership that the Oregon beaches were preserved for public use. The main attractions here are hiking, an ancient forest, photography, fishing, surfing and viewing of both wildflowers and wildlife.

Facilities: Picnic tables, primitive campground sites (closed in winter) and restrooms.

For further information, contact: Site Manager, 8300 Third Street, Nehalem, OR 97130, ☎ (503) 368-5943.

Saddle Mountain State Park

Location: From Tillamook, drive 3 miles north on US 101 to US 26, then 10 miles east to prominently marked Saddle Mountain Road; from there, go 7 miles to the developed area.

At the beginning of the developed area – after seven twisting miles – is the trailhead of the highest peak in this part of the Coast Range. The trail is steep, gaining more than 1,600 feet in just three miles; it takes over four hours to negotiate, roundtrip. People are warned not to attempt this climb unless they are in good shape and sure-footed, because conditions above the timberline are very hazardous. On a clear day, hikers to this point can see 50 miles of the Oregon and Washington coastlines, as well as Mt. Hood, Mt. St. Helens and Mt. Rainier.

This mountain top was a refuge for plants during the Ice Age, and it remains the only habitat in the Coast Range for more than 300 species of flora. The wildflower display here between May and August is nationally famous. The surrounding forests are home to deer, elk and black bears.

Saddle Mountain State Park is comprised of 2,911 acres; its main attractions are hiking, photography, and rare plants and flowers.

Facilities: Picnic tables, restrooms and a primitive campground with 10 tent sites. Closed in winter.

For further information, contact: Tillamook OPRD Office, 2505 Highway 101 North, Suite A, Tillamook, OR 97141, ☎ (503) 842-5501.

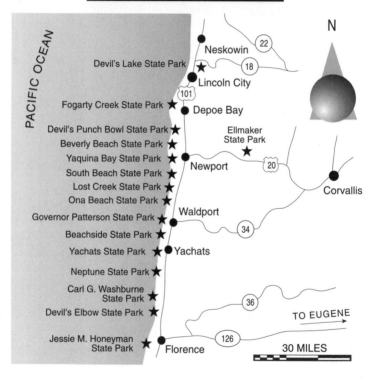

Central Coast

𝒯he central coast is replete with state parks. Both Lincoln City and Newport (the coast's second largest city) draw large numbers of tourists. State park campgrounds provide accommodations close to this region's major populations. There are also many day-use parks that offer easy access to miles of inviting, uncrowded beaches.

Beachside State Park

Location: Off US 101, 4 miles south of Waldport.

The campground at Beachside State Park has the only oceanfront sites of all the parks along the Oregon Coast (with the exception of a few summer sites at Cape Lookout). It is small, with only 16.7 acres. The Beachside sites are available year round, but there are not many of them, so reserve early for summer. There is a small creek between the campground and the day-use area, with beach access available on either side of the park.

This is an excellent spot for crabbers, clammers and rock fishermen. Walking is popular as well, due to the beach's hard, smooth sand. Tent and RV sites also are available.

Facilities: Picnic tables, campgrounds, hiker/biker camps, wheelchair-accessible restrooms with showers, and horseshoe pits. Open overnight, year-round.

For further information, contact: Site Manager, Box 1350, Newport, OR 97365, ☎ (503) 563-3023.

Beverly Beach State Park

Location: Off US 101, 7 miles north of Newport.

Beverly Beach State Park, comprised of 130 acres, boasts the third-highest overnight use of any Oregon state park. This is due in part to its proximity to many activities in the Newport area. Beach access joins a section of the Oregon Coast Trail; the five miles of beach is easily traveled, except for a small section north of Yaquina Head, which must be walked at low tide.

There is a quarter-mile nature trail (foot traffic only) between two campsites. Here you may glimpse some excellent examples of rain forest and wetlands habitat. The main attractions are hiking, fishing, kite flying, surfing and beachcombing.

Facilities: Picnic tables, campgrounds with electrical hookups, tent sites, wheelchair-accessible restrooms with showers, group camps, a playground and firewood. Open year-round.

For further information, contact: Site Manager, Star Route North, Box 684, Newport, OR 97365, ☎ (503) 265-7655.

Carl G. Washburne State Park

Location: Off US 101, 14 miles north of Florence.

Open overnight year-round, this park is popular with Oregonians due to its proximity to beaches and Sea Lion Caves. Agates and other colorful rocks are plentiful on the beach; in the distance is Cape Perpetua.

The park was built as a memorial to Eugene businessman Carl G. Washburne, Oregon Highway Commissioner from 1932-1935. He and his family once resided in a small home in the northeast corner of the property.

There is a four-mile loop trail through several habitats which can be hiked on two trails and the beach. The park is home to elk herds, and black bears are occasionally sighted.

People interested in seeing a good forest habitat should visit the nearby Audubon Tenmile Creek Preserve. This can be reached by taking the next inland road north from the park and following Tenmile Creek into the Siskiyou National Forest for five miles.

Facilities: Facilities at this 1,089-acre park include picnic tables; a campground with 58 full hookups, two tents, and six primitive sites; a hiker/biker camp; firewood; and restrooms with showers. The main attractions are hiking, beachcombing, clamming and elk viewing.

For further information, contact: Carl G. Washburne State Park, c/o The Campground, Florence, OR 97439, ☎ (503) 238-7488.

Devil's Elbow State Park

Location: Off US 101, 13 miles north of Florence.

This year-round, day-use park offers a spectacular view of Cape Cove. It is bounded on the north by Heceta Head, and on the south by a rocky cape that contains Sea Lion Point. Picnic tables are scattered at the edge of the sea, allowing visitors to enjoy the view while eating lunch.

One of the Oregon coast's most photographed features, the Heceta Head Lighthouse, sits at the tip of the northern headland. Built in 1894, it is named for Spanish navigator Bruno Heceta. The view from the picnic area does not include the lighthouse, but the renovated assistant lighthouse keeper's residence can be seen. Named Heceta House, the 1893 dwelling is now a historic landmark. The lighthouse itself can be photographed from turnouts on the south cape.

A half-mile trail affords travelers a good view of both structures. Near the beginning is a side trail down to the rocky shore, which is accessible at low tide.

The park's main attractions are the lighthouse, hiking, beach access and numerous photographic opportunities. To the south are the Sea Lion Caves. During the winter months, wild sea lions can be seen lingering inside their huge caves. During spring and summer, they inhabit the rock ledges.

Facilities: Facilities in this 546-acre park include wheelchair-accessible restrooms and picnic tables. There is a summer day-use fee for vehicles.

For further information, contact: Coos Bay OPRD Office, 365 N 4th Street, Suite 1, Coos Bay, OR 97420, ☎ (503) 269-9410.

Devil's Lake State Park

Location: Campground is off US 101 in Lincoln City; the day-use area is ¾-mile east of the city, on East Devil's Lake Road.

This park is in two separate units, with elaborate camping available. Located on the western shores is a campground with 68 tent sites and 32 RV sites. Although none of the campsites has a view, they all feature showers. In addition, they are serviced by both a café and a laundromat. This is the only campground on the Oregon coast located in the middle of a city. A wetland area separates the campsites from the lake. Wildlife viewing is plentiful here, with herons, cormorants and ducks on the lake. The boat ramp is situated at the East Devil's Lake day-use unit, on the east side of the lake.

Hikers can access the Cascade Head Natural Area to the north via Three Rocks Road, north of the Salmon River. Wildlife are frequently viewed in this forest and wetland habitat, with elk spotted crossing the river during winter.

Facilities: Facilities at this 104-acre state park include the campground, picnic tables and restrooms with solar showers. The primary attractions are fishing, hiking, boating and wildlife viewing.

For further information, contact: Devil's Lake State Park, 1542 NE Sixth Street, Lincoln City, OR 97367, ☎ (503) 994-2002.

Devil's Punch Bowl State Park

Location: Off US 101, 8 miles north of Newport.

At the center of Devil's Punch Bowl State Park is a huge "punch bowl." Comprised of sedimentary rock and basalt, it is located just west of the small community of Otter Rock. Most likely it was shaped by wave action after the collapse of the roof over two sea caves. It empties and fills with the tides.

This small park is an official whale-watching site staffed by Hatfield Marine Science Center volunteers during whale migrations.

During minus tides, the marine gardens can be easily accessed via a rebuilt trail. Here tiny fish swim in tidepools, while sea anemones cling to rocks in the waves. The number of visible species varies the closer you get to the sea. Collecting of marine life is not allowed.

Facilities: Facilities at this four-acre park include picnic tables, wheelchair-accessible restrooms and a small playground. The marine gardens comprise the park's main attraction; many also come for the unusual geology, as well as the whale watching, hiking, and photographic opportunities.

For further information, contact: Oregon Parks and Recreation Department, 1115 Commercial Street NE, Salem, OR 97310-1001, ☎ (503) 378-6305.

Ellmaker State Park

Location: Approximately 18 miles east of Newport, off of US 20.

This land – donated by Harlan D. Ellmaker – is a perfect rest stop on the highway between Newport and Corvallis. Ellmaker, who once worked for the US Forest Service, called the parcel his "Garden of Eden." The park's 77 acres are divided by the Tumtum River and the highway, but the developed part is on the north side. Here, four picnic tables surround a grassy meadow – an ideal respite for weary travelers.

Facilities: Restrooms and picnic tables. Day use; open year-round.

For further information, contact: Oregon Parks and Recreation Department, 1115 Commercial Street NE, Salem, OR 97310-1001, ☎ (503) 378-6305.

Fogarty Creek State Park

Location: Off US 101, 2 miles north of Depoe Bay.

This park is a beautiful place to watch the surf hurl into the rocks jutting out into the sea. There are walkways on both sides of the creek through which visitors can access the beach. Picnic tables inland are perfect for lunching beachcombers. At various points, there are arched foot-bridges where the stream can be crossed, as well as a number of enticing paths for hikers. After years of logging, there is a regrowth of pine, Sitka spruce and western hemlock.

Facilities: Consisting of 142 acres, this day-use park is open year-round. Both picnic tables and restrooms are available; there is a summer day-use fee for vehicles. Beachcombing and hiking are especially popular here.

For further information, contact: Oregon Parks and Recreation Department, 1115 Commercial Street NE, Salem, OR 97310-1001, ☎ (503) 378-6305.

Governor Patterson State Park

Location: Off US 101, 1 mile south of Waldport.

A tiny park 10 acres in size, Governor Patterson State Park is named after Governor Isaac L. Patterson, a noted champion of scenic areas.

Oregon Coast Trail hikers can cross the Alsea Bay Bridge here and resume walking on the beach. A nearly eight-mile stretch can be hiked to just north of Yachats, with only a few minor creek crossings. Open year-round for day use only, the park's primary attractions are hiking and beach access.

Facilities: Picnic tables and restrooms.

For further information, contact: Oregon Parks and Recreation Department, 1115 Commercial Street NE, Salem, OR 97310-1001, ☎ (503) 378-6305.

Jessie M. Honeyman State Park

Location: Both sides of US 101, 3 miles south of Florence.

Surrounding Cleowax Lake, Jessie M. Honeyman State Park is one of the most popular and complete parks on the Oregon coast. With 520 acres, the park features not only a large campground, but three lakes for various water sports and numerous trails for exploring. Of special interest are the sand dunes, hiking trails, and photo opportunities.

On the east side of the highway is Woahink Lake, which contains a group camp, boat ramps, picnic tables and a cordoned-off area for swimming. West of the highway are Lake Cleowax, the campground, and a breathtaking view of sand dune formations that slide into the lake. Smaller than Woahink, this lake also offers swimming, fishing and boating.

There are many paths and trails accessing the various parts of Honeyman State Park. The dune parking area is connected to the campground by a trail that follows a wetland area along Lily Lake, the third park lake, which is covered with water lilies.

Three miles away is the Darlington Wayside. Here, one can view a swampy wetland from an observation platform, watching a thick growth of cobra-lily plants trap and digest insects.

Facilities: Campground with 66 full hookup sites and 240 tent sites; a hiker/biker camp; group camps; a boat ramp, a dock and a restaurant. There is a summer day-use fee for vehicles. Open overnight, year-round.

For further information, contact: Oregon Parks and Recreation Department, 1115 Commercial Street NE, Salem, OR 97310-1001, ☎ (503) 378-6305.

Lost Creek State Park

Location: Off US 101, 7 miles south of Newport.

Oregon has a legacy of saving its beaches for the public, and this park is a perfect example of that legacy. It boasts access to a straight, long stretch of marvelous sandy beach. There is a large parking area with a path that drops downhill and presents a clear view of Yaquina Head in the distance. The small portion of the park that consists of shoreland occupies both sides of the highway, running along a section of the Oregon Coast Trail which can be hiked from Yaquina Bay to Ona Beach State Park. (This is a perfect access point for those who prefer to hike a shorter distance.)

Facilities: This 34-acre park is open year-round for day use, with the primary attractions being the beaches and trails. Facilities here do not include water, but there are picnic tables and pit toilets.

For further information, contact: Oregon Parks and Recreation Department, 1115 Commercial Street NE, Salem, OR 97310-1001, ☎ (503) 378-6305.

Neptune State Park

Location: Off US 101, 3 miles south of Yachats.

Neptune State Park has a gorgeous beach and is located near Cummin's Creek Wilderness, east of US 101. The park is split by the highway; one side houses a visitor center staffed by the US Forest Service and offering information about Cape Perpetua Scenic area to the north. Also available here are trail maps outlining the many hiking opportunities between the park and the scenic area. Across the highway is a section of the Oregon Coast Trail which runs between the park and the visitor center. Many shorter trails begin across from the visitor center and wind along the coastline. The activities of choice are hiking and wildlife viewing, with the park's beach access especially prized. Inland is a forest that is home to giant Sitka spruce trees and multitudes of ferns and wildlife.

Alsea Indians originally inhabited this area; they frequently harvested its many shellfish beds. The first white visitor was Captain James Cook, who sighted the nearby cape on St. Perpetua's Day in 1778, naming it accordingly.

Facilities: The 302-acre park is intended for day use, year-round. It features picnic tables and wheelchair-accessible vault toilets, though no water is available.

For further information, contact: Oregon Parks and Recreation Department, 1115 Commercial Street NE, Salem, OR 97310-1001, ☎ (503) 378-6305.

Ona Beach State Park

Location: Off US 101, 8 miles south of Newport.

Ona Beach State Park, named after the Indian word for "razor clam," is a 237-acre day-use park that is open year-round. East of the highway is a park boat ramp for fishermen or paddlers. There are hiking paths that lead through the picnic area to a footbridge across Beaver Creek, providing beach access. The beach stretches a couple of miles south to Seal Rock. A portion of the Oregon Coast Trail can be hiked from Newport to Seal Rock, with only a short stretch to the highway to cross Beaver Creek. The main attractions here are boating, fishing and beachcombing.

Facilities: Picnic tables, a boat ramp and restrooms.

For further information, contact: Oregon Parks and Recreation Department, 1115 Commercial Street NE, Salem, OR 97310-1001, ☎ (503) 378-6305.

South Beach State Park

Location: Off US 101, 2 miles south of Newport.

Because of its proximity to Newport, South Beach offers a campground close to a lot of action. There are many pathways leading from the campground to the beach, most of them relatively short walks of a half-mile or less. The longest path – which is also the farthest north – boasts a view of the Yaquina Bay Lighthouse, the Yaquina Head Lighthouse and the Yaquina Bay Bridge. It also veers off to the Cooper Ridge Nature Trail, where a bench affords a chance to savor the view of spruces, pines and an abundant growth of rhododendrons.

Nearby is the Hatfield Marine Science Center, which has a public wing housing an aquarium. At the popular "touch" pool, visitors can actually feel the surface of a fish or crab. Next door is the Oregon Coast Aquarium, where visitors can experience outdoor exhibits set on beaches, shores and in the forest. There are streams full of trout, a sea otter pool and sea lions in caves. This park offerse an extremely educational look at coastal ecosystems. Main attractions at the 434-acre park are the nature trails, beaches and fishing areas.

Facilities: Picnic tables, a campground with 250 electrical sites, a hiker/biker camp, wheelchair-accessible restrooms with showers, playground and horseshoe pit. Open year-round.

For further information, contact: Oregon Parks and Recreation Department, 1115 Commercial Street NE, Salem, OR 97310-1001, ☎ (503) 378-6305.

Yachats State Park

Location: Off US 101; west at Yachats sign, on north side of the river.

This 93-acre park is set at the point where the Pacific Ocean and the north side of the Yachats River meet. Because of this – as well as its location within the town of Yachats – the park has been designated for public use, rather than development. The name *Yachats* is derived from the Indian for "at the foot of the mountain" – applicable in this case, due to the park's geographical setting below Cape Perpetua. Popular activities here include fishing, birdwatching and photography.

Facilities: Picnic tables and restrooms. Day use; open year-round.

For further information, contact: Oregon Parks and Recreation Department, 1115 Commercial Street NE, Salem, OR 97310-1001, ☎ (503) 378-6305.

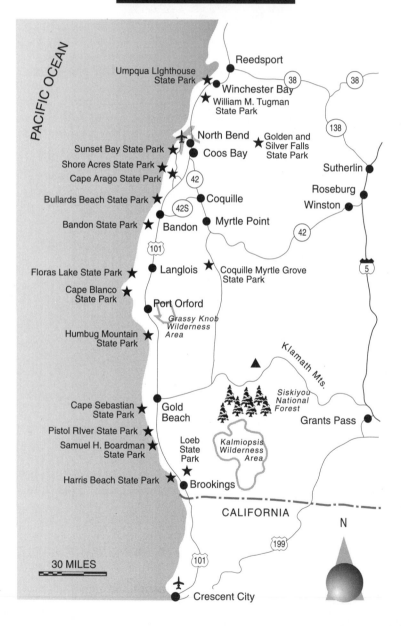

South Coast

PACIFIC OCEAN

Reedsport

Umpqua Lighthouse
State Park

Winchester Bay

38

38

William M. Tugman
State Park

138

North Bend

Golden and
Silver Falls
State Park

Sunset Bay State Park

Coos Bay

Shore Acres State Park

Sutherlin

Cape Arago State Park

42

Roseburg

Bullards Beach State Park

42S

Coquille

Winston

Bandon State Park

Bandon

Myrtle Point

42

101

Floras Lake State Park

Langlois

Coquille Myrtle Grove
State Park

Cape Blanco
State Park

Port Orford

Grassy Knob
Wilderness
Area

Humbug Mountain
State Park

Klamath Mts.

Siskiyou
National
Forest

Cape Sebastian
State Park

Gold
Beach

Grants Pass

Pistol River State Park

Loeb
State
Park

Kalmiopsis
Wilderness
Area

Samuel H. Boardman
State Park

Harris Beach State Park

Brookings

CALIFORNIA

N

30 MILES

199

101

Crescent City

Yaquina Bay State Park

*Location: Off US 101 in Newport; turn west
at the north end of Yaquina Bay Bridge.*

Sitting on a bluff overlooking the entrance to the bay is Yaquina Bay State Park. The primary attraction here is the Yaquina Bay Lighthouse. Now a historic landmark and museum, it is open on weekends, even in the winter.

Outside are picnic tables and trees, offering a peaceful place to stop for lunch. Numerous paths offer views of vegetation and rhododendrons. The main attractions are the museum and gift shop, with kite flying, photography and hiking popular diversions. Agates can be found on the north end of the beach. Nearby Newport offers restaurants and art galleries. The park is comprised of 32 acres.

Facilities: Picnic tables and restrooms. Day use; open year-round.

For further information, contact: Oregon Parks and Recreation Department, 1115 Commercial Street NE, Salem, OR 97310-1001, ☎ (503) 378-6305.

South Coast

*M*any who travel to Oregon believe the south coast has the most spectacular scenery on the Oregon coast. Indeed, this section features numerous rocky headlands and natural bridges, as well as the finest sportfishing available. The climate here is temperate year-round, with an occasional sunny day in the middle of winter and a stormy season. Of course, blue skies are sometimes accompanied by a lot of wind – especially in the summer.

This region boasts a small human population, which makes for more animal life in its natural habitat. Black bears are spotted inland, looking for berries. Deer are plentiful as well. Gray whales heading south in the winter can be spotted from vantage points on the coastal headlands. Humpback whales are occasionally sighted on the south coast as well. The high points are an excellent place to watch the surf action, as the waves hit the rocks on the oldest part of the Oregon Coast.

Bandon State Park

Location: Just south of Bandon, off Beach Loop Road.

There are many entrances to this 893-acre, day-use park, which is open year-round and stretches up to five miles south of Bandon.

Closest to downtown Bandon is a parking area that overlooks Face Rock, reputedly an Indian maiden who was the daughter of Chief Siskiyou. A distinctive area landmark, the Face Rock area houses picnic tables and wheelchair-accessible restrooms. A trail leads downstairs to the beach. This vantage point is great for birdwatching; over 300 species are seen in the area. Each spring, tufted puffins return, resplendant in their full plumage.

South of Face Rock is Devil's Kitchen, which features a hillside spot with benches overlooking the sea. Two paths wind from there to the beach, with the south path leading to a covered picnic area by a creek. The third and fourth areas have beach access, but no facilities; the former can only be accessed by a steep sand dune.

Well-known in Oregon for its cranberry crop, Bandon is home to people who love the winter. These same people have organized a group that gives talks and slide shows. Activities popular in this area include hiking, beachcombing and storm watching.

Facilities: Devil's Kitchen – restrooms; benches.

For further information, contact: Oregon Parks and Recreation Department, 1115 Commercial Street NE, Salem, OR 97310-1001, ☎ (503) 378-6305.

Bullards Beach State Park

Location: Off US 101, 2 miles north of Bandon.

Drive north of Bandon for a couple of miles, and you'll find a great place to fish, crab, bike or spend the night. Named for the Bullards, early settlers in the Bandon area, the park is situated between the Coquille River and the Pacific Ocean.

There are several hiking trails and a seven-mile horse trail. Visitors may also meander through woods and open fields on a three-mile path to the Coquille River Lighthouse, situated on the North Jetty. Abandoned since 1939, the lighthouse was designed to serve as a coastal light and harbor. Restored in 1976, it was placed on the National Park Service's Register of Historic Places. Open daily as a museum, it is visited often.

Fishing for steelhead, Chinook and coho is excellent in this area. At the mouth of the Coquille River is Bandon Marsh, a National Wildlife Refuge that contains 285 acres of salt marsh. Many species of birds, mammals and fish reside here. The main attractions are the lighthouse and Bandon Marshes, with fishing and photography popular activities.

Facilities: Comprised of 1,290 acres, this overnight, year-round park has a campground with 92 full hookup and 10 electrical sites, wheelchair-accessible restrooms with showers, a playground, hiker/biker camp, boat ramp and horse camp.

For further information, contact: Oregon Parks and Recreation Department, 1115 Commercial Street NE, Salem, OR 97310-1001, ☎ (503) 378-6305.

Cape Arago State Park

Location: 14 miles southwest from US 101, in Coos Bay.

Originally part of the Simpson Estate, this 134-acre park was given to the state in 1932. Climbing to 200 feet at its highest elevation, it is backed by cliffs and a forest. The area to the south has no road. Offshore is Simpson Reef; this is comprised of rocks that break the surface of the water, providing a home for seals and sea lions.

There are coves in the north, south and center of this park. All of these afford beach access, although North Cove is closed between March and July to protect seal and sea lion pups. In the summer, visitors may take guided walks of South Cove down a steep trail surrounded by high cliffs. Of special interest are the fishing areas, trails and beaches. Three miles of the Oregon Coast Trail can be accessed a short distance to the north.

Facilities: Picnic tables and restrooms. Open for day use, year-round.

For further information, contact: Oregon Parks and Recreation Department, 1115 Commercial Street NE, Salem, OR 97310-1001, ☎ (503) 378-6305.

Cape Blanco State Park

Location: Travel 4 miles north of Port Orford on US 101,
turn west and drive 5 miles to the park.

Located at Oregon's westernmost point, this park includes beaches to both the north and south; it is comprised of 1,880 acres. There is an abundance of flora here, including both huckleberry and salmonberry. Many people hunt mushrooms here as well.

Near the Sixes River is a road to the historic Hughes House. Patrick Hughes came to the cape in 1860, searching for gold in the black sand beach to the south. After being occupied for 110 years, the Hughes House is all that remains of the original ranch compound. Restored by the Friends of Cape Blanco and open from May to September, it is now on the National Register of Historic Places.

Hikers can access the Oregon Trail from the southern end of the campground. After a short distance on the road, the trail reaches the beach and continues to Paradise Point Wayside, crossing the Elk River along the way. Only possible during low tide in the summer, the crossing is difficult even then. Nearby is the Camp Blanco Lighthouse, the oldest active lighthouse on the Oregon Coast. Closed to the public, it is easily viewed from the park.

Facilities: Picnic tables, the campground (which has 58 electrical sites, one accessible to wheelchairs), restrooms with showers, a year-round horse camp with corrals, and a boat ramp on the Sixes River. The campground is closed in winter.

For further information, contact: Oregon Parks and Recreation Department, 1115 Commercial Street NE, Salem, OR 97310-1001, ☎ (503) 378-6305.

Cape Sebastian State Park

Location: Off US 101, 7 miles south of Gold Beach.

At 700-plus feet, Cape Sebastian is probably the highest south coast overlook accessible by a paved public road. Visibility on a clear day extends at least 45 miles in either direction. A trail leads from the parking area through two miles of beautiful spring wildflowers until it reaches the ocean. The 1,100-acre park attracts tourists interested in hiking, beach access and photography.

Sebastian Vizciano discovered this cape in 1603, and named it after the patron saint of the day of his discovery.

Facilities: Chemical toilets; no water is available. Day use only; open year-round.

For further information, contact: Oregon Parks and Recreation Department, 1115 Commercial Street NE, Salem, OR 97310-1001, ☎ (503) 378-6305.

Coquille Myrtle Grove State Park

Location: 3 miles east from Myrtle Point on Oregon Highway 42, then 11 miles south on the road to Powers.

This beautiful grove of myrtle wood trees along the banks of the Coquille River was given to the state in 1950. The trees are prized for their hardwood and used to make bowls and plates, as well as furniture. This tiny park has only seven acres.

Fishermen can access the river by a winding old dirt road. The main attractions here are the trees and fishing.

Facilities: Picnic tables and vault toilets; no water is available. Open year-round for day use.

For further information, contact: Oregon Parks and Recreation Department, 1115 Commercial Street NE, Salem, OR 97310, ☎ (503) 378-6305.

Floras Lake State Park

Location: Off US 101, 4 miles south of Langlois, west on Airport Road to its end.

This park is for the adventurous type who is comfortable in the wilderness. Though scheduled for development in the future, it is relatively untouched for the moment. Visitors come here for the beach and the many photo opportunities.

During World War II, park land was leased to the county; the Navy built a road and airport there. In 1971, the State Board of Aeronautics took over the land for the Curry County Airport.

Two trails run north from the airport runway, but both are difficult to traverse, as the cliffs are fragile. The park offers no access to Floras Lake, but coastal windsurfing is popular there.

Facilities: The 1,300-acre park is open for day use, year-round. There are no facilities.

For further information, contact: Oregon Parks and Recreation Department, 1115 Commercial Street NE, Salem, OR 97310-1001, ☎ (503) 378-6305.

Golden and Silver Falls State Park

Location: 24 miles northeast of Coos Bay; from US 101 at the south end, follow signs to Allegany, and continue 10 additional miles to the park.

Known mostly for its spectacular waterfalls and old-growth wilderness, this coastal range park is an excellent spot to take pictures. The last five miles to the park take you down an extremely narrow gravel road used by loggers. It is best to visit on weekends or holidays, as it is difficult to share the road. At the end of the road is the park picnic area.

Of particular interest are the park's waterfalls. Though each is approximately 100 feet high, they are very distinctive from each other. Silver Falls is unusual in appearance but more visually appealing, due to its semicircular flow around a head near the top. The tremendous roar of Golden Falls makes it, too, an awe-inspiring view. Each waterfall can be reached by two half-mile trails. Its main attractions are the waterfalls and the old-growth forest, both of which are prime photo opportunities.

Facilities: The 157-acre park is open for day use, year-round. There are picnic tables and pit toilets, but no water is available.

For further information, contact: Oregon Parks and Recreation Department, 1115 Commercial Street NE, Salem, OR 97310-1001, ☎ (503) 378-6305.

Harris Beach State Park

Location: Off US 101, 2 miles north of Brookings.

Visitors come to Harris Beach State Park for the huge rock sculptures rising from its beach. Many climb it; others photograph it.

Picnic tables sit on stone terraces overlooking the ocean. The beach is perfect for walking and collecting seashells and rocks. Sometimes the ocean pushes large pools onto the beach, making perfect little swimming areas for children of all ages. Trails access many parts of this 175-acre expanse. Popular activities here include photography, beachcombing and hiking.

The park was named after George Scott Harris, a Scottish native who obtained the property in 1871 with an eye to raising sheep and cattle there.

Facilities: Picnic tables, a campground with 34 full hookups, plus 53 electrical and 69 tent sites, a hiker/biker camp, wheelchair-accessible restrooms with showers, and a playground. Open overnight, year-round.

For further information, contact: Oregon Parks and Recreation Department, 1115 Commercial Street NE, Salem, OR 97310-1001, ☎ (503) 378-6305.

Humbug Mountain State Park

Location: Off US 101, 6 miles south of Port Orford.

The scenery is plentiful at this park, whose 1,840 acres consist of mountains, beaches and forest. A four-mile stretch of beach here is accessed through the west end of a walkway running through the campground. A tip: this spot is an excellent place to view the sunset. Of particular interest here are the hiking trails, the beach, and the many photographic opportunities.

There is a separate day-use area south of the campground. Here, meadows are surrounded by tall trees, making this a perfect site for picnicking. At 1,750 feet, Humbug Mountain is the highest point on the south coast of Oregon. The Civilian Conservation Corps built a difficult three-mile trail to the summit in 1934. This trail winds through a rain forest where the climate is moderate and ideal for hiking in any season. Snow is rare, even on the summit.

Past the fee booth on the walkway east is a 2½-mile Recreation Trail that follows the old highway. It crosses a creek, with forest up one side and down the other.

Facilities: Picnic tables, a campground with 30 full hookups and 78 tent sites, a hiker/biker camp, wheelchair-accessible restrooms with showers, and firewood. Closed in winter.

For further information, contact: Oregon Parks and Recreation Department, 1115 Commercial Street NE, Salem, OR 97310-1001, ☎ (503) 378-6305.

Loeb State Park

Location: From US 101 at the south end of Brookings,
follow North Bank Chetco River Road for 10 miles northeast.

The camping areas in Loeb State Park are located in a beautiful grove of old-growth myrtlewood trees, with some sites fronting the Chetco River. These trees are not so plentiful anymore, and their preservation was ensured by the purchase of this park. There is also a group of redwood trees at the northern edge of their habitat. There are 320 acres in the park.

Driftboats can be launched at the picnic area, which fronts the gravel bar of the river. The entry to the day-use area offers trailhead parking; brochures with hiking maps are available. The ¾-mile Riverview Trail links the Redwood Nature Trail to the Siskiyou National Forest. Other hikes in the vicinity are available as well. The main attractions are the myrtlewood grove and the redwoods; swimming and photography lure tourists here, too.

Facilities: Campground with 53 electrical sites, picnic tables, a hiker/biker camp, wheelchair-accessible restrooms and firewood. Open year-round.

For further information, contact: Oregon Parks and Recreation Department, 1115 Commercial Street NE, Salem, OR 97310-1001, ☎ (503) 378-6305.

Pistol River State Park

Location: Off US 101, 11 miles south of Gold Beach.

When traveling down the hill south from Cape Sebastian, one is treated to a spectacular view of Pistol River State Park. Beach access is possible from the north parking area at Myers Beach; be prepared for an expansive and awesome seascape of huge rocks jutting up from the sea.

The south parking area offers no beach access, but binoculars afford a great view of birds in the estuary. The park extends south to Crook Point, but has not been developed in that protected area.

Comprised of 440 acres, this park is open for day use, year-round. Many visitors come to take photos, birdwatch and beachcomb.

Facilities: Chemical toilets, but no water. Day use only.

For further information, contact: Oregon Parks and Recreation Department, 1115 Commercial Street NE, Salem, OR 97310-1001, ☎ (503) 378-6305.

Samuel H. Boardman State Park

Location: Off US 101, 4 miles north of Brookings.

Samuel H. Boardman, the first Oregon state parks superintendent (1929-1950), worked tirelessly to acquire this land for a spectacular coastal park in Curry County. Initially proposed as a national park, the idea never took hold; thus, this state park honoring Boardman was established.

There are a number of unusual seascapes here, and it is not uncommon to find small beaches at the base of steep canyons. Many people believe this to be one of the finest stretches of coastline in the world. The park is for day use only, but nearby Harris Beach State Park is open for camping. This arrangement allows visitors time to explore the numerous trailheads of the Oregon Coast Trail, which winds for seven miles through the park. There are many vehicle stops that afford trail access.

Facilities: This 1,450-acre park is open year-round, with picnic tables and wheelchair-accessible restrooms available in certain areas. The main activities here are hiking and photography.

For further information, contact: Oregon Parks and Recreation Department, 1115 Commercial Street NE, Salem, OR 97310-1001, ☎ (503) 378-6305.

Shore Acres State Park

Location: From US 101 in Coos Bay, follow signs 12 miles southwest.

Once the home of shipping magnate and North Bend founder Louis J. Simpson, this stretch of coastline is truly superb. While on a timber cruise in 1905, Simpson discovered this spot and purchased it for a country home. In 1906 he built a mansion for his wife Cassie in what is now Shore Acres State Park. Wave action is now eroding their concrete tennis courts.

The old homesite is now occupied by a glass-enclosed observation building with exhibits outlining the history of the place. Here, the view of the cliffs is the same as that once seen from the family mansion.

Among this park's most attractive features are its incredible gardens, which contain hydrangeas, roses, rhododendrons and wisteria. Kept in immaculate condition by the Oregon state parks system, the gardens are open during daylight hours. In winter months, the observation building is an excellent place in which to track storms.

Shore Acres is connected to Cape Arago State Park and Sunset Bay State Park by a three-mile section of the Oregon Coast Trail. The trail is open year-round and extends from the beach up to the cliff tops.

Facilities: This 734-acre park is open year-round for day use. Facilities include picnic areas, the observation shelter, gift shop and wheelchair-accessible restrooms. The main attractions are the botanical garden, the beaches and the hiking trail.

For further information, contact: Oregon Parks and Recreation Department, 1115 Commercial Street NE, Salem, OR 97310-1001, ☎ (503) 378-6305.

Sunset Bay State Park

Location: Off US 101, follow signs 12 miles from Coos Bay.

This park's day-use area is set in a cove south of the Coos Bay inlet, offering protection from the wind. North and south of the beach are steep bluffs that leave only a narrow passage to the sea. After being warmed by the summer sun, the shallow cove water is ideal for limited swimming.

This park was once part of the Simpson Estate. In 1913, after their home at Shoreacres was constructed, the Sunset Bay Inn was built.

The campground is on the east side of the road in a forested area. South of the Big Creek highway crossing is a path going under the road to the picnic area. This park includes a three-mile section of the Oregon Coast Trail, with a beautiful view of the Cape Arago Lighthouse in the distance. There are 395 acres. The most popular activities here are hiking, swimming, photography and skin diving.

Facilities: Picnic tables, a campground with 29 full-hookup, 34 electrical, and 75 tent sites, wheelchair-accessible restrooms with showers, a bathhouse and a playground. Open overnight, year-round.

For further information, contact: Oregon Parks and Recreation Department, 1115 Commercial Street NE, Salem, OR 97310-1001, ☎ (503) 378-6305.

Umpqua Lighthouse State Park

Location: From US 101 on Discovery Drive,
travel about 1 mile south of Winchester.

This park is centered on Lake Marie, between the highway and the ocean. It is comprised of 450 acres. Both the park and the adjacent lighthouse are named after the Umpqua Indians; they are located at the mouth of a river by the same name.

Lake Marie is a favorite summer spot for canoeing and small rafts. North of the lake is a whale-watching area with exhibits on the different species.

There is a 1.3-mile hiking trail that circles the lake and connects to three campground loops leading downhill to the lake.

The Umpqua Lighthouse can be seen from the day-use area, and the walk there is not difficult. However, the immediate vicinity is fenced and visitors are not allowed. The original lighthouse, built in 1854, was toppled by sand erosion and a new one constructed in 1894. The light at the top is visible for 20 nautical miles.

Nearby, a few miles east of Reedsport, is the Dean Creek Viewing Area. From this scenic overlook, visitors can see Roosevelt Elk as they move down from the higher elevations in winter. These can be spotted in early morning, at the bottom of the Umpqua River.

Visitors come primarily to see the lighthouse; they also indulge in hiking, boating, fishing and photography.

Facilities: Picnic tables, a campground with 22 full hookups and 42 tent sites, restrooms with showers, and a boat ramp. Closed in winter.

For further information, contact: Oregon Parks and Recreation Department, 1115 Commercial Street NE, Salem, OR 97310-1001, ☎ (503) 378-6305.

William Jugman State Park

Location: Off US 101, 8 miles south of Reedsport.

Picnic spots dot the waterfront and lawn of this park's day-use area, offering the choice of either sun or shade. A walkway connects these to the campground, which is studded with spruce, pine and cedar trees.

On the east side of the highway is Eel Lake, an excellent venue for freshwater fishing. Once a brook lake for trout, it became filled with logging debris. After it was cleaned out, it was given to the state for park protection and public enjoyment.

Coho salmon travel upstream from Eel Lake to spawn in the fall and winter. In 1978, a fish trap was established here to collect Coho eggs for hatcheries. After that is accomplished, the fish are allowed to travel upstream to spawn. Visitors are permitted to watch the salmon in the trap.

The park was named after William M. Tugman, the first chairman of the State Parks and Recreation Advisory Committee in 1957. He was a firm believer in the wise use of Oregon's natural resources. South of the campground and across the highway is the Umpqua Dunes Trail, one of the best dune spots for hiking. Since ORVs are banned in the area, a quiet, safe experience is assured. There are 560 acres in the park.

Facilities: Picnic tables, a group picnic shelter, a campground with 115 electrical sites, a hiker/biker camp, wheelchair-accessible restrooms with showers, and a boat ramp with pier. Open overnight, but closed in winter.

For further information, contact: Oregon Parks and Recreation Department, 1115 Commercial Street NE, Salem, OR 97310-1001, ☎ (503) 378-6305.

Willamette Valley

As pioneers traveled west on the Oregon Trail, many headed for the Willamette Valley. The valley is named for the Willamette River, which divides it from the city of Portland. The region is enclosed by the Coast Range on the west and the snow-capped Cascade Mountains on the east. The proximity of both the coast and the mountains makes this is a wonderful place to live or vacation.

Oregon's population is centered primarily around Portland, with the state capital of Salem an hour south along I-5. The more populated cities are surrounded by a lot of rural land and many rivers flowing out of the mountains. Years ago, ferries were used to cross these waters and sternwheelers were common on the Willamette River. Many covered bridges were constructed over the valley's creeks with timber from the area. (Because of the amount of rain, the bridges lasted longer if they had covers.)

Because of the lush soil and excellent growing conditions, fruit and vegetables are plentiful here; hence, the many roadside stands. There are also "U-Pick" farms – where travelers can pick their own fruit – in different parts of the valley. World-class wines are made in numerous area wineries, and the northwest section of Portland offers excellent microbrews. State parks throughout the valley help preserve the region's heritage. They also provide access to rivers, lakes and natural areas close to urban communities.

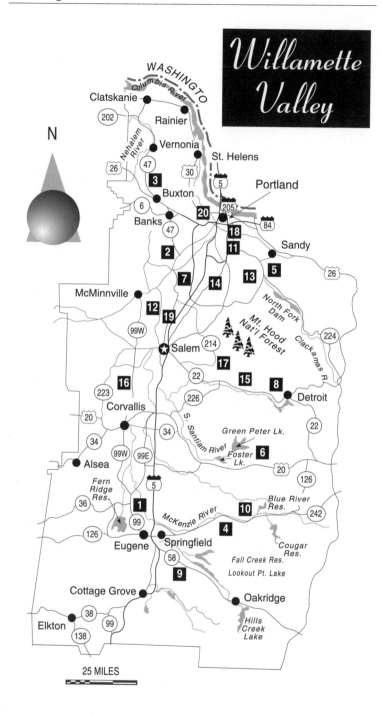

Willamette Valley

WASHINGTO

Columbia River

Clatskanie
202
Rainier

N

Nehalem River

Vernonia
47
St. Helens
30
26
47
3 Buxton
6
Banks
47
2
20
18
11
Portland
205
5
84
Sandy
26
7
14
13
5
McMinnville
12
19
224
99W
North Fork Dam
Mt. Hood Nat'l Forest
Clackamas R.
Salem 214
17
22
15
8
Detroit
16
226
223
22
Corvallis
20
Green Peter Lk.
34
34
6
Foster Lk.
99W 99E
20
126
Alsea
S. Santiam River
Fern Ridge Res.
36
Blue River Res.
242
1
10
99
McKenzie River
4
Cougar Res.
Eugene
Springfield
58
Fall Creek Res.
Lookout Pt. Lake
9
Cottage Grove
Oakridge
38
Hills Creek Lake
99
Elkton
138

25 MILES

For further information, contact: Oregon Parks and Recreation Department, 1115 Commercial Street NE, Salem, OR 97310-1001, ☎ (503) 378-6305.

Armitage State Park

Location: From I-5, take Coburg Road 5 miles north of Eugene.

Situated on the south banks of the McKenzie River, Armitage State Park offers a welcome retreat from Eugene. Walking paths are abundant in the park, and it is often used for picnics and reunions.

Facilities: This 55-acre, day-use park is open year-round. It offers picnic tables, a boat ramp, wheelchair-accessible restrooms, a group picnic shelter and horseshoe pits. The main activities are fishing and boating, and there is a day-use fee for vehicles.

For further information, contact: Oregon Parks and Recreation Department, 1115 Commercial Street NE, Salem, OR 97310-1001, ☎ (503) 378-6305 or (503) 686-7592.

Bald Peak State Park

Location: Off US 99W, 9 miles northeast of Newberg.

This small, 26-acre day-use park is open year-round. It offers a spectacular view from the summit of Bald Peak, which is accessible from a paved road. Good views of Mount Hood, Mount Adams, Mount St. Helens, and all of the Cascade Range can be seen from an area facing northeast. The agricultural land of the Tualatin and Willamette Valleys is visible from the front of the park. Though the southwest side of the park is forested, a path circles back to the

1. Armitage State Park
2. Bald Peak State Park
3. Banks/Vernonia State Park
4. Ben and Kay Dorris State Park
5. Bonnie Lure State Park
6. Cascadia State Park
7. Champoeg State Park
8. Detroit Lake State Park
9. Elijah Bristow State Park
10. Howard J. Morton State Park
11. Mary S. Young State Park
12. Maud Williamson State Park
13. Milo McIver State Park
14. Molalla River State Park
15. North Santiam State Park
16. Sarah Helmick State Park
17. Silver Falls State Park
18. Tryon Creek State Park
19. Willamette Mission State Park
20. Willamette Stone State Park

summit. The main attractions here are the views, which are a photographer's dream.

Facilities: Picnic tables and toilets, but water is not available.

For further information, contact: Oregon Parks and Recreation Department, 1115 Commercial Street NE, Salem, OR 97310-1001, ☎ (503) 378-6305.

Banks / Vernonia State Park

Location: Off Highway 47, between Banks and Vernonia.

Between Banks and Vernonia is a 21-mile stretch of abandoned railway. Originally used to haul logs, lumber, freight and passengers, this is being converted to a pathway with many accessible trailheads. There is gravel and paving on one side of the wide trail; this is intended for use by hikers and bicyclists. Horseback riders can use the dirt side. However, motorized vehicles are not allowed on the trail.

Facilities: Restrooms. This area is open for day use, year-round.

For further information, contact: Oregon Parks and Recreation Department, 1115 Commercial Street NE, Salem, OR 97310-1001, ☎ (503) 378-6305.

Ben and Kay Dorris State Park

Location: Off US 126, 31 miles east of Springfield.

Situated 80 feet above the McKenzie River, this wooded park is a popular fishing and picnic venue. Overnight camping was once allowed here and vehicles were restricted. But because of heavy use by fishermen, overnight camping is no longer allowed and vehicles now have direct access to the river.

Downhill from the picnic area is a paved path that leads to the boat launch. A huge rock formation forms a base from which fishermen throw their lines into the clear water. Another path leads from the west end of the picnic area to the river, through a heavily forested Douglas fir area. Boating and fishing are popular here.

The park acreage was donated by Ben and Kay Dorris.

Facilities: Picnic tables, a boat ramp, a group picnic shelter and wheelchair-accessible restrooms. There is a day-use fee for vehicles. Open for day use, year-round.

For further information, contact: Oregon Parks and Recreation Department, 1115 Commercial Street NE, Salem, OR 97310-1001, ☎ (503) 378-6305.

Bonnie Lure State Park

*Location: County Road 24028, 6 miles north
of Estacada on the Clackamas River.*

Used primarily by the few locals who can find this obscure spot, this 94-acre day-use park offers a parking area and picnic tables. (Both of these are located immediately past a one-lane bridge across Eagle Creek.) Paths along the Clackamas River are easily accessed. Hiking, boating and fishing are especially popular here.

Facilities: Picnic tables and a portable toilet, but no water. Open year-round.

For further information, contact: Oregon Parks and Recreation Department, 1115 Commercial Street NE, Salem, OR 97310-1001, ☎ (503) 378-6305.

Cascadia State Park

Location: Off US 20, 14 miles east of Sweet Home on the South Santiam River.

Originally purchased in 1895 by George Geisendorfer, this parcel of land near the South Santiam River was originally earmarked for a resort. The state parks system bought it in 1941.

Known for its soda springs with mineral water, this park is crisscrossed by walkways connecting the day-use and picnic areas. The day-use section is very large, with beautiful, open meadows. Rocks here form excellent swimming holes at the point where the Santiam River flows down the Cascades. A path winds to the river from the day-use area. Nearby on Highway 20 are the Green Peter and Foster Lake reservoirs, both of which offer excellent boating and fishing. The park is comprised of 250 acres.

Facilities: Picnic tables, group picnic shelters, a campground with 26 sites, group campsites and wheelchair-accessible restrooms. Open overnight; closed in winter.

For further information, contact: Oregon Parks and Recreation Department, 1115 Commercial Street NE, Salem, OR 97310-1001, ☎ (503) 378-6305.

Champoeg State Park

Location: From I-5, take Exit 278 and drive 5 miles west.

Situated along the south bank of the Willamette River, the 615-acre Champoeg State Park was the home of the Calapooya Indians until 1811, when fur traders from the Hudson's Bay Company built a warehouse there. The name means "Field of Roots" in Chinook; it refers to the camas roots eaten by the native Americans at their salmon feasts. The early settlers were attracted to this area because of the boat access. In 1843, they voted to break away from the British and Hudson's Bay Company rule to establish the first pro-American provisional government on the Pacific coast.

An 1861 flood destroyed most of the town's buildings, and the settlement was abandoned by the late 1800s. There is a visitor center with exhibits explaining how the Indians, explorers, French Canadian fur traders and the settlers co-existed here. The grounds also contain several historic buildings, including the Manson Barn, built in 1862, and the restored Newell House.

The main attractions here are the Newell House and the log cabin museum; visitors also enjoy hiking, boating and fishing.

Facilities: Picnic tables, a group picnic shelter, a campground with 48 electrical and six tent sites, an RV group camp, wheelchair-accessible campsites, restrooms with showers, firewood, a dock, exhibit information, a visitor center and a gift shop. There is a summer day-use fee for vehicles. Open overnight, year-round.

For further information, contact the park office at (503) 678-1251 or the Oregon Parks and Recreation Department, 1115 Commercial Street NE, Salem, OR 97310-1001, ☎ (503) 378-6305.

Detroit Lake State Park

Location: Oregon Highway 22, 2 miles west of Detroit.

Detroit Lake is a spot that attracts many boating and fishing enthusiasts, due to its close proximity to most locations in the Willamette Valley. The lake was created by the construction of the Detroit Dam on the Santiam River in the 1950s. Early settlers of nearby Detroit hailed from Michigan; hence, the names of both the park and the lake. The Mongold day-use area is situated 1½ miles west of the campground.

Located within the Willamette National Forest, this 104-acre park was once a Forest Service campground. It is now leased by the state. In the center of the lake is a small island which is not part of the park. Called Piety Knob, it features 12 primitive campsites, but no water.

This is an incredibly popular hiking spot – during the summer it is very crowded, especially on weekends.

Facilities: Picnic tables, a campground with 107 full hookups, 70 electrical sites and 134 tent sites, wheelchair-accessible restrooms with showers, boat ramps, fishing docks, and moorage docks. There is a summer day-use fee for vehicles. The park is open overnight, but the campground is closed in winter.

For further information, contact the park office at (503) 854-3406 or the Oregon Parks and Recreation Department, 1115 Commercial Street NE, Salem, OR 97310-1001, ☎ (503) 378-6305.

Elijah Bristow State Park

Location: Oregon Highway 58, 17 miles southeast of Eugene on the Middle Fork of the Willamette River.

Two of Oregon's past governors, Tom McCall and Bob Straub, supported a plan to acquire and preserve a 250-mile stretch of river frontage along the Willamette River. The purpose was to promote public access and long-term recreational use.

Elijah Bristow State Park is one of the major parks along the Willamette River Greenway System, authorized by the Oregon

Legislature in 1973. Named for one of the first white settlers in Lane County, it was originally called Dexter State Park.

Facilities: This 850-acre park is open year-round for day use. Its focal points include 16 miles of equestrian trails, as well as hiking and biking paths. Picnic tables, group picnic areas and wheelchair-accessible restrooms are also available.

For further information, contact: Oregon Parks and Recreation Department, 1115 Commercial Street NE, Salem, OR 97310-1001, ☎ (503) 378-6305.

Howard J. Morton State Park

Location: Off OR 126, 40 miles east of Eugene.

This tiny (25 acres) day-use park is difficult to find; it is not identified by the usual state park sign. Instead, a large wooden sign was installed at the request of Mrs. Winifred Morton, who donated the park in honor of her husband. The bequest was made with the provision that no improvements be made and no trees cut, except to make way for a small picnic area. This park's main asset is its remote location; hikers also prize the nearby Olallie Trail.

Facilities: Picnic tables and a chemical toilet, but no water. Open year-round.

For further information, contact: Oregon Parks and Recreation Department, 1115 Commercial Street NE, Salem, OR 97310-1001, ☎ (503) 378-6305.

Mary S. Young State Park

Location: OR 43, 9 miles southwest of Portland.

Comprised of 130 acres, this park is a haven for Portland residents who need to escape for a pleasant day on the water. Close to the road is a cleared area where children can play. The park contains a half-mile hiking trail and a two-mile biking trail, both of which travel through a forest of Douglas firs, maple and oak to the Willamette River.

The most popular activities here are hiking, bicycling and fishing. However, the rules are very precise: no fires, no pets, and no kegs of beer!

Facilities: Picnic tables and wheelchair-accessible restrooms. Open year-round for day use.

For further information, contact: Oregon Parks and Recreation Department, 1115 Commercial Street NE, Salem, OR 97310-1001, ☎ (503) 378-6305.

Maud Williamson State Park

Location: OR 221, 12 miles north of Salem.

Comprised of 24 acres, this day-use park is open year-round. At one time, overnight camping was allowed; now, the park is used primarily as a rest stop and for picnics. Tall, beautiful Douglas Firs offer shade during a hot day of traveling. The park still houses a historic farmhouse that was once occupied by Maud Williamson, the donor of this land. The park was established in memory of her mother.

Facilities: Picnic tables and restrooms.

For further information, contact: Oregon Parks and Recreation Department, 1115 Commercial Street NE, Salem, OR 97310-1001, ☎ (503) 378-6305.

Milo McIver State Park

Location: Off OR 211, 5 miles west of Estacada on the Clackamas River.

Located just 20 miles from Portland, this beautiful 950-acre park offers a place for gatherings and picnics, as well as overnight camping. The majority of the park, including the campground, is located up and away from the river. There are large, grassy areas which accommodate many people. There is also a strip where model airplane enthusiasts can launch and land their planes.

The park's southern section contains 4½ miles of equestrian trails; wildlife and vegetation is plentiful. The Oregon Department of Fish and Wildlife operates a fish hatchery in the south day-use area. Over one million Chinook salmon are raised and released here each year. Hikers are welcome, too, and there is a hiking-only trail at the north end of the park. The main attractions here are the model airplane strip, the equestrian and hiking trails, and the fish hatchery.

Facilities: Group picnic shelter, a campground with 45 electrical sites, group tent camping, wheelchair-accessible restrooms and a boat ramp. There is a summer day-use fee for vehicles. Closed during the winter.

For further information, contact: Oregon Parks and Recreation Department, 1115 Commercial Street NE, Salem, OR 97310-1001, ☎ (503) 378-6305.

Molalla River State Park

Location: Canby Ferry Road, 2 miles northwest of Canby.

Originally the home of the Molalla Indians, this 565-acre park – which is located along the Molalla River – was developed as part of the Willamette River Greenway System. It is used chiefly by locals as a recreation area. The water joins the Willamette River to the north; the road past the park gives you access to the Canby Ferry, which crosses the river. It's a short trip, but the ferry is not always running.

Water sports are popular here, and the water is always full of boats and skiers. A 1½-mile hiking trail borders the river and descends to a beach. The latter is a good place for fishing, but no picnic facilities are available.

A unique feature of this park is its great blue heron rookery, best spotted by following the flight of one of these magnificent birds as it returns to its nest.

Facilities: Boat ramp, picnic tables and restrooms. Day use; open year-round.

For further information, contact: Oregon Parks and Recreation Department, 1115 Commercial Street NE, Salem, OR 97310-1001, ☎ (503) 378-6305.

North Santiam State Park

Location: OR 22, 4 miles west of Mill City on the North Santiam River.

Located on the north bank of the river, this park offers a comfortable picnic setting, as well as the feeling of wilderness. Much of the 120-acre park is natural; the ground is covered with vegetation and surrounded by untrimmed maple and fir trees.

The water here is clear and green, and fishermen flock to this beautiful section. Though there is no official boat ramp, there is a gravel bar along the river from which some launch their small boats. There is a also hiking trail through the woods, and one that follows the river. Fishing is popular here as well.

Facilities: Picnic tables and restrooms. Open year-round for day use.

For further information, contact: Oregon Parks and Recreation Department, 1115 Commercial Street NE, Salem, OR 97310-1001, ☎ (503) 378-6305.

Sarah Helmick State Park

Location: Off US 99W, 6 miles south of Monmouth.

Statuesque old firs, maples and willows make picnicking delightful at this park on the Luckiamute River. The first land given to the Oregon State Highway Commission for park purposes, this tract was donated by Sarah Helmick and her son James in 1922. Sarah and her husband traveled from Iowa to Oregon via the Oregon Trail in 1845.

When the park was first established, it was used as an overnight rest stop for travelers on the old Pacific Highway 99. The fishing here is reportedly worthwhile. The park has 75 acres.

Facilities: Picnic tables and restrooms. Open year-round for day use.

For further information, contact: Oregon Parks and Recreation Department, 1115 Commercial Street NE, Salem, OR 97310-1001, ☎ (503) 378-6305.

Silver Falls State Park

Location: OR 214, 26 miles east of Salem.

At nearly 9,000 acres, this is Oregon's largest state park; it was once even considered for national park status. It contains sections of old-growth forest as well as young timber. While Silver Falls features only small creeks, these become 10 waterfalls in a lush, narrow canyon.

This park has something for everyone. It is so large that a map is needed to recognize the isolated locations of the conference center, the Howard Creek Horse Camp, the youth camp and Upper Smith Creek. There are old and new ranch structures with dormitories, and cooking equipment is available by reservation for reunions or group affairs. There are also eight cabins at Upper Smith Creek that can house 20 people.

The main attraction here is a seven-mile hiking trail that leads to 10 waterfalls of varying heights. Spring is the best time to view these, and there are many other access points if a shorter hike is desired. There is also a 14-mile equestrian trail, a three-mile jogging trail, and a four-mile bike trail. Activities here include biking, horseback riding, fishing, and swimming.

Visitors may learn about park history at the Nature Lodge; a group tour is available to take visitors on nature walks or answer questions.

Facilities: 53 electrical and 51 tent sites, wheelchair-accessible restrooms with showers, a group tent or trailer camp with meeting hall, rustic group lodging, a nature lodge (with a snack bar in summer), and group picnic shelters. Open overnight; closed in winter.

For further information, contact the park office at (503) 873-8681 or the Oregon Parks and Recreation Department, 1115 Commercial Street NE, Salem, Oregon 97310, ☎ (503) 378-6305.

Tryon Creek State Park

Location: Off I-5, Terwilliger Boulevard, Lake Oswego.

During the 1960s, local residents realized that this large, undeveloped parcel of land would soon be purchased for real estate interests. Located in the suburbs of Portland, Tryon Creek flows through a forested canyon near the wealthy community of Lake Oswego. In 1969, a group called "Friends of Tryon Creek" was formed. Its main purpose was to raise funds for the purchase of more land. With help from the state, a state park was soon established to preserve the area for native plants and animals. The group went on to design and finance the Nature Center. Members also continue to work with the State Parks Department to host events and maintain the center.

Comprised of 630 acres, this park is open year-round for day use. Of particular interest are the trails. These include eight miles of hiking trails, 3½ miles of equestrian trails, a three-mile bike trail and an all-abilities, barrier-free trail and nature study area.

Facilities: Picnic shelter, wheelchair-accessible restrooms, exhibit information and a gift shop.

For further information, contact: Oregon Parks and Recreation Department, 1115 Commercial Street NE, Salem, OR 97310-1001, ☎ (503) 378-6305.

Willamette Mission State Park

Location: Wheatland Ferry Road, 8 miles north of Salem.

Willamette Mission is another of the five greenway state parks located along the Willamette River. The land was used in 1834 by the Reverend Jason Lee to set up an Indian Methodist mission school. In 1844, land on the river's west bank was purchased by Daniel Matheny, who operated a ferry across the Willamette River. A ferry still operates here; it can be used to travel to the park.

The 1,686-acre park contains the world's largest cottonwood tree, which can be viewed by hiking the signed trail from the park road.

Facilities: Picnic tables, a boat ramp, wheelchair-accessible restrooms, fishing piers and exhibit information. There is a summer day-use fee for vehicles. Day-use only; open year-round.

For further information, contact: Oregon Parks and Recreation Department, 1115 Commercial Street NE, Salem, OR 97310-1001, ☎ (503) 378-6305.

Willamette Stone State Park

Location: 4 miles west of Portland, on Skyline Boulevard.

This 1.6-acre piece of forested land contains the monument marking the Willamette Meridian, the focal point for all Northwest township surveys. A trail leads from the parking area to the monument.
Facilities: The park is open year-round for day use, but there are no restrooms or water. The principal attraction is the monument.

For further information, contact: Oregon Parks and Recreation Department, 1115 Commercial Street NE, Salem, OR 97310-1001, ☎ (503) 378-6305.

Columbia Gorge

The Columbia Gorge between Washington and Oregon has the greatest concentration of waterfalls in North America. The Oregon side boasts no fewer than 75, with the highest and most visited location being Multnomah Falls, east of Portland. (This is visible from the Scenic Highway.) Some of the more spectacular falls are only accessible via State Parks trails. Latourell Falls, the second highest in the Columbia Gorge, drops 249 feet in Guy W. Talbot State Park. Other gorge waterfalls worth visiting include Bridal Veil, John B. Yeon and Shepperd's Dell.

The Columbia River Scenic Highway, built in 1913 and starting at Troutdale, was the only road on the Oregon side of the river for 37 years. Portlanders who have only a short time to entertain visitors often head east to see the breathtaking 70-mile stretch between Troutdale and The Dalles.

Artifacts found in the gorge put humans there roughly 10,000 years ago. A Captain Gray was the first white man to arrive here, in 1792. The river was named for his ship, the *Columbia Rediviva*. Folksinger Woody Guthrie was hired by the federal government in 1941 to write a song to sell the public on the benefits of the Bonneville Dam. He is said to have reached the peak of his creativity while penning 26 relevant tunes.

The Columbia Gorge National Scenic Area Act, passed by Congress in 1986, made provisions for bicyclists, pedestrians and people in wheelchairs. The park's popularity has increased significantly due to the influx of windsurfers attracted by the strong summer winds. Hood River also has the world's highest density of sailboarding shops. For information about sailboarding, wind and the weather in general, call (503) 387-WIND.

The metal Bridge of the Gods crosses the Columbia River at Cascade Locks, a National Historic Site. Rising above the gorge in the middle of this region is the fantastic Mt. Hood, the highest peak of the Cascade range.

Many natural wonders await visitors to this area; it is a part of Oregon that shouldn't be missed.

Ainsworth State Park

Location: US 30 (Scenic Highway; I-84 exit 35), 37 miles east of Portland.

Visitors interested in this area's many waterfalls can use Ainsworth State Park's campground as a base. It is one of only three parks in the gorge area that allows overnight camping; it also offers access to many of the over 60 miles of gorge trails. The Columbia River Scenic Highway is so narrow, however, that only small vehicles should be used here. This area is a photographer's delight, especially given its close proximity to the many gorge trails. The day-use area of the park is located along the scenic highway.

Facilities: This 155-acre park features picnic tables, a campground with 45 full hookup sites, restrooms with showers, a dumping station, and firewood.

For further information, contact: Oregon Parks and Recreation Department, 1115 Commercial Street NE, Salem, OR 97310-1001, ☎ (503) 378-6305.

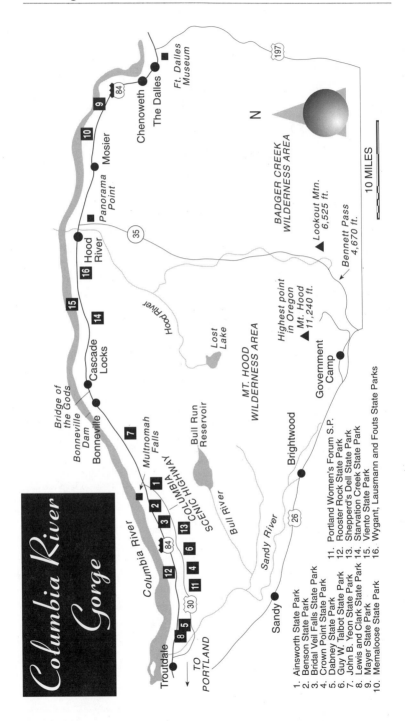

Columbia River Gorge

1. Ainsworth State Park
2. Benson State Park
3. Bridal Veil Falls State Park
4. Crown Point State Park
5. Dabney State Park
6. Guy W. Talbot State Park
7. John B. Yeon State Park
8. Lewis and Clark State Park
9. Mayer State Park
10. Memaloose State Park
11. Portland Women's Forum S.P.
12. Rooster Rock State Park
13. Shepperd's Dell State Park
14. Starvation Creek State Park
15. Viento State Park
16. Wygant, Lausmann and Fouts State Parks

Benson State Park

Location: I-84 (eastbound access only), 30 miles east of Portland.

Named after Simon Benson, a main benefactor of the Columbia River Scenic Highway, this 272-acre, day-use park is used mainly for picnicking, swimming, boating and fishing. Future development is planned for the area east of Multnomah Falls, along the Scenic Highway. This will include hiking, biking and horse trails.

A small lake dominates the park; it's an excellent place to swim on a hot summer day. The park is closed from November through the middle of March.

Facilities: Picnic tables, wheelchair-accessible restrooms, and a boat ramp on the Columbia at Dalton Point (westbound access only). There is a summer day-use fee for vehicles.

For further information, contact: Oregon Parks and Recreation Department, 1115 Commercial Street NE, Salem, OR 97310-1001, ☎ (503) 378-6305.

Bridal Veil Falls

Location: US 30 (Scenic Highway), 16 miles east of Troutdale.

This 15-acre day-use park has a small picnic area adjacent to its parking lot; it also contains an all-abilities, half-mile interpretive trail. The vegetation is varied here, and wildflowers abound. Many spots along this trail offer unique vistas of the Columbia River Gorge and numerous photographic opportunities.

For an excellent view of the falls, take the moderately steep dirt path in back of the restrooms. This descends and crosses Bridal Veil Creek before leading to a platform overlooking the waterfall. This is a two-tier falls; water is present here year-round.

Facilities: Picnic tables and wheelchair-accessible restrooms.

For further information, contact: Oregon Parks and Recreation Department, 1115 Commercial Street NE, Salem, Oregon 97310, ☎ (503) 378-6305.

Crown Point State Park

Location: US 30 (Scenic Highway), 11 miles east of Troutdale.

Crown Point was the site of the dedication of the Columbia River Scenic Highway in 1916. Designed as a rest stop, Vista House was built 725 feet above the Columbia at Crown Point in 1917. The highway was dedicated as a monument to early pioneers; photos of the road's construction are on display in the rotunda, which boasts interior floors, stairs and a basement of Alaskan marble. The interior of the dome is lined with eight carved panels of different designs. Vista House was registered as a National Historic Landmark in 1974. "Friends of the Vista House" was formed in 1987; it is a group of locals residents interested in the preservation of this landmark.

Historic photos, exhibits and an information center (manned by volunteers from May to mid-October) are available on the main floor. The upper level offers a panoramic view of the Columbia Gorge. The park is comprised of 307 acres.

Facilities: Restrooms, the Vista House, a gift shop, information center and historic exhibits. Open for day use, year-round.

For further information, contact: Oregon Parks and Recreation Department, 1115 Commercial Street NE, Salem, OR 97310-1001, ☎ (503) 378-6305.

Dabney State Park

Location: US 30 (Scenic Highway), 4 miles east of Troutdale on Sandy River.

Located on the north bank of the Sandy River, Dabney State Park features a hiking path that measures 1½ miles round trip. Smaller trails branch off from the path to three parking areas next to picnic locations; these are spaced apart for privacy. Picnicking, hiking and fishing are popular diversions here.

Facilities: Picnic tables and wheelchair-accessible restrooms. There is a summer day-use fee for vehicles, and no dogs or alcohol are allowed.

For further information, contact: Oregon Parks and Recreation Department, 1115 Commercial Street NE, Salem, OR 97310-1001, ☎ (503) 378-6305.

Guy W. Talbot State Park

Location: US 30 (Scenic Highway), 12 miles east of Troutdale.

This 378-acre park is home to Latourell Falls, at 249 feet the second highest waterfall in the Columbia Gorge. A paved 150-yard trail winds toward to the base, a nice, shady spot where the cooling spray from the water can be felt. There is a wooden bridge in front of the falls; this enables visitors to cross the creek to another trail leading to the picnic area. The main attractions are the waterfall, the hiking trails and photographic venues.

Facilities: Picnic tables and restrooms. Day-use; open year-round.

For further information, contact: Oregon Parks and Recreation Department, 1115 Commercial Street NE, Salem, OR 97310-1001, ☎ (503) 378-6305.

John B. Yeon State Park

Location: US 30 (Scenic Highway), 40 miles east of Portland (I-84, exit 35).

Named after John B. Yeon, a Portland citizen instrumental in the development of the Columbia River Scenic Highway, this 284-acre park offers many hiking opportunities. In addition to hiking, it also has many photographic venues, such as nearby Bonneville Dam.

Bonneville Dam houses a fish hatchery, ladder, and a visitor center. There are underwater windows for fish viewing; these offer closeup peeks of salmon and steelhead.

Facilities: Parking pullover and exhibit information; however, neither water nor restrooms are available. Day use only; open year-round.

For further information, contact: Oregon Parks and Recreation Department, 1115 Commercial Street NE, Salem, OR 97310-1001, ☎ (503) 378-6305.

Lewis and Clark State Park

Location: Off I-84, 16 miles east of Portland.

Situated on the edge of the Sandy River (close to Portland at the beginning of the Columbia River Scenic Highway), this park is a good place to begin exploration of the gorge area. Fishing is plentiful here; depending on the season, salmon, steelhead or shad can be caught. A short smelt run occurs in the spring, when these fish come up from the Columbia River to spawn.

The park was named after Lewis and Clark, leaders of the famous expedition to Oregon in 1805. Though they hoped to find the Sandy navigable, Lewis and Clark instead came across the rapids and waterfalls that descended from Mount Hood. They had missed the Willamette River, and backtracked with an Indian guide to explore that area.

Comprised of 56 acres, the park once housed a campground, but this was closed due to vandalism. Signs warn against alcohol use and unsupervised swimming. The main attractions here are the nature trail, as well as boating and fishing. The Lewis and Clark Nature Trail circles the edge of this park, and there is a wonderful spot to picnic that is surrounded by shade trees.

Facilities: Picnic tables, a boat ramp, wheelchair-accessible restrooms, and historical exhibits. Day use only; open year-round.

For further information, contact: Oregon Parks and Recreation Department, 1115 Commercial Street NE, Salem, OR 97310-1001, ☎ (503) 378-6305.

Mayer State Park

Location: Off I-84, 10 miles west of The Dalles.

Mayer State Park is located in three different areas, all of which may be accessed from Exit 76 off I-84. East Mayer is mainly a day-use parking area that is popular with windsurfers due to the strong wind on the river. West Mayer, back the other direction across the freeway at the edge of the Columbia, offers good fishing and boating. Alternatively, it's a quiet spot to sun yourself. The third area, Rowena Crest Overlook, is reached by traveling approximately 10 miles on the Columbia River Scenic Highway to an elevation of 1,000 feet. Park property is not included all along this drive, but the scenery is pleasant and the view of the gorge from the overlook is expansive. This is also the site of the Tom McCall Nature Preserve. Named after one of Oregon's more popular governors (and one committed to preserving the landscape), this area offers one of the finest wildflower blooms from the end of February through May. The park has 677 acres.

The main attractions in these three diverse areas are windsurfing, hiking, nature study and beach access.

Facilities: Picnic tables, restrooms, a boat ramp and beach access. There is a summer day-use fee for vehicles. Open for day use, year-round.

For further information, contact: Oregon Parks and Recreation Department, 1115 Commercial Street NE, Salem, OR 97310-1001, ☎ (503) 378-6305.

Memaloose State Park

Location: I-84 (westbound access only), 11 miles west of The Dalles.

Memaloose State Park sits on a hillside overlooking the Columbia River, with a view of Washington in the distance. Named after the Chinook word *memaloose* – meaning "island of the dead," because of its proximity to two islands used as sacred burial spots – this park was nearly destroyed by fire in the drought of 1992. The fire raged severely and people were evacuated, but the campground survived and many of the large trees are still standing.

This is still a popular fishing spot, though it cannot rival the excellent salmon runs once enjoyed at Celilo Falls (now buried by the construction of The Dalles Dam). Nevertheless, some Native Americans still fish here today. Operating from platforms built on rocks in the water, they catch their fish in nets suspended from long poles. Native Americans have fished the Columbia River for 10,000 years, but salmon fishing has declined 75% since 1910.

The main attractions in this 337-acre park are the sacred Native American burial grounds on a Columbia River island; windsurfing; and the nearby Deschutes Recreation Area.

Facilities: Picnic tables at the highway rest stop, a campground with 43 full hookup sites and 67 tent sites, wheelchair-accessible restrooms with showers, and a dumping station. The campground is closed in winter.

For further information, contact: Oregon Parks and Recreation Department, 1115 Commercial Street NE, Salem, OR 97310-1001, ☎ (503) 378-6305.

Portland Women's Forum State Park

Location: US 30, Scenic Highway, 10 miles east of Troutdale.

This 7.25-acre state park is the best spot for taking pictures of the Columbia Gorge and Vista House. A 50-ton boulder at the parking area entrance is adorned with plaques honoring individuals and acts of historic importance to the area.

Half of the park land was originally donated by the Portland Women's Forum, representatives of the area's primary women's organizations. This group worked to preserve the natural beauty of the Columbia Gorge for many years. The main attractions at this park are the views and the photographic venues.

Facilities: The park is open year-round for day use, with exhibit information and parking, but no restrooms.

For further information, contact: Oregon Parks and Recreation Department, 1115 Commercial Street NE, Salem, OR 97310-1001, ☎ (503) 378-6305.

Rooster Rock State Park

Location: I-84, 22 miles east of Portland.

Rooster Rock is a 200-foot climb at the west end of this park by the same name. It attracts geologists, artists and rock climbers; it also serves as a guide for boaters. Lewis and Clark passed through this area on their expedition west in 1805.

This is a popular spot because of its proximity to Portland. The sandy beaches make an excellent venue for family picnicking and swimming. At the eastern end of the park are a stairway and paths that lead to secluded beaches. Here, in the area 100 yards east of the stairway, nude sunbathing is permitted. Windsurfing is also popular in this region; the east wind, combined with the river's westward flow, provide excellent conditions here.

Facilities: Picnic tables, group picnic shelters, wheelchair-accessible restrooms, a sandy beach, a boat basin and exhibit information. The main activities here are fishing, boating, swimming, windsurfing and hiking. Open for day use, year-round.

For further information, contact the Park Office at ☎ (503) 695-2261; for wind information, call ☎ (503) 695-2220. Information may also be obtained from the Oregon Parks and Recreation Department, 1115 Commercial Street NE, Salem, OR 97310-1001, ☎ (503) 378-6305.

Shepperd's Dell State Park

Location: US 30, Scenic Highway, 13 miles west of Troutdale.

This park is large (519 acres), but mostly rocky and inaccessible. There is a short trail that drops into the canyon for a better view of the waterfall at the point where Young's Creek flows into it. George G. Shepperd donated the land as a memorial to his wife.

Facilities: Parking is limited; there are no restrooms and no water. Open for day use, year-round.

For further information, contact: Oregon Parks and Recreation Department, 1115 Commercial Street NE, Salem, OR 97310-1001, ☎ (503) 378-6305.

Starvation Creek State Park

Location: I-84 (eastbound access only), 10 miles west of the Hood River.

This 153-acre park was named after an incident that occurred in 1885-85, when passengers on an Oregon-Washington Railroad & Navigation train were snowbound here for several days. While no one actually starved, the park, creek and its waterfall got its name from the lack of food during that incident. The main attractions here are a short trail to the waterfall, another trail to Viento Campground, and various photographic opportunities.

Facilities: Picnic tables and restrooms. Open year-round for day use.

For further information, contact: Oregon Parks and Recreation Department, 1115 Commercial Street NE, Salem, OR 97310-1001, ☎ (503) 378-6305.

Viento State Park

Location: I-84, 8 miles west of Hood River.

This is a another popular spot for windsurfers. However, the access point for enthusiasts of this sport lies across the railroad tracks between the Columbia River and the park. A "no trespassing" sign warns that this is private property owned by the railroad. But a fence opening leads to trails along the river beach.

This park serves as a camp for people participating in the windsurfing competitions in the gorge. The main attractions at this 248-acre park are windsurfing and the short trail to the Columbia River and Viento Lake.

Facilities: Picnic tables, a campground with 58 electrical sites and 17 tent sites, and wheelchair-accessible restrooms with showers. Closed in winter.

For further information, contact: Oregon Parks and Recreation Department, 1115 Commercial Street NE, Salem, OR 97310-1001, ☎ (503) 378-6305.

Wygant, Lausmann and Fouts State Parks

Location: I-84 (eastbound access only), 6 miles west of Hood River.

Exit 58 eastbound from I-84 provides access to these three parks. The only sign directs visitors to Mitchell Point Overlook at the eastern end; this is also the direction to Seneca Fouts State Park. This road leads only to these three parks. Public access was cut off to Wygant State Park, which can now be reached only by trail.

It is hard to differentiate where one park ends and the next begins. At the western end, Vinzenz Lausmann State Park is identified by a memorial plaque. The relatively unknown Wygant Trail is located in Wygant State Park, which can be accessed from the old Columbia River Scenic Highway.

The three parks total 919 acres, and are open for day use, year-round. The main attractions are the views, the photographic venues, and a six-mile hiking trail.

Facilities: Picnic tables and pit toilets, but no water.

For further information, contact: Oregon Parks and Recreation Department, 1115 Commercial Street NE, Salem, OR 97310-1001, ☎ (503) 378-6305.

Eastern Oregon

E astern Oregon parks allow you to follow the Oregon Trail and imagine the lives of miners and cowboys in the old frontier. Information shelters in several parks recount the experiences of Oregon Trail pioneers who traveled west through this section of the state in their covered wagons. This 20-year pioneer movement began in Independence, Missouri, and is considered one of the largest voluntary human migrations ever. Because of the need to traverse the mountains before winter, the wagons left as soon as spring arrived. During the crossing of the plains the ride was not too difficult, but the hardships were not far away. By some estimations, cholera, Indian attacks, loss of direction and just plain exhaustion killed as many as 25,000 immigrants. When they reached a fork in the trail at Fort Hall in eastern Idaho, these travelers were faced with a big decision. Should they head south to California, and the lure of gold, or continue west to Oregon, and the promise of fertile farmland? Several of the pioneers' old campsites are part of the state parks system.

Many of the parks feature geological oddities. Massive rock formations rise from canyon walls. Along the state's boundary is Hell's Canyon, the deepest gorge in our country. Wallowa Lake is dammed by a terminal moraine, and surrounded by glacial lateral moraines. Almost all of the campgrounds are located on a river, lake or reservoir, providing many recreational opportunities.

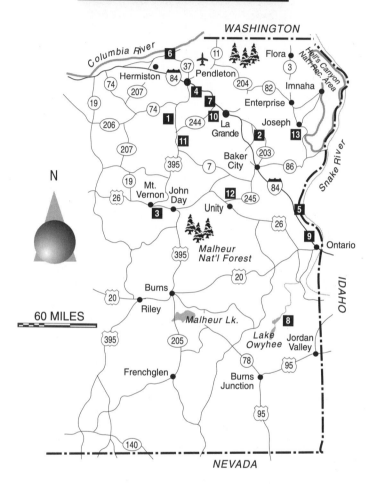

Eastern Oregon

1. Battle Mountain State Park
2. Catherine Creek State Park
3. Clyde Holliday State Park
4. Emigrant Springs State Park
5. Farewell Bend State Park
6. Hat Rock State Park
7. Hilgard Junction State Park

8. Lake Owyhee State Park
9. Ontario State Park
10. Red Bridge State Park
11. Ukiah-Dale Forest State Park
12. Unity Lake State Park
13. Wallowa Lake State Park

Battle Mountain State Park

Location: US 395, 9 miles north of Ukiah.

This tract was the site of the Bannock War, thought to be the last major Indian uprising in the Pacific Northwest. As white people moved in, the Bannock, Paiute and Snake Indians fought and were defeated by the troops of General Oliver Howard here in the Blue Mountains.

Consisting of 420 acres, this park is open for day use. Visitors are attracted to this site primarily for its history.

Facilities: Picnic tables and restrooms. It is closed in the winter, however, due to snow.

For further information, contact: Oregon Parks and Recreation Department, 1115 Commercial Street NE, Salem, OR 97310-1001, ☎ (503) 378-6305.

Catherine Creek State Park

Location: OR 203, 8 miles southeast of Union.

This is a quiet, serene place in which to pull up and relax. It's also a good spot to fish, being situated beside a mountain stream just a short distance from the Wallowa-Whitman National Forest. There are two picnic spots southeast of the camping area, and the creek is accessible from both. Catherine Creek State Park has 168 acres. The main activity here is the fishing.

Facilities: Picnic tables, a campground with 18 primitive sites, restrooms and firewood. Closed in winter.

For further information, contact: Oregon Parks and Recreation Department, 1115 Commercial Street NE, Salem, OR 97310-1001, ☎ (503) 378-6305.

Clyde Holliday State Park

Location: US 26, 7 miles west of John Day.

This 20-acre park is set in the middle of Grant County, which is prime gold and cattle country. Gold was discovered in Canyon Creek in the 1860s, and the area became prosperous. Cattle ranching is still the main local industry; the animals are frequently spotted as they're moved through towns.

Picnic tables here overlook the John Day River, with the Strawberry Mountains in the background. There are campsites near the river, but none have a river view. The main attractions here are geologic pursuits and fishing.

Nearby – 30 miles west of the park – are the John Day Fossil Beds. Here, visitors can watch geologists preparing fossils for display. The Kam Wah Chung Museum, located in John Day, preserves the structure that served the area's Chinese miners during the gold mining days. It is open during business hours from May to October.

Facilities: Picnic tables, a campground with 30 electrical sites, restrooms with showers, a hiker/biker camp, horseshoe pits and firewood. Closed in winter.

For further information, contact: Oregon Parks and Recreation Department, 1115 Commercial Street NE, Salem, OR 97310-1001, ☎ (503) 378-6305.

Emigrant Springs State Park

Location: I-84, 26 miles southeast of Pendleton.

Pine trees are plentiful in this park, providing excellent shade for picnicking. Primarily a day-use park during the 1930s, this tract gained a campground in the 1950s (although it is closed in the winter). There is a covered wagon display en route to the overnight camp, and Oregon Trail information may be obtained at the north end. The Totem Bunk House, which features two units with bunk beds, is available for rental. The main attractions are the Oregon Trail exhibits and a nature trail; the park has 20 acres.

Facilities: Picnic tables, a group picnic shelter, a campground with 18 full hookups and 33 tent sites, the Totem Bunk House, restrooms with showers, group tents, a meeting hall, a play area and firewood.

For further information, contact: Oregon Parks and Recreation Department, 1115 Commercial Street NE, Salem, OR 97310-1001, ☎ (503) 378-6305.

Farewell Bend State Park

Location: Off I-84, 25 miles northwest of Ontario.

Missionary Marcus Whitman guided the first large wagon train through this piece of land in 1836. At the entrance to the park are the remains of an old pioneer wagon.

Several park paths lead to the Snake River, where quiet spots for catfish and bass fishing may be found. Wildlife lovers can expect to see deer and antelope here; on hot, dry summer days, geese and ducks feed on the vegetation-covered river banks. The main attractions here are the Oregon Trail exhibit, as well as swimming, fishing and boating venues.

Nearby is the National Historic Oregon Trail Interpretive Center, established in 1992 in celebration of the 150th birthday of the Oregon Trail. The center houses artifacts, photographs, a theater, and diaries of Oregon Trail pioneers. This historical perspective is rounded out by exhibits on mining, Native Americans, explorers and fur traders, the area's natural history, and the General Land Office. An interpretive trail just over four miles long passes covered wagons, a campsite and a gold mine.

Facilities: Boat ramp, a campground with 53 electrical sites (and a separate area with 43 primitive sites), group tent camping, restrooms with showers, a dumping station and firewood. There is a summer day-use fee for vehicles. The park is open overnight, year-round.

For further information, contact: Farewell Bend State Park, Star Route, Huntington, OR 97907, ☎ (503) 869-2365.

Hat Rock State Park

Location: Off US 730, 9 miles east of Umatilla.

The rock for which this park is named resembles a man's silk hat; it was noted as a landmark by Lewis and Clark. The 756-acre park is located on the south shore of a lake formed by the Columbia River's McNary Dam. Swimming, hiking and fishing are plentiful; access to the Columbia is through a boat dock.

The weather is hot and dry here, and in the summer it is not unusual to have temperatures of greater than 100°. Nearby on McCormack Slough is the Umatilla Wildlife Refuge. Critical wildlife habitats were destroyed by the John Day Dam, but other wetlands were created to support more than 180 species of birds.

Facilities: Picnic tables, a boat ramp, and restrooms. The main attractions are boating, fishing, swimming and Hat Rock itself. Open for day use, year-round.

For further information, contact: Hat Rock State Park, Route 3, Box 3783, Hermiston, OR 97838, ☎ (503) 567-5032.

Hilgard Junction State Park

Location: Off I-84, 8 miles west of LaGrande on the Grande Ronde River.

Hilgard Junction State Park is an excellent place for river rafters to put their crafts in the water. The Grande Ronde starts in the Blue Mountains to the southwest and continues to the northeast, where it combines with the Snake River, just north of the Oregon border. This section of the river, which is located in the valley, is reasonably calm.

Oregon Trail exhibit information is available here, as the park is located along the Oregon Trail route. Beautiful picnic and camping areas are situated near the tree-lined stream; these appeal to children and fishermen alike. The park is comprised of 23 acres.

Facilities: Picnic tables, a campground with 18 primitive sites, wheelchair-accessible restrooms, and a dumping station. The chief activities here are the rafting access, the Oregon Trail exhibit, and the fishing venues. Open overnight, year-round.

For further information, contact: Oregon Parks and Recreation Department, 1115 Commercial Street NE, Salem, OR 97310-1001, ☎ (503) 378-6305.

Lake Owyhee State Park

Location: Off OR 201, 33 miles southwest of Nyssa.

Part of the fun of going to Lake Owyhee State Park is the colorful drive into the park. Sculptured rock borders the Owyhee River, a major tributary of the Snake, and the journey takes you through a one-lane rock tunnel. Birds and wildlife are plentiful, especially in the early morning hours. During the last four miles, the road becomes winding and narrow. The park is comprised of 730 acres.

Boating and water-skiing are popular here; fishermen also scrounge for bass, trout and crappie. The river is only navigable after a considerable snowmelt. But occasionally – in April or May – rafters can traverse this most remote of Oregon rivers.

A separate picnic area is located one mile north of the camping area. The views are wonderful from the upper campsites, but on hot days, these spots can be very uncomfortable. Shadier lower campsites offer relief from the heat. The terrain here is rough, but the beautiful canyon colors make exploring worthwhile. People come here mostly to take photos and enjoy fishing, water-skiing and boating.

Facilities: Picnic tables, a boat ramp and dock, a campground with 10 electrical sites and 30 tent sites, restrooms with showers, a dumping station and a fish-cleaning station. Closed in winter.

For further information, contact: Oregon Parks and Recreation Department, 1115 Commercial Street NE, Salem, OR 97310-1001, ☎ (503) 378-6305.

Ontario State Park

Location: I-84, 1 mile north of Ontario on the Snake River.

Located just across the border from Idaho, this 35-acre park contains a mile or so of river frontage where vegetation is plentiful. The area is perfect for boating on a hot summer day after a picnic by the river; fishing is popular here as well.

Facilities: Picnic tables, a boat ramp, and wheelchair-accessible restrooms. Day use only, year-round.

For further information, contact: Oregon Parks and Recreation Department, 1115 Commercial Street NE, Salem, OR 97310-1001, ☎ (503) 378-6305.

Red Bridge State Park

Location: OR 244, 16 miles southwest of La Grande.

Situated a few miles west of Hilgard Junction, this small park offers another tree-filled rest stop. Overnight use is no longer available, but campers can stay at Hilgard Junction and journey over to Red Bridge to fish. Despite the park's name, the bridge that crosses the Grande Ronde River is no longer red. The 37-acre park is open for day use, year-round.

Facilities: Picnic tables and wheelchair-accessible restrooms.

For further information, contact: Oregon Parks and Recreation Department, 1115 Commercial Street NE, Salem, OR 97310-1001, ☎ (503) 378-6305.

Ukiah-Dale Forest State Park

Location: US 395, 3 miles southwest of Ukiah
on the north fork of the John Day River.

Located at the north end of the huge Unity-Dale Forest, this is the only developed portion of an enormous protected tract. Popular activities here include fishing and nature study. Nearby is the 130-mile Blue Mountain Scenic Byway, which offers many recreational options, and numerous opportunities to view wildlife.

Facilities: Overnight campground with 25 primitive sites. Open year-round.

For further information, contact: Oregon Parks and Recreation Department, 1115 Commercial Street NE, Salem, OR 97310-1001, ☎ (503) 378-6305.

Unity Lake State Park

Location: OR 245, 53 miles east of John Day.

Unity Lake State Park was created on a small lake shore peninsula. The lake itself was formed from a dam constructed on the Burnt River for agricultural irrigation. There is lake access for both visitors and fishermen; trees have also been planted here, most of them containing bird houses.

Comprised of 39 acres, this park is used primarily by locals for picnicking and reunions. Its main attractions are fishing, swimming and boating. Nearby is the 106-mile Elkhorn Drive scenic byway. This offers many recreational opportunities, including campgrounds, picnic grounds and wildlife viewing on Phillips Lake.

Facilities: Picnic tables, a boat ramp, a campground with 21 electrical sites, a hiker/biker camp, firewood, a dumping station and restrooms with showers.

For further information, contact: Oregon Parks and Recreation Department, 1115 Commercial Street NE, Salem, OR 97310-1001, ☎ (503) 378-6305.

Wallowa Lake State Park

Location: Off OR 82, 6 miles south of Joseph.

Wallowa Lake State Park is one of Oregon's most outstanding state parks. There is something for everyone in this pristine setting, located within a hidden valley. The snow-topped Wallowa Mountains are a beautiful sight as they rise 10,000 feet at the southern end of four-mile Wallowa Lake. The entire park is situated at the edge of the scenic Wallowa-Whitman National Forest.

Both the lake and the park are named for a Nez Percé Indian word meaning "fish trap." The Indians caught salmon and trout by hand, having trapped them first with a network of sticks. When white settlers first arrived in the area, they were befriended by the Nez Percé Indians, who both hunted and fished here. The Treaty of 1855 was supposed to protect this land for them, but other Nez Percé uprisings in 1877 prompted Chief Joseph to flee with his tribe towards Canada. That journey was cut short in Montana, where he was forced to surrender. The great chief's burial place is located along the lake as visitors enter the park.

The 166-acre park is divided into two units. The campground and one day-use area (with provisions for swimming) are located on the lake. The other day-use area is situated a mile to the south, on the Wallowa River. Wildlife abounds here, and it is not unusual to see deer wandering around the campsites. Birds are prevalent around Wallowa Lake, and a list of the local species is available in the park. Modern fishing techniques are used to catch landlocked salmon and trout in Wallowa Lake; the lake also hosts a number of other water sports, including canoeing. Some claim this body of water is home to the "Wallowa Lake monster," a beast that varies in size depending on the sighting. The Monster Observation and Preservation Society (MOPS) was established to keep track of the creature, which has reportedly been glimpsed over several centuries.

Nature trails abound in the park; these form the basis of the Oregon State Volkswalk. There are many paths, varying in length and difficulty. One is particularly unusual: just a short walk from the path with the steepest vertical lift in North America, a four-passenger gondola carries you from the edge of Wallowa Lake to the top of Mount Howard. The view from here encompasses four states. Two miles of trails looping the summit allow for further exploration of the area. The main activities here are hiking, fishing, wildlife viewing, boating and swimming.

Nearby is the Hell's Canyon National Recreation Area, with the deepest gorge in North America. The landscape varies, but the terrain is mainly undeveloped. The Snake River offers rafting in varying degrees of intensity, depending on which direction is traveled.

Facilities: Picnic tables, group picnic sites, a boat ramp, a campground with 121 full hookups and 89 tent sites, group club and tent camping, wheelchair-accessible restrooms with showers, a dumping station and firewood. There is a summer day-use fee for vehicles, and a water sports rental concession is available. Open overnight; closed in winter.

For further information, contact: Oregon Parks and Recreation Department, 1115 Commercial Street NE, Salem, OR 97310-1001, ☎ (503) 378-6305.

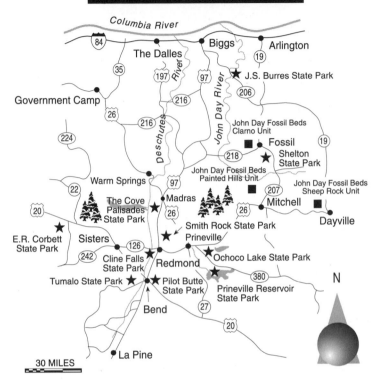

Central Oregon

*O*ne's perspective of Oregon's climate and terrain is drastically altered when traveling east of the Cascades' north/south ridge. The water essential to survival in this arid land is a common theme in many recreation areas here. The transformation is abrupt as green, wet, western Oregon changes into dry desert and sagebrush country. A feeling of the Old West lingers here; there is not much rain, and summer temperatures remain in the high 80s and 90s. The Newberry Crater houses two lakes – Paulina and East Lake – and winter brings cross-country skiers and snowmobilers to the area.

The Deschutes and John Day Rivers, both scenic waterways, are prominent parts of this landscape. Easy access to the Columbia occurs at the mouth of the Deschutes, and the river's whitewater rapids attract serious rafters.

The Kah-Nee-Ta resort on the Warm Springs Indian Reservation is open to visitors wishing to experience Native American culture. Here they can sleep in a teepee, or attend tribal powwows; a gambling casino is also in the works.

Other park waterways feature a number of natural attractions. There are several reservoirs on the Crooked River where water sports can be enjoyed. Lakes Billy, Ochoco, Prineville and Chinook are popular with fishermen, water-skiers and boaters. Due to past volcanic activity and the resulting rock upheaval, rockhounds flock here for agates, obsidian and much more. The steep-walled gorge carved by this river draws many climbers to Smith Rock, located outside of Redmond. Towering rocks offer a challenge to experienced and beginning climbers alike; some of the climbs are rated among the most difficult in the world.

Cline Falls State Park

Location: OR 126, 4 miles west of Redmond on the Deschutes River.

This tiny, nine-acre park is just a narrow strip of river frontage along a quiet section of the Deschutes River. It is used primarily in the summer, for picnicking, fishing or swimming. North of the park are the falls, and across the highway are a series of swimming holes enclosed by boulders.

The park is open for day use only, but closed in winter. Facilities include picnic tables and restrooms.

For further information, contact: Oregon Parks and Recreation Department, 1115 Commercial Street NE, Salem, OR 97310-1001, ☎ (503) 378-6305.

Cove Palisades State Park

Location: Off US 97, 15 miles southwest of Madras.

The second largest state park in Oregon, Cove Palisades is central Oregon's most visited facility. It has 4,130 acres. Originally situated at the bottom of Crooked River Canyon, the park had to be moved, or risk flooding. Lake Billy Chinook, formed in 1963 when Round

Butte Dam was constructed, is surrounded by public and private land. The lake was named after a local Indian guide who helped Oregon explorer Captain John Fremont. Today, it is a popular spot for boating, water-skiing and fishing.

Facilities: Three day-use areas with picnic tables, two campgrounds with 87 full hookups, 91 electrical sites, 94 tent sites, restrooms with showers, group camps, firewood, and boat ramps. In addition, there are boat and equipment rentals, and a handicapped-accessible marina with supplies. Popular activities here include swimming, water-skiing, boating, fishing, photography and geologic pursuits. There is a summer day-use fee for vehicles. Open overnight; closed in winter.

For further information, contact: Oregon Parks and Recreation Department, 1115 Commercial Street NE, Salem, OR 97310-1001, ☎ (503) 378-6305.

E.R. Corbett State Park

Location: Off US 20, 14 miles west of Sisters.

This park is completely undeveloped, and accessible only by hiking in almost two miles. The land was donated by Henry L. Corbett in memory of his son, who was lost during World War II. The donor's wishes that the park remain a wilderness have been carried out to a "T" – a sign at the park's entrance emphasizes that the road is only to be traveled by foot, horse, or bike. This area is used primarily for hiking and, in winter, cross-country skiing. Consisting of 63 acres, this park is open year-round for day use. However, no facilities are available.

For further information, contact: Oregon Parks and Recreation Department, 1115 Commercial Street NE, Salem, OR 97310-1001, ☎ (503) 378-6305.

J.S. Burres State Park

Location: OR 206, 25 miles northwest of Condon on the John Day River.

This small, seven-acre park is situated along the John Day Scenic Waterway. It was preserved in order to give the public a scenic view of the river, as well as fishing access. The park's Cottonwood

Bridge is one of the few spots where rafters can haul out after the 70-mile trip from Clarno.

Facilities: Picnic tables and pit toilets, although no water is available. Open year-round for day use.

For further information, contact: Oregon Parks and Recreation Department, 1115 Commercial Street NE, Salem, OR 97310-1001, ☎ (503) 378-6305.

John Day Fossil Beds National Monument

Location: Clarno is located 20 miles west of Fossil; Painted Hills,
9 miles northwest of Mitchell; and Sheep Rock, 6 miles west of Dayville.

Congress established John Day Fossil Beds National Monument in 1975. It encompasses 14,000 acres in three separate units. Visitors can follow trails into the badlands and examine fossils displayed at the visitor center while scientists continue field investigations and the painstaking analysis of the monument's vast fossil record.

All three units provide a variety of opportunities for recreation and study. Eastern Oregon holds many unexpected elements: pine-forested mountains; glades preserving tall native grasses and wildflowers; deep canyons, trout streams, and small coves of pinnacled badlands. Also intriguing are its hidden landscapes – the fossil remains of the jungles, savannas, and woodlands that once flourished here. The badlands of the John Day Valley are fossil beds. These sedimentary rocks preserve a 40-million-year-record of plant and animal life.

Clarno Unit

Within this unit are significant fossil sites not yet open to the public. In the Clarno Nut Beds, more than 300 plant species have been found. The Hancock Mammal Quarry has yielded unusual ancient fauna still under investigation. Sites of interest are:

Palisades. The cliffs of the Clarno Palisades were formed when a succession of ash-laden mudflows (lahars) inundated a forested landscape. Two trails begin at the base of the Palisades. Winding up through the lahars, they afford observation of embedded plant remains. Picnic facilities and water are available.

The Hancock Field Station. Operated by the Oregon Museum of Science and Industry, this station offers several programs for those interested in the geology, paleontology, and ecology of central Oregon. For further information, contact: Hancock Field Station, Fossil, OR 97830, ☎ (503) 763-4691.

Scenic drives. The routes between Clarno and Painted Hills – and between Clarno and Sheep Rock – pass through colorful scenery and interesting geological features. At the visitor center, travelers may obtain road logs that interpret the geology of these routes.

Painted Hills Unit

Areas of interest include the following:

Picnic area. This landscaped area features restrooms, water, shaded picnic tables, and exhibits.

Painted Hills Overlook. This area's color-splashed hummocks and hills are the eroded remnants of the lower John Day Formation. The weathering of volcanic ash under varying climatic regimes resulted in vividly-hued rock layers of red, pink, bronze, tan and black.

Carroll Rim Trail. A moderately strenuous ¾-mile trail rewards the hiker with an outstanding view of the Painted Hills and Sutton Mountain.

Painted Cove Trail. A short path winds around a crimson hill, permitting a close view of the popcorn-textured clay stones that characterize the Painted Hills. A printed trail guide is available at the trailhead.

Leaf Hill Trail. An exhibit describes the hill from which large quantities of plant fossils have been removed for scientific study. (Research continues here today.) Much of what is now known about eastern Oregon's ancient forests was learned at this site. Walking on the hill is strictly prohibited.

Sheep Rock Unit

Sites to see in this area:

Visitor Center. This facility is the monument's principal information center. It features museum exhibits of fossils recovered from the

John Day Basin. The shaded lawn of the visitor center is a favorite picnic area.

The monument is an area of active research; fossils are continually being collected from all units. Visitors may view a laboratory in which specimens are prepared for scientific study and for use in future exhibits.

Sheep Rock Overlook. A short distance south of the visitor center is a vista of Sheep Rock, a colorful part of the John Day Formation.

Blue Basin. One way to experience the fossil beds is to walk along the Island in Time interpretive trail, extending a half-mile into blue-green canyons. The more strenuous three-mile Overlook Trail climbs to the rim of Blue Basin, affording spectacular views of the valley's badlands. Off-trail hiking in Blue Basin is strictly prohibited.

Cathedral Rock. This large block of the John Day Formation slid down from the high bluff to the west. A geologically "recent" event, the slump caused a re-routing of the John Day River, which now forms a horseshoe bend around the base of Cathedral Rock.

Foree Area. A picnic site and two short trails here offer views of sculpted John Day Formation sediments capped by enormous flows of Picture Gorge Basalt.

River Access. Pedestrian access to the John Day River is provided at several points along Oregon 19. Be careful when pulling off or onto the road.

Facilities: The visitor center, located in the Sheep Rock Unit, is open daily from March through October. During the winter, it is closed on weekends and holidays. The trails and picnic facilities are open all year. There are no campgrounds within the monument, but nearby national forests, state parks, and private facilities offer a variety of campsites. Lodging, food, and gasoline are available in nearby communities. Water is available all year at the visitor center, and at all picnic areas during the summer.

For further information, contact: John Day Fossil Beds National Monument, 420 West Main Street, John Day, OR 97845, ☎ (503) 575-0721.

Ochoco Lake State Park

Location: US 126, 1 mile west of Prineville.

Situated on a bluff overlooking the north shore of the Ochoco Reservoir, this park contains both a campground and a day-use area. Created by the construction of the Ochoco Dam, its water was harnessed from Ochoco Creek – a tributary of the Crooked River – in the 1920s. Both the park and the creek were named after the Paiute Indian word for willow, a tree common in the region.

Because the reservoir is relatively small, rowboats are the main mode of transportation. The trout fishing is reportedly good here.

Comprised of almost 10 acres, this park is open overnight (but the campground is closed in winter). Facilities include picnic tables, a campground with 22 primitive sites, a hiker/biker camp, and a boat ramp. The activities of choice here are fishing, boating and hiking. There is also good rock hunting in the area adjacent to the lake.

For further information, contact: Oregon Parks and Recreation Department, 1115 Commercial Street NE, Salem, OR 97310-1001, ☎ (503) 378-6305.

Pilot Butte State Park

Location: US 20, east of Bend.

Terrance Hardington, a prominent citizen of Bend, was one of many donors of this land atop Pilot Butte – hence the plaque installed at the park's dedication. The butte, which rises 500 feet above its surroundings, served as a landmark to pioneers traveling west. There is a narrow, steep road that reaches to the top. Hikers like to climb it on foot, even in hot weather. And for good reason: the view of the distant Cascade Mountains is spectacular. The park has 101 acres.

Facilities: Open for day use, year-round. There are no restrooms or water.

For further information, contact: Oregon Parks and Recreation Department, 1115 Commercial Street NE, Salem, OR 97310-1001, ☎ (503) 378-6305.

Prineville Reservoir State Park

Location: Off US 26, 17 miles southeast of Prineville.

Prineville Reservoir is the by-product of the construction of Bowman Dam, built west of the park in 1961 for irrigation and flood control. Famous for its huge bass, the reservoir covers 310 acres and is an excellent spot for year-round fishing. Boating, swimming and water-skiing are popular here as well. This area is also the destination for many Oregon rockhounds. The attraction: semi-precious stones such as agates and thundereggs. The park covers 365 acres.

Facilities: Picnic tables, a campground with 22 full hookup and 48 tent sites, restrooms with showers, a bathhouse, group camps, firewood, a boat ramp and a fish-cleaning station. Open overnight; closed in winter.

For further information, contact the park office at ☎ (503) 447-4363, or the Oregon Parks and Recreation Department, 1115 Commercial Street NE, Salem, OR 97310-1001, ☎ (503) 378-6305.

Shelton State Park

Location: OR 19, 10 miles southeast of Fossil.

Located in a section of central Oregon that is quiet and secluded, this particular oasis is tucked away in the forest. As such, it's a pleasant place to stop and camp. A creek runs through the 180-acre park, cooling off the nearby sites.

Facilities: Picnic tables, a campground with 36 primitive sites, firewood, and pit toilets. Open overnight; closed in winter.

For further information, contact: Oregon Parks and Recreation Department, 1115 Commercial Street NE, Salem, OR 97310-1001, ☎ (503) 378-6305.

Smith Rock State Park

Location: Off US 97, 9 miles northeast of Redmond, on the Crooked River.

A spectacular array of beautiful, multi-colored rocks form a canyon carved by the Crooked River. This park's geological wonders attract many visitors, including some of the best rock climbers in the world. The number of straight vertical climbs is impressive; some of them are as difficult as any in the United States. This park is also a popular spot for hikers. There are seven miles of signed dirt trails, accessed from a bluff overlooking the river. To reach the major trails, take a footbridge across the river.

Wildlife is plentiful here, with sightings of many species of birds frequent. Climbers are asked not to disturb the nests found high in the rocks; in the hot summer months, all visitors should look out for rattlesnakes. In early spring, the wildflowers make for some breathtaking photography. The main attractions are the unique rock formations, the hiking trails, the fishing venues, the river, and the photographic and rock climbing opportunities. The park has 623 acres.

Facilities: Picnic tables, an area for tents, showers, and restrooms. There is a summer day-use fee for vehicles, and drinking water is only available in the picnic area. Open for day use, year-round.

For further information, contact: Oregon Parks and Recreation Department, 1115 Commercial Street NE, Salem, OR 97310-1001, ☎ (503) 378-6305.

Tumalo State Park

Location: Off US 20, 5 miles northwest of Bend on the Deschutes River.

Located on the Deschutes River, this park is so close to Bend that locals can drop by for a quick dip in the riverbend hole on a hot summer day. The day-use area is a massive section of lawn, and trees and wildlife are plentiful. The main attractions at this 330-acre park are swimming and fishing. Nearby is the High Desert Museum, which features acres of nature trails, as well as exhibits showing wildlife in their natural habitats. Across the road is the Lava Lands Visitor Center. Here, visitors can learn about the region's volcanic happenings, and then set out to see them.

Facilities: Picnic tables, a campground with 21 full hookups and 68 tent sites, restrooms with showers, a group picnic shelter, group tenting, a hiker/biker camp and firewood. Open overnight; closed in winter.

For further information, contact: Oregon Parks and Recreation Department, 1115 Commercial Street NE, Salem, OR 97310-1001, ☎ (503) 378-6305.

Southern Oregon

*V*isitors are drawn to this region for its rivers, lakes and history. Crater Lake National Park is the only national park located in southern Oregon. The spectacular Rogue River flows from its source within the park. An extremely important waterway, it attracts many rafters. A wildlife safari near Winston is famous for its wild animals. Another major river, the North Umpqua, is located east of Winston and across the freeway. This waterway is popular for steelhead fishing, rafting and kayaking.

Ashland is home of the nationally known Shakespearean Festival. Nearby – in Applegate Valley – is the town of Jacksonville. Each summer, music lovers of all types flock here for the Peter Britt Music Festival.

Though not as populous as the northern half of the state, this area offers a wide array of scenic treasures that make a visit worthwhile.

Casey State Park

Location: OR 62, 29 miles northeast of Medford.

The Rogue River flows through Casey State Park. During the salmon migration upriver, this park's waterway is filled with fishermen. Because the reservoir at Lost Creek Dam determines the amount of water that flows through the park, the rafting here varies. The water is usually filled with boats, either fishing craft or rafts.

There is a sign for the Rogue River Trail at the east edge of the park; the area offers hikes of all lengths. The park is open for day use, year round; it has 80 acres.

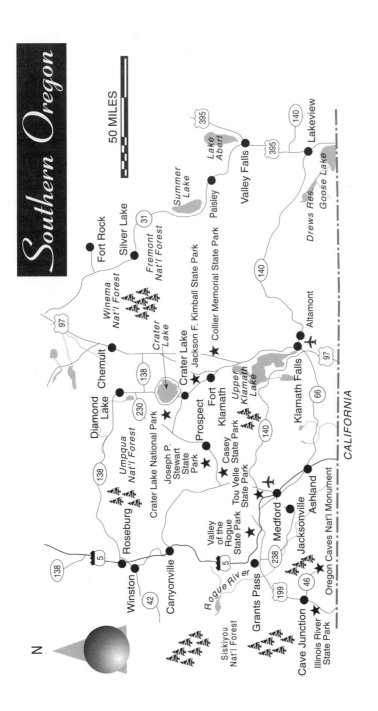

Southern Oregon

50 MILES

N

Facilities: Picnic tables, a boat ramp and restrooms.

For further information, contact: Oregon Parks and Recreation Department, 1115 Commercial Street NE, Salem, OR 97310-1001, ☎ (503) 378-6305.

Collier Memorial State Park

Location: US 97, 30 miles north of Klamath Falls.

This park is located a few miles southeast of the boundary to Crater Lake National Park, which contains a huge lake formed in a collapsed volcano. The campground at Crater Lake is often full during peak season, so the Collier campground may be a wise alternative.

A portion of this land was donated by Alfred and Andrew Collier in 1945, as a memorial to their parents. The Colliers started to establish a logging museum here, donating much equipment from the time of ox-powered logging up to the present. The collection is thought to be one of the best in the country. An original logger's homestead has been turned into a gift shop and information center staffed by volunteers. North of the museum, at the edge of Spring Creek, there are some log cabins. A short trail along the creek leads to picnic areas at both ends.

Collier Memorial's main attractions are the logging museum and exhibits, the gift shop, the pioneer cabins and the fishing venues. The park is comprised of 856 acres.

Facilities: Picnic tables in two day-use areas, a campground with 50 full-hookup trailer sites and 18 tent sites, restrooms with showers, firewood and a dumping station. Open overnight; closed in winter.

For further information, contact: Oregon Parks and Recreation Department, 1115 Commercial Street NE, Salem, OR 97310-1001, ☎ (503) 378-6305.

Crater Lake National Park

Location: Northeast of Medford, off of State Highway 62.

Crater Lake National Park attracts admiration from all over the world. The interaction of people with this region can be traced to a period well before Crater Lake's designation as a national park.

A two-lane highway encircles the lake, with entrances to the park from the north (off State Highway 138) or from the south (off State Highway 62). One spur departs from Rim Drive on the east side of the lake, taking visitors to the Pinnacles Overlook and Lost Creek Campground. This road ends at the Pinnacles, requiring travelers to return to Rim Drive.

History

The Native American connection dates to before the eruption of Mount Mazama. Archaeologists have discovered sandals and other artifacts buried under layers of ash, dust, and pumice from the eruption of this mountain approximately 7,700 year ago. To date, there is little evidence to indicate that Mount Mazama was a permanent human home; however, it may have been used as a temporary campsite. Accounts of the eruption are found in legends told by the Klamath Indians. (These are the descendants of the Makalak people, who lived in an area southeast of the present park boundary.) Because information was passed down orally, there are many different versions. The Umpqua people have a similar story, using different spirits.

It is doubtful that early explorers learned of Crater Lake from the native inhabitants, because this place is sacred to most Native Americans in both Oregon and Northern California. Therefore, European contact is believed to be fairly recent.

It was the spring of 1853 when a party of gold miners made their way here in search of the legendary "Lost Cabin" mine. The trip was financed by 21-year-old John Wesley Hillman, who had recently returned to Oregon from a successful trip to the California gold fields. On June 12, three members of the party came upon a large body of water sitting in a huge depression. Hillman exclaimed that it was the bluest water he had ever seen. Another party member, Isaac Skeeter, suggested the name "Deep Blue

Lake." This was the first of several names given to the lake over the years. The miners soon returned to Jacksonville, where they reported the discovery of the lake. However, fear of unknown regions to the north – combined with slim prospects for gold – meant the discovery was soon forgotten.

Another party of Oregon prospectors ventured into this area in 1862. Their leader, Chauncy Nye, subsequently wrote a short article for the Jacksonville-based *Oregon Sentinel*. His article stated, "The waters were of a deeply blue color, causing us to name it `Blue Lake.'"

Responding to hostilities between settlers and Native Americans, the US Army established Forth Klamath seven miles southeast of the park in 1863. This led to the construction of a wagon road from Prospect, in the Rogue River Valley, to the newly established Fort Klamath. On August 1, 1865, the lake was "rediscovered" by two hunters working with the road crews. Several soldiers and civilians journeyed to see the now-legendary lake. One of these, a Sergeant Orsen Stearns, was so struck that he climbed down into the caldera and became the first non-Native American to reach the shore of Crater Lake. Captain Sprague soon joined him, and suggested the name "Lake Majesty."

In July, 1869, newspaper editor Jim Sutton and several others decided to explore Lake Majesty by boat. By August, a canvas boat had been constructed and lowered onto the lake. Five people reached Wizard Island and spent several hours exploring the cinder cone. Sutton wrote an article describing the trip for his Jacksonville newspaper. It is he who is credited with the lake's final name, "Crater Lake" – appropriate, given the crater on top of Wizard Island.

Having read about Crater Lake as a young boy, William Steel vowed he would someday set eyes upon it. When he finally arrived in 1885, he was so impressed that he felt the lake should be set aside for the enjoyment of the general public. He would spend the next 17 years trying to push this idea through Congress. During this time, he helped Captain Clarence Dutton of the US Geological Survey prove the lake's scientific significance. Crater Lake was discovered to be the deepest lake in the United States.

A growing conservation movement in the 1890s worked to Steel's advantage, emphasizing appropriate use of land still in the public domain. By 1893, the lake had received partial protection, becoming part of the Cascade Range Forest Reserve (land now managed by the US Forest Service).

William Steel finally saw his dream come true in 1902, when President Theodore Roosevelt signed the bill establishing Crater Lake as the country's sixth national park.

Steel's early efforts paved the way for this area to be protected for the public. It is up to this generation to keep his dream alive, ensuring that future generations are able to enjoy this area just as we are today.

Topography

Today the calm beauty of Crater Lake belies the violent earth forces that formed it. Crater Lake lies inside the top of an ancient volcano known as Mount Mazama. This dormant volcano is just one in a group of 13 major cones atop the crest of the Cascades. Dominating the landscape of the Northwest, these volcanic peaks extend from Lassen Peak in Northern California to Mount Garibaldi near Vancouver, British Columbia.

The volcanoes of the Cascade Range are visible evidence of what geologists call "plate tectonics." In this process, the continents move over the Earth's surface as large land plates. As they move, the continents and the adjacent sea floor either move apart or push into one another. When a plate carrying oceanic crust pushed into what is now the northwestern United States, it was forced under the "stronger" continental plate. Tremendous pressures were exerted on the oceanic plate, causing it to deform and even melt. This melted rock is called magma. Lighter and more fluid than the surrounding rock, it tends to rise. Volcanic eruptions eventually force the magma back onto the surface, where it is then called lava. This process created the Cascade Range, including Mount Mazama.

Mount Mazama began to form about 450,000 years ago. As time passed, overlapping layers of lava flowed from several vents in the volcano, building up one giant composite volcano. The mountain was estimated to have been around 12,000 feet in elevation prior to its collapse. It resembled Mount Shasta in North California. Mount Mazama's most violent eruption occurred about 7,700 years ago. A column of hot gas and magma was ejected high into the air. This magma fell to the earth as fragments of frothy white pumice and volcanic ash. Ash from this eruption can be found as far away as Alberta, Canada.

Explosions on the northern side of Mount Mazama produced fast-moving flows of hot ash. Finally, as the magma chamber was emptying and the mountain's underlying support was lost, the walls of the volcano began to collapse. The top of the mountain "disappeared" in just a few days!

Minor eruptions continued inside the newly formed caldera. These flows created Wizard Island, which rises 700 feet above the lake's surface today. Over the course of approximately 1,000 years, rain and snow filled the caldera, creating the nation's deepest lake at 1,932 feet.

Hiking

Please note that the steep terrain of Crater Lake National Park means time, length and difficulty are not directly related. Times given are estimates of how long it takes to complete the trail and return to the trailhead. Trails listed as "strenuous" should be attempted only by people in good physical condition. The following is just a partial listing of day hikes.

⋄   **Short hikes (15 to 45 minutes):**

Sun Notch Viewpoint
Time: 20 minutes
Length: A quarter-mile, one way
Elevation: 7,000-7,115 feet
Difficulty: Moderate
Trailhead: Four miles east of Park HQ on East Rim Drive (marked by a sign).
Features: Overlook of Crater Lake and Phantom Ship. Use caution near steep edges.

Godfrey Glen
Time: 30 minutes
Length: One mile
Elevation: 6,000-6,050 feet
Difficulty: Easy, but some uneven ground and rocks
Trailhead: 1) east Rim Drive, a half-mile from HQ; or 2) across road from Park Headquarters parking lot.
Features: Small brook, lush vegetation, and spectacular blooms of wildflowers in summer.

⋄ **Medium hikes (One to two hours):**

The Watchman
Time: One hour
Length: .7 mile, one way
Elevation: 7,400-8,056 feet
Difficulty: Difficult, steep
Trailhead: "The Corrals," 3.7 miles northwest of Rim Village on West Rim Drive.
Features: Wildflowers and small animals. Great view of the lake.

Discovery Point
Time: One hour
Length: 1.3 miles, one way
Elevation: 7,050-7,150 feet.
Difficulty: Easy
Trailhead: West end of Rim Village parking area.
Features: Views of Crater Lake, and a plaque commemorating John Wesley Hillman's 1853 "discovery."

Annie Creek Canyon
Time: One hour and 15 minutes
Length: 1.7-mile loop
Elevation: 5,800-6,000 feet
Difficulty: Moderate
Trailhead: Amphitheatre at Mazama Campground
Features: Deep stream-cut canyon, creek habitats, wildflowers and occasional animals.

Cleetwood Cover
Time: One hour
Length: 1.1 miles, one-way
Elevation: 6,850-6,176 feet
Difficulty: Strenuous, 11% grade
Trailhead: Parking area 4½ miles east of North Junction
Features: Access to lake shore and boat landing.

⋄ **Longer hikes (two hours or more):**

Garfield Park
Time: Two or three hours
Length: 1.7 miles, one way
Elevation: 7050-8060 feet
Difficulty: Difficult
Trailhead: Parking area just west of North Junction. Clearly marked.
Features: Excellent view of Crater Lake, Phantom Ship and wildflowers.

Mt. Scott
Time: Three hours
Length: 2½ miles, one way
Elevation: 7,450-8,929 feet
Difficulty: Strenuous
Trailhead: 14 miles east of Park HQ, across East Rim Drive from road to Cloudcap junction.
Features: Highest point in park, lake view, and a panorama of the eastern part of the park and the Klamath Basin.

Closed Areas

Camping and open fires are prohibited in certain areas of the park, to preserve specific fragile spots. While you may not camp in these areas, you may visit them as a day user. Closed areas include those that are:

◇ Within one mile of any paved road, nature trail, or developed area.
◇ Within a quarter-mile of Boundary Springs or Sphagnum Bog.
◇ Within 100 feet of any water source between Rim Drive and Crater Lake.
◇ Atop Mt. Scott or along the trail to its summit, or within any meadow.
◇ Within 100 feet of any trail or other camping party, except when using a designated campsite.

Camping

There are two developed campgrounds at Crater Lake. Mazama Campground is located near the Annie Springs Entrance Station. Lost Creek Campground is accessed by taking East Rim Drive to the Pinnacles Road. Campsites are all available on a first-come, first-served basis. No reservations are taken, and there are no group campsites. Camping opportunities are also available at several locations outside the park.

Mazama Campground. This 198-site campground is operated by the Crater Lake Lodge Company. Fees are $11 per night. Fresh water, flush toilets, a dump station, pay showers, and laundry facilities are all available. However, there are no utility hookups. Fires are permitted in designated fireplaces only. Firewood may be purchased at the Mazama Store. Campers are allowed to collect only dead and downed wood. Mazama Campground remains open through mid-October, weather permitting.

Lost Creek Campground. A 16-site, tents-only campground, Lost Creek is operated by the National Park Service. It typically opens by early July and closes for the season in mid-September. Fees are $10 per night. Sites fill by early afternoon, so campers should select them upon arriving in the park.

Sinnott Memorial Overlook

Built in 1930 and 1931, the Sinott Memorial Overlook is located below the caldera rim at Rim Village. A short but steep path consisting of 39 steps begins near the Rim Visitor Center. The overlook is open daily from mid-June through September; however, it is staffed on an unscheduled basis. Ranger talks are given at 11 a.m., 12:30 p.m., 2:00 p.m., and 3:30 p.m. daily from June 25 through Labor Day, weather permitting.

For visitor safety and the protection of this historic structure, tourists are required to use the established walkway when accessing the overlook. Do not climb on the structure's roof.

For further information, contact: Crater Lake National Park, PO Box 7, Crater Lake, OR 97604, ☎ (503) 594-2211, extension 402.

Illinois River State Park

Location: US 199, 1 mile south of Cave Junction.

Situated on the Illinois River, this park is a perfect place to stop for lunch or just a rest. On a hot summer day, the river invites visitors to jump in and cool off or sit on the bank and fish. Some old roads through the park's wilderness areas are still available for exploration. Comprised of 368 acres, this park is open for day use, year-round. Its main activities are fishing and picnicking.

Facilities: Picnic tables and restrooms.

For further information, contact: Oregon Parks and Recreation Department, 1115 Commercial Street NE, Salem, OR 97310-1001, ☎ (503) 378-6305.

Jackson F. Kimball State Park

Location: OR 232, 3 miles north of Fort Klamath.

This is a quiet little park, just off the main route to Crater Lake. A tiny primitive campground and picnic area sit under tall trees along the Wood River. Should Crater Lake be overpopulated in peak season, this park offers an alternative campground.

Nearby is the Sky Lakes Wilderness Area. Here, more than 200 shallow lakes sit on a plateau at the crest of the Cascades. Numerous trails connect the lakes, with the best time for exploring between late June and October, due to the lack of snow. The main activities at this 19-acre park are hiking and fishing.

Facilities: Picnic tables and a campground with six primitive sites and pit toilets; no water is available. Open overnight; closed in winter.

For further information, contact: Oregon Parks and Recreation Department, 1115 Commercial Street NE, Salem, OR 97310-1001, ☎ (503) 378-6305.

Joseph P. Stewart State Park

Location: OR 62, 35 miles northeast of Medford.

Joseph P. Stewart State Park serves as the entrance to the recreation area at Lost Creek Reservoir, on the upper stretch of the Rogue River. Situated at the western edge of the Cascade Mountains, the lake is surrounded by canyon walls. The reservoir is open to fishermen year-round, and is stocked with bass and trout. Boating, water-skiing, hiking, photography and swimming are also very popular here. The park is comprised of 910 acres.

The campground features some sites with views overlooking the water at the upper end of the lake. Picnic areas of varying sizes are nestled among the trees in the day-use area. A swimming spot here is separated by buoys from the rest of the lake.

Paved bicycle trails closer to the highway allow cyclists to travel between the day-use area and the campground. Numerous hiking trails offer connections to other paths, including the Rogue River Trail.

Facilities: Picnic tables, a campground with 151 electrical sites and 50 tent sites, group camps, firewood, a dumping station, electric kitchen shelters, a boat ramp with docks, a marina and a fish-cleaning area. Closed in winter.

For further information, contact: Oregon Parks and Recreation Department, 1115 Commercial Street NE, Salem, OR 97310-1001, ☎ (503) 378-6305.

Oregon Caves National Monument

Location: 20 miles southeast of Cave Junction on OR 46.
The park is 50 miles south of Grants Pass, and 76 miles northeast of Crescent City, California, via US 199.

Oregon Caves may surprise you. Small in size, it is rich in diversity. That richness can be found both underground, amidst narrow, winding passageways; and above ground, where old- growth forest harbors a fantastic array of animals and plants found nowhere else. Visitors will discover a land rich in conifers, wildflowers, birds, and amphibians. An active marble cave and underground stream reveal the interior of one of the world's most diverse geologic realms.

OR 46 is a narrow, mountainous road with sharp curves; drive at a safe and legal speed, and leave trailers at the Illinois Valley Visitor Center or at the Grayback Campbround in Siskiyou National Forest.

History

As his last match flickered out, 24-year-old hunter Elijah Davidson found himself in the total blackness of the cave. Davidson was chasing after his dog Bruno, who in turn was pursuing a bear. One following the other, the dog and bear entered a dark hole high on the mountainside. Davidson stopped at the mysterious dark entrance. He could see nothing, but an agonizing howl pulled him into the cave to save his dog. Now the matches were gone, and Davidson was in total darkness. Fortunately, he was able to wade down a gurgling, ice-cold stream and find his way back into daylight. Bruno soon followed. That was in 1874.

Later, other brave souls ventured deeper into the cave, returning home to tell of its great beauty and mystery. In 1907, a party of influential men – including Joaquin Miller, the "poet of the Sierras" – visited the cave. Charmed, Miller wrote of the "Marble Halls of Oregon." The ensuing publicity alerted federal officials to the possibility of preserving the cave. In 1909, President William Howard Taft proclaimed a 480-acre tract "Oregon Caves National Monument." By 1922, an automobile road reached the park. Twelve years later, a six-story hotel – the Chateau – was constructed here. The very same year, Oregon Caves National Monument was transferred from the Forest Service to the National Park Service.

Workers blasted tunnels and widened passages in the cave during the 1930s. They put waste rock in side passages, covering many limestone formations. Changes in air flow patterns altered the growth of formations, causing greater swings in temperature. Freezing water now cracked rock layers. The introduction of lights promoted the growth of algae, which turned sections of the cave green and dissolved some formations. Smoke from torches and lint from visitors' clothing blackened other portions.

Since 1985, the National Park Service has removed more than a thousand tons of rubble in an effort to restore the cave. Transformers, asphalt trails, and cabins have been demolished to prevent sewage or oils from leaking from the surface into the cave. Thousands of previously-buried formations were uncovered. Today, crystal-clear water again cascades over white marble. Some broken formations have been repaired with epoxy and powdered marble. Air locks have restored natural cave winds by blocking airflow in artificial tunnels, while bleach sprays keeps the algae under control. A new lighting and trail system will reduce evaporation and unnatural elements which have attracted surface insects and driven out native species. Not everything has been or can be restored. For example, the cave decorations hang in a delicate balance, with the amount of carbon dioxide in the air and water. A global increase of this gas – caused largely by deforestation and the burning of fossil fuels – is affecting this balance. Still, visitors can now see a renewed cave, a valuable benchmark against which we can measure human impacts, now and in years to come.

Topography

A tour through Oregon Caves is an adventure in geology and underground life. All six of the world's major rock types and a myriad of calcite formations decorate the cave. Visitors will find striking parachute-like flowstone at Paradise Lost, and what appear to be giant ribs as you squeeze through the Passageway of the Whale. Tiny rimstone dams resemble miniature waves on the sea. Minute mushrooms grow on the massive root of a Douglas fir. Cave creatures are often secretive, but you may see daddy long-legs, crickets, moths, and bats.

The drip, drip, drip of water decorates the cave, creating its bizarre and eerie sculptures. It is the water's movement – seeping, dripping, flowing – and the number of crystals coming out of each drop that dictates the shape and size of the calcite formations. (This is the same mineral found in chalk, cement, and eggshells.) These formations can be dissolved just as easily as they were created. Rising warm air condenses on the cold ceiling. Acidified by carbon dioxide in the cave, this water does the dissolving. "Cave ghosts" – nubbins of former stalactites – are all that remain.

The temptation to reach out and touch these formations can be overwhelming. However, they break easily, and oils in your skin will discolor them. Look, but do not touch. The cave is cool, wet, and slippery in places, with temperatures in the 40s year-round. Be sure to wear rubber-soled shoes and warm clothing. During the summer, be prepared to wait as long as 90 minutes for a cave tour.

Some formations provide valuable information about the cave. Water evaporated by the influx of air leaves a residue of bumpy cave "popcorn." Just as hikers use moss on the north side of trees, cavers use popcorn as a compass to find new passages, or – when lost – their way out. "Moonmilk" is made of tiny calcite crystals, but has the look and feel of cottage cheese. From early times, this substance was used to heal wounds in livestock. Because it cured infections almost overnight, people called it "gnome's milk" – an apparent gift from the nether world. But some folklore is true. Moonmilk is created by the same type of bacteria used to make today's antibiotics.

Touring the Caves

A tour of Oregon Caves has been a tradition for Oregon visitors for more than 100 years. Today, tours are conducted by the Oregon Caves Company, a private concession. A fee is charged. The route through the cave is about a half-mile of often low and narrow passages, with more than 500 steps; it lasts about 75 minutes. Persons with walking, breathing, or heart problems should avoid the tour. Special regulations restrict entry to the cave, and some small children may be barred from the tour (short-term child care is available). The first room is accessible to those using canes, walkers, and manually-operated wheelchairs. However, visitors may not bring tobacco, gum, food, drinks, or flashlights into the cave.

Camping. There is no campground in this park. However, the Forest Service operates two campgrounds in the adjoining Siskiyou National Forest. These are open from late May through mid-September. Grayback and Cave Creek campgrounds are located along OR 46. Cave Creek cannot accommodate large vehicles. Neither campground has showers or utility connections.

Hiking Trails. These reach most of the park, but are not maintained during snowy weather. Trails at elevations of 3,800-5,500 feet require hikers to be in good physical condition. Interested parties should check with park rangers before setting out.

Facilities: Accommodations and food are available at The Oregon Caves Chateau (see the next entry for more information), a six-story hotel with dining room, soda fountain, and coffee shop. Completed in 1934, it is an excellent example of how buildings can blend in with nature through the use of local materials. It has even been listed on the National Register of Historic Places. The Chateau operates from mid-June through early September.

For further information, contact: Oregon Caves Company, 20000 Caves Highway, Cave Junction, OR 97523, ☎ (503) 592-3400.

Oregon Caves Chateau

The Oregon Caves Chateau, a National Historical Landmark, offers full service lodging with all the amenities, including a fine dining room that is open from May 23 through September 6. During the winter months, the Chateau operates as a bed and breakfast. Enjoy a quiet evening around the roaring fire as the snow falls silently on the mountain. There are no jangling phones or blaring TVs, but there is plenty to do. Those visitors not interested in parlor games may walk the trails – one of which passes the largest Douglas Fir tree in Oregon.

During the summer, the hotel's coffee shop – complete with an original 1930s soda fountain – serves both breakfast and lunch. The latter is an ideal time to try the shop's famous club sandwich, reportedly the talk of southern Oregon.

For further information, contact: Oregon Caves Chateau, PO Box 128, Cave Junction, OR 97523, ☎ (503) 592-3400.

Tou Velle State Park

Location: Off OR 62, 9 miles north of Medford.

This 54-acre park, set on both sides of the Rogue River, is often used by Jacksonville residents for picnics, reunions and fishing. A boat take-out is located under the bridge on the north side of the river. The park also features numerous picnic areas, and excellent fishing for steelhead and salmon.

To the east is a wildlife refuge area featuring a number of different species; this can be accessed by a loop trail.

Nearby Jacksonville is a National Historic Landmark, due to its preservation of Victorian homes and businesses. The Peter Britt Music Festival is held here every summer.

Facilities: Picnic areas, a reservation-only group shelter, restrooms, a boat ramp and a horseshoe pit. A summer day-use fee is charged for vehicles. Open for day use, year-round.

For further information, contact: Oregon Parks and Recreation Department, 1115 Commercial Street NE, Salem, OR 97310-1001, ☎ (503) 378-6305.

Valley of the Rogue State Park

Location: I-5, 12 miles east of Grants Pass on the Rogue River.

Located downstream on the Rogue River, this 277-acre park gives good river access and serves as a base for excursions through the Rogue Valley. The only campground along I-5, it is a very popular park. The day-use area is used extensively as a rest stop for I-5 travelers. The picnic area features an occasional table with a river view, and boat access is close by.

The composition of the Rogue River varies greatly, but this area is relatively calm and extremely scenic. The famous 40-mile Rogue

River Trail travels the roadless section of the river, and may be accessed at the Grave Creek Bridge. This is the entry point for rafters and kayakers wishing to float the more difficult waters downstream. Permits are required to traverse this section; a commercial operator can also be hired to help you on your trip.

Facilities: Picnic tables, a group picnic shelter, a boat ramp, a campground with 97 full hookups, 55 electrical and 21 tent sites, wheelchair-accessible restrooms with showers, a dumping station, group camps and firewood. Open year round.

For further information, contact: Oregon Parks and Recreation Department, 1115 Commercial Street NE, Salem, OR 97310-1001, ☎ (503) 378-6305.

Washington

Introduction

It seems as if everyone started beating a path to the state of Washington in the late 1980s and 1990s. Yet even with the overwhelming increase in visitors, the state's unspoiled beauty remains exactly that – unspoiled. Fortunately for outdoor recreation buffs, Washington is a bit isolated from the rest of the country. The Pacific Ocean forms the state's western boundary, and the Columbia River separates Washington from Oregon for most of the southern border, with Idaho serving as the eastern border. Major cities are few and far between, with almost six driving hours between Spokane and Seattle.

Visitors will be awed by the sheer beauty of this state. Washington boasts not only towering evergreens but snowcapped mountains, natural lakes and the Pacific Ocean. Recreational opportunities are limitless. While the eastern portion of the state is treeless, brown and flat – hence, its reputation as the "dry side of the mountains" – you can expect colder winters, more snow, more wind and a little less rain. Much of the area is actually desert, with less than 12 inches of rainfall each year.

The "wet side of the mountains" – or western Washington – is filled with natural wonders virtually unmatched elsewhere in the world. Winter snowfalls are generally light and melt quickly. But don't be discouraged. Mt. Rainier is the perfect spot to spend time if you are a snow lover. Winters with at least 70 feet of snow are not unusual. Cascade ski areas open in November, with an eight-month ski season not uncommon.

To experience the best of this outdoor paradise, there is no better place to start than in Washington's state and national parks. Roosevelt elk, black bears, deer, bald eagles and marmots can be seen from a distance as you walk the park trails. Mountain goats reign supreme in Olympic National Park. Bring your tent, sleeping bag, skis, mountain bike and binoculars. You won't have a moment to spare.

General Information

Park Hours

Although most parks are open year-round, some close during the winter. To make sure your camping plans don't come to an early end, contact the Public Affairs Office for the latest schedule and activity information at ☎ (360) 902-8563; TDD (360) 664-3133.

Hours of summer operation are from 6:30 a.m. to dusk, with winter hours from 8 a.m. to dusk. Campers may check in any time after 3 p.m., up until 10 p.m. "Quiet hours" begin at 11 p.m. and ending at 6:30 a.m.

Campsite Information and Reservations

You can stay a maximum of 10 consecutive days in any one park, and most parks have some sites that can accommodate both a vehicle and a trailer up to a combined length of 32 feet. During the winter season the maximum stay is 15 days.

Of the parks offering camping, nearly 75% have tent sites, which include a campstove, picnic table, nearby running water, sink, garbage disposal and flush toilet.

A new central facility, **Reservations Northwest,** handles reservations for many campgrounds in both Washington and Oregon. They have a nationwide toll-free number. Contact:

Reservations Northwest
PO Box 500
Portland, OR 97207
☎ (800) 452-5687

For general information, specific questions, and information on special facilities (such as equestrian facilities), contact:

Washington State Department of Parks and Recreation
7150 Cleanwater Lane
PO Box 42650
Olympia, WA 98504-2650
☎ (800) 233-0321 (nationwide)

In addition, Fort Worden has its own year-round reservation system for campsites and houses. Contact Fort Worden directly at ☎ (360) 385-4730.

Fees

Fees are as follows: "standard" sites (with campstove, picnic table, nearby running water, garbage disposal and a flush toilet), $8; "utility" sites (includes the standard site amenities, plus electricity and possibly running water), $12; "primitive" sites (no flush toilet, and no guarantee of any other standard amenities), $4 for those that cannot accommodate a motorized vehicle (or a site used by campers who are hiking or biking), and $5.50 for those with motorized vehicle access.

A $4 fee is charged per night for a second vehicle, unless it is towed by another recreational vehicle. Extra vehicles must be parked in designated campsites or extra vehicle parking spaces only.

Fees are reviewed annually by the Washington State Parks and Recreation Commission, and are subject to change.

Marine Facilities

Washington State Parks offer many marine facilities for boaters. Some of these are accessible by car, while others are accessible by either private boat or state ferry. In some cases, you can get there either by private boat or Seattle tour boat; still others are accessible only by private boat. Fees are charged for use of the moorage facilities at certain marine parks. The fees apply from 3 p.m.-8 a.m., May 1 through Labor Day, and year-round at certain parks. For boats under 26 feet in length, the charge is $3.50; for longer boats,

.the charge is $5.50. Seasonal permits or year-round permits are available at some of the parks. For more information on the boat moorage program or for a listing of all public marine facilities, write or call the Washington State Department of Parks and Recreation; the address and phone number are on the previous page.

Equestrian Facilities

Horseback riding is enjoyed by many people, and several Washington State Parks have equestrian facilities ranging from trails to arenas. Riding is also permitted on the ocean beaches within the seashore conservation area. (This area extends north to Moclips, and south to Ilwaco.) Although no fees are charged to use trails in state parks, they may be charged by private concessionaires who operate facilities within a state park. Equestrian campers pay the applicable camping fee based on the site occupied. Because most state parks are developed for camping and picnicking, horses are permitted only in the designated areas. To ensure the safety of all park visitors, the following regulations have been adopted by the Washington State Parks and Recreation Commission:

- ◇ Horses are permitted only in the designated areas.
- ◇ Horses are not permitted in swimming areas, campgrounds or picnic areas.
- ◇ Horses must be ridden in a manner that does not endanger the life or limb or any person; they may not be tied insecurely or left unattended.

Except where prohibited by statute or rule, horses are permitted year-round on and along the ocean beaches within the seashore conservation area. Loading and unloading horses is prohibited in state park beach-approach parking lots, and on or near any recreational facilities.

Clam beds extend 500 feet from the water's edge to the edges of dunes or cliffs, or where marked. Horses are permitted only on the uppermost, hard-packed sand area between the clam beds and the landward limit.

Equestrian access is permitted at the intersection of any access road and the beach, or on any equestrian trail designated by the commission. Upland owners are also allowed equestrian access to and from their property, except for commercial purposes.

Horses shall be led or walked through areas of heavy pedestrian concentration, at all beach-approach intersections, and along the drivable beach areas. At all times, equestrian traffic shall yield the right of way to pedestrians on the ocean beaches.

For a list of equestrian trails within the state parks system, contact the Washington State Department of Parks and Recreation (address and telephone number are in the section titled Campsite Information and Reservations on pages 102-103.

Bicycle Camping

Many campers reach the parks by bicycle. All camping parks have areas for hikers and bicyclists, in addition to regular campsites. These campsites offer accommodations for bicyclists at a lower cost than standard sites, and are often inaccessible to motorized vehicles. To ensure that overnight accommodations are available, contact the park in advance of your arrival. The park staff should also be able to advise if space is available for groups in primitive campsites, or if the group camp can be used.

For a list of state parks with primitive campsites, hostels, and parks that provide good group destinations, contact the Washington State Parks and Recreation Commission.

Ocean Beaches

Under Washington state law, the ocean beaches have been designated public recreation areas. Many services – both publicly and privately operated – enhance your enjoyment of these venues. Check with area chambers of commerce for suggestions regarding the beach activities and accommodations you prefer.

Some popular forms of seashore recreation include beachcombing, clam digging, horseback riding, sunbathing, picnicking, wading and swimming, scuba diving and skin diving, surf fishing, children's sand play, marine life observation, birdwatching and just enjoying the view.

All types of beach activity must be considered by the Washington State Parks and Recreation Commission in its management of this valuable resource. Where conflicts exist between different user groups (or where some recreational activity represents a threat to the beach ecology), appropriate regulations provide for the needs of all concerned.

Beaches are fun, but there are hazards. The following safety suggestions are offered:

⋄ *Tides.* Check the action when walking or driving on the beach, to ensure you don't get marooned. Outgoing tides are hazardous, especially for swimmers.

⋄ *Wash Areas.* Don't underestimate the depth of the water when driving through areas where the tide ebbs and flows. A wash that is only inches deep may prove to be a gulch capable of trapping the wheels of your vehicle.

⋄ *Surf.* Drifting logs, which sometimes wash ashore, can be very dangerous. Don't be caught in the path of a log concealed in a high wave.

⋄ *Sand.* Invisible soft spots caused by tidal action often lurk in the hard, wet sand. Logs buried in drifted sand create another type of hazard for drivers. Gap road surfaces and firm, wet sand usually provide sufficient traction for vehicle wheels; dry sand rarely does.

⋄ *Currents.* Powerful currents and undertow may be hidden in the surf. If you enter the water, do so with a companion and take every precaution.

⋄ *Driving Dos and Don'ts.* "Drivable beach" is defined as the area of firm, wet sand upland from the clam beds over which the tide ebbs and flows daily. This area is considered hard enough to support the weight of an ordinary passenger vehicle and provide traction for the tires.

The dry sand area is everything upland from the waterline, except for this strip of firm, wet sand, which is designated as drivable beach.

You will find that the beach varies in width from 200 to 600 feet due to tide action. Extreme caution must be exercised to avoid driving on clam beds exposed by low tides. A good rule of thumb is to drive on the uppermost level of wet packed sand closest to the dry sand. A razor clam bed is defined as that portion of Pacific Ocean beaches westerly of a line 500 feet seaward and parallel to the base of the primary dune or cliff.

When you operate a motor vehicle on the ocean beach, you are subject to the same rules and regulations as a driver on a city street. You must have a valid driver's license and your vehicle must be licensed. Remember, too, that the vehicle must be "street legal."

Parking is permitted only on the landward 100 feet of drivable beach (within the area of firm, wet sand). No overnight parking or camping is allowed anywhere on the open beach. Camping space is provided in state parks and privately operated campgrounds.

The maximum speed limit on the beaches is 25 mph, with the exception of the Long Beach area, which is 35 mph. Drivers must slow down in the vicinity of pedestrians or any actual or potential hazard. Do not squirrel, circle, cut figure eights or race your vehicle. You are urged to watch out for children and animals. Remember that pedestrians always have the right of way, even on the drivable beach area. There are pilings located every .20 mile between the Benner Access and Chancew a la Mer, in the Ocean City area. These were installed to protect the clam beds. Drive only on the landward side of them.

Season and legal limits are set by the State Fisheries Department. A license – available locally – is required to dig clams. Consult Fisheries regulations before you try your luck.

Each Ocean Beach Access (OBA) features a "Beach Information" sign that is visible as you approach the beach. Please read it; some areas of the beach may be open to pedestrians only.

Hunting and Fishing

Wildlife is protected in state parks; hunting is not permitted. Fishing – as well as the digging of clams, oysters and geoducks – may be enjoyed on the saltwater beaches of many state parks during the legal season. The pertinent regulations are those established by the Department of Fish and Wildlife. Contact the following for information about seasons, dates, limits and licenses:

Saltwater fishing/shellfish	☎ (360) 902-2200
Freshwater fishing	☎ (360) 902-2737
Shellfish beach closures	☎ (800) 562-5632

1. Alta Lake State Park
2. Battle Ground Lake State Park
3. Bay View State Park
4. Beacon Rock State Park
5. Belfair State Park
6. Birch Bay State Park
7. Bogachiel State Park
8. Bridgeport State Park
9. Brooks Memorial State Park
10. Camano Island State Park
11. Central Ferry State Park
12. Chief Timothy State Park
13. Conconully State Park
14. Crawford State Park
15. Crow Butte State Park
16. Curlew Lake State Park
17. Dash Point State Park
18. Deception Pass State Park
19. Dosewallips State Park
20. Fay-Bainbridge State Park
21. Federation Forest State Park
22. Flaming Geyser State Park
23. Fort Canby State Park
24. Fort Casey State Park
25. Fort Ebey State Park
26. Fort Flagler State Park
27. Fort Simcoe Historical State Park
28. Fort Ward State Park
29. Fort Worden State Park
30. Goldendale Observatory State Pk.
31. Grayland Beach State Park
32. Horsethief State Park
33. Ike Kinswa State Park
34. Illahee State Park
35. Iron Horse State Park
36. Jones Island State Park
37. Kanaskat-Palmer Recreation Area
38. Kitsap Memorial State Park
39. Kopachuck State Park
40. Lake Chelan State Park
41. Lake Cushman State Park
42. Lake Easton State Park
43. Lake Sammamish Park
44. Lake Sylvia State Park
45. Lake Wenatchee State Park
46. Larrabee State Park
47. Leadbetter Point State Park
48. Lewis & Clark State Park
49. Lewis & Clark Trail State Park
50. Lime Kiln Point State Park
51. Lincoln Rock State Park
52. Lyons Ferry State Park
53. Manchester State Park
54. Maryhill State Park
55. Millersylvania State Park
56. Moran State Park
57. Mount Spokane State Park
58. Ocean City State Park
59. Old Fort Townsend State Park
60. Olmstead Place State Park
61. Osoyoos Lake Veterans
    Memoriall Park
62. Paradise Point State Park
63. Peace Arch State Park
64. Pearrygin Lake Staet Park
65. Penrose Point State Park
66. Potholes State Park
67. Potlatch State Park
68. Posey Island Marine State Park
69. Rainbow Falls State Park
70. Riverside State Park
71. Rockport State Park
72. Sacajawea State Park
73. Saint Edward State Park
74. Saltwater State Park
75. Scenic Beach State Park
76. Schafer State Park
77. Seaquest State Park
78. Sequim Bay State Park
79. South Whidbey State Park
80. Spencer Spit State Park
81. Squaxin Island State Park
82. Steamboat RockState Park
83. Sucia Island State Park
84. Sun Lakes State Park
85. Tolmie State Park
86. Turn Island State Park
87. Twanoh State Park
88. Twin Harbors State Park
89. Wallace Falls State Park
90. Wenberg State Park
91. Yakima Sportsman State Park

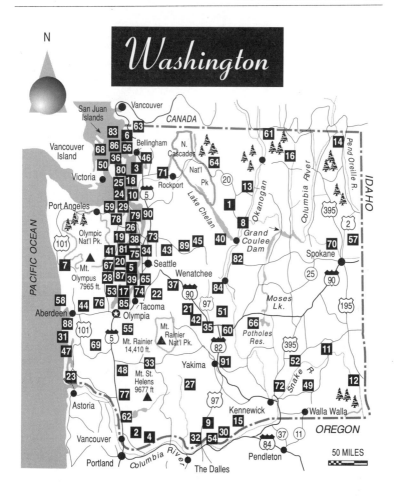

Washington State Parks

Alta Lake State Park

Location: 2 miles southwest of Pateros, off Highway 153 (a short distance southwest of the confluence of the Methow and Columbia Rivers).

Alta Lake is a water-oriented park popular for swimming, boating, water-skiing and sunbathing. The surrounding area offers hunting, hiking, backpacking and sightseeing. The Columbia, Methow and Okanogan Rivers, plus many lakes, provide year-round sports fishing, as well as boating, rafting, hunting and backpacking.

Snowmobiling and cross-country skiing are also popular here during winter.

State game department fish hatcheries are located at Winthrop and Wells Dam. Tourists may view migrating fish climbing the fish ladders at Wells Dam. Besides regulating fishing there, the game department also stocks Alta Lake annually.

Fort Okanogan Interpretive Center is located 15 miles north of the park, on Highway 97. The center, which is situated at the site of the early fort, depicts early fur trade in the northwest.

Facilities: 184 standard campsites and 16 utility campsites, all with tables and stoves. Swimming beach, picnic shelter, boat launch, and bathhouse are located in the day-use part of the park. There is also a hiking trail, trailer dumping facility, and comfort stations with hot showers.

For further information, contact: Alta Lake State Park, 40 Star Route, Pateros, WA 98846, ☎ (509) 923-2473.

Battle Ground Lake State Park

Location: The foothills of the Cascade Mountains, 3 miles northeast of Battle Ground and 19 miles northeast of Vancouver.

This state park is a haven for geology buffs. The lake's origin is volcanic. It is believed to be a caldera (a basin formed when the cone of a volcano collapses). Globular chunks of lava called "lava bombs" have been found in the park, where they landed years ago when the volcano exploded. There is a good view of the top of the active volcano – Mt. St. Helen's – from the northwest corner of the park.

History

This area was named for a battle which never occurred between escaped Klickitat Indians and soldiers from nearby Fort Vancouver. The year was 1855; the Indians promised Captain Strong they would return after burying Chief Umtuch, who was accidently killed. Captain Strong agreed, and returned to the fort without his "prisoners." Because he refrained from using force to return the Indians, the captain was presented with a petticoat for "bravery and courage." Henceforth, this area became known as Strong's Battle Ground.

Activities

Battle Ground Lake State Park offers many types of recreational activities. The spring-fed lake is stocked annually with rainbow trout, small-mouth bass and catfish. There are 10 miles of roads and trails to explore, and a self-guided nature trail that is also popular. Supervised swimming is allowed in the lake during the summer. Horseback riding is permitted.

Flora & Fauna

Photography and plant and flower study are favorite activities here. In addition, the park offers a wide array of wildlife. Rabbits and deer are common here, as well as three species of woodpeckers: the pileated woodpecker, the flicker and the sapsucker. You might also see bluejays, crows, ospreys, grouse, pheasants, chickadees and robins.

Facilities: 35 non-hookup vehicle or tent campsites, 15 walk-in tent sites, group camp area with four camping shelters for up to 32 people, and day-use kitchen shelter that accommodates groups of 20 to 150. Shelters are available by reservation only. The day-use area has 48 picnic tables, covered kitchen, play area, horseshoe pits, a modern bathhouse, restrooms with hot showers, a concession building, and a trailer dump station.

For further information, contact: Battle Ground Lake State Park, 18002 NE 249th Street, Battle Ground, WA 98604. ☎ (360) 687-4621.

Bay View State Park

Location: Padilla Bay in Skagit County, 8 miles west of Burlington.

Bay View State Park has been a favorite recreation area since the mid-1800s. The tract is surrounded by several fresh and saltwater lakes and affords plenty of fishing, camping and beachcombing opportunities.

History

The original inhabitants of Bay View were Indians, although the Spaniards were the first recorded people to sail into Padillo Bay. Spain sent explorers into Puget Sound waters in 1792 in an attempt to secure claims on the Pacific Northwest. However, Captain George Vancouver was ordered by Great Britain to explore and map the region that same year.

It was Captain Vancouver who named many of these islands, mountains and waterways. His reports were published and available to the public long before those of the Spaniards. Yet, to this day, several islands and waterways retain their Spanish names. It is an appropriate testament to Spain's determined yet futile efforts to secure the Puget Sound territory. Great Britain finally triumphed in the diplomatic struggle when Spain relinquished all claims to the far northwest.

Activities

Today, Bay View State Park features over 1,300 linear feet of saltwater frontage. There are seven lakes nearby, which make beachcombing, bird watching, crabbing, and water-skiing the park's most popular attractions. Salmon fishermen flock to the Samish, a well-protected salmon river flowing into Padilla Bay just north of Bay View. Steelhead anglers can test their skills at the Skagit River, which flows from the town of Mount Vernon into Skagit Bay, south of the park.

Douglas fir, willow, red cedar, alder and maple trees abound in this park, creating a peaceful, relaxed environment year-round. Bicyclists on their way to La Conner often stay here because of its convenient location, only eight miles north of that city. Other visitors enjoy the park while attending community events such as parades, pageants, barbecues, rodeos, fairs and holiday celebrations.

Facilities: Camp area – 100 tent sites, nine trailer spaces with full hookups, four pit toilets, 14 water standpipes, comfort station, 12 extra parking spaces for visitors and boat trailers. Day-use facilities – the 6½-acre area can accommodate 300 people, with parking for 150 cars. It has 59 picnic tables, an outdoor fireplace, two electric stoves, picnic shelter, one kitchen shelter, one kitchenette, two comfort stations, two pit toilets and a horseshoe pit.

For further information, contact: Bay View State Park, 1093 Bay View Edison Road, Mt. Vernon, WA 98273, ☎ (360) 757-0227.

Beacon Rock State Park

Location: The gorge of the mighty Columbia River,
35 miles east of Vancouver on State Route 14.

Beacon Rock is the world's second-largest monolith (Gibraltar is the first). Composed of basalt, Beacon Rock is actually the eroded core of a volcano. Formed by years of wear from the nearby river, the "throat" of the volcano is still recognizable in the form of Beacon Rock.

History

The Indian name for the massive monolith was "Che-Che-Optin," but the meaning has been lost. Indians canoeing the last of the Cascade Rapids (where Bonneville Dam now stands) knew upon reaching Beacon Rock that there were no more obstructions in the river. They had arrived at tidewater, and the Pacific Ocean was only 150 miles west. Thus, the rock became a "beacon" to the early explorers traveling the Columbia. For years, the rock was known as Castle Rock; it was renamed by the Board of National Geographic Names, who restored it to Beacon Rock, the name given to it by Lewis and Clark in 1805.

There is no record of a successful ascent of this 848-foot rock until 1901. Henry J. Biddle built the original trail over a two-year period, beginning in 1816 (after purchasing the rock). A panoramic view of the Columbia can be seen from the top of Beacon Rock. Islands, rugged basaltic cliffs and waterfalls can also be seen.

Activities

Among the many activities available here is a chance to either climb or hike to the top of the 848-foot Beacon Rock. For those who prefer hiking, there is a well-maintained, 4,555-foot trail from the base of the rock to the top. The trail has a 15% grade; handrails line most of the ascent, making the climb brisk but safe. There is a continuous panoramic view of the Columbia River gorge. There are 7½ miles of trails to Rodney Flats, Hardy Falls, and Hamilton Mountain. In addition, 14 miles of Off-Road Vehicle (ORV) roads are open to the public.

Climbing Beacon Rock

For those who wish to attempt this climb, there are several simple safety facts to keep in mind. Only advanced climbers should attempt to scale this rock.

Access to the rock. A trail east of the roadside rest area leads to the southeast corner of the rock. Climbers are restricted to the south side of the rock.

Registration. The Washington State Parks and Recreation Commission has officially adopted a policy requiring all climbers to register prior to climbing. Registration instructions are posted on the information bulletin board at the trailhead to the rock. (This is located to the east of the roadside rest area.) Climbers must also check in at the registration area after their climb.

Rescue efforts are always difficult on this rock – sometimes impossible. Local authorities responsible for such efforts may pursue legal avenues to recover costs.

All climbers should be aware of the following dangers:

- ⬦ High winds, with accompanying chill factors, can come up suddenly.
- ⬦ Watch for occasional rockfall, caused by other climbers or by hikers on the trail above.
- ⬦ Be alert to other rockfall.
- ⬦ There are many route finding problems; allow sufficient time for your climb, so that you don't get caught in darkness.
- ⬦ Fixed pitons are often old and unreliable; do not trust them.
- ⬦ Poison oak is prevalent, particularly at the rock's base.
- ⬦ Rescue is difficult, and you may be responsible for the cost.

Area climbing clubs have identified the following items as minimum equipment for all climbers:

- ⬦ Hard hat.
- ⬦ Two 150' climbing ropes.
- ⬦ Appropriate and adequate clothing for weather conditions and emergencies.

- ◇ Rappel equipment.
- ◇ Proper climbing footwear.
- ◇ Headlamp (for longer routes).

If you do not have all of this equipment, you are not prepared to climb Beacon Rock. Don't take unnecessary risks.

Oregon Rock, a guide that details climbing routes on Beacon Rock, is available at local climbing stores. Check with the park manager for nearby locations.

For additional information or assistance, contact the park manager or local climbing clubs. Two of the latter are listed below:

Mazamas	Ptarmigans
909 NW 19th	PO Box 1821
Portland, OR 97209	Vancouver, WA 98660

Facilities: Picnicking, camping, hiking, fishing, boating, rock climbing and swimming, 33 non-hookup campsites with kitchens and shelters, modern restrooms, hot showers, boat launch area and moorage facilities.

For further information, contact: Beacon State Park, MP 34.83 L, State Road 14, Skamania, WA 98648, ☎ (509) 427-8265.

Belfair State Park

*Location: The lower portion of Hood Canal,
three miles west of Belfair on State Highway 300.*

Belfair State Park includes over 3,000 feet of freshwater shoreline on Big Mission and Little Mission Creeks, and over 1,300 feet of saltwater shoreline on the canal. Picnicking, beachcombing, camping, scuba diving, crabbing and rock collecting are popular activities here.

History

This area was once a meeting place for countless generations of Indians, as evidenced by the numerous arrowheads found during the park's construction. The state first acquired this tract in 1949; it was named after the nearby community of Belfair. The town was originally named "Clifton," but the post office asked that it be changed due to the great number of Cliftons living there. The

Postmistress, Mrs. Murray, chose the name "Belfair" from *St. Alamo*, a book she was reading at the time.

Flora & Fauna

This park is typical of a seashore area. Native Douglas fir, red cedar, madrone and alders form the upper story of the ground cover, while ferns, wild berries and sea grasses cover the forest floor. Wildlife here includes squirrels, seagulls, ducks geese, woodpeckers and a variety of other birds. Belfair State Park is close to other attractions as well, including Bremerton, home of the Naval Shipyard, and the Itsap Peninsula. The numerous small communities on the peninsula host festivals and special events throughout the summer.

Facilities: 194 campsites, 47 of which have full hookup capabilities; tables and stoves are located at each site. The park has modern restrooms with hot showers and a trailer dumping station. The day-use portion of the park features picnic sites, a swimming beach and a large parking area. Fuel can be purchased at the park office.

For further information, contact: Belfair State Park, Route 2, Box 2520, Belfair, WA 98528, ☎ (360) 275-0668.

Birch Bay State Park

Location: 10 miles south of Blaine.

History

The land now known as Birch Bay State Park was first inhabited by Semiahmoo Indians, who gathered shellfish, waterfowl and edible plants from the bay shore. Named "Birch Bay" in 1792 by a botanist with Captain George Vancouver's expedition, the area became a logging center in the 1850s.

Today, you can see remnants of the Indians' shellfish beds and huge fir stumps left over from logging days. You can also explore the 193 acres of Puget Sound shoreline, as well as the marshes and forests that attracted the Semiahmoos.

Activities

The resort community of Birch Bay is a unique blend of curio shops, boat, bicycle and cottage rental facilities, and many other recreational outlets. Mt. Baker, a 45-minute drive southeast, offers hiking, sightseeing and varied winter sports.

Activities in the park include crabbing, clamming, beachcombing, scuba diving, water-skiing, shore fishing, picnicking, and camping. There is also a quarter-mile hiking trail that follows a freshwater marsh.

The park's campsites are pre-assigned, with reservations available from the Friday before Memorial Day through Labor Day.

Facilities: 167 campsites, 20 of which have water and electrical hookups, modern restrooms with showers located in each camp loop, and trailer dump station near the main entrance. The day-use area is complete with tables, barbecue grills, group fire rings, three open picnic shelters with electricity, full-facility restrooms, and plenty of lawn space for recreational activities.

For further information, contact: Birch Bay State Park, 5105 Helwig Road, Blaine, WA 98230, ☎ (360) 371-2800.

Bogachiel State Park

Location: Six miles south of Forks on State Highway 101.

Bogachiel State Park is comprised of 199 acres, 21 of which are developed. This park's unusual name is derived from a Clallum Indian word meaning "muddy waters." However, the water in Bogachiel River is clear most of the year.

Activities

There are a variety of recreational opportunities at this park. In addition to camping and picnicking, you can enjoy swimming, drift and paddleboating, and fishing in the Bogachiel River. Flowing along the south boundary of the park, this waterway is famous for its steelhead – both summer and winter runs. Other fish to look for here include salmon and various trout, such as rainbow, cutthroat and Dolly Varden.

A nature trail winds through the moss-covered growth, which is typical of a rain forest. Here, you will find hemlocks, sitka spruce, alders, lichens, huckleberries, skunk cabbage and several varieties of mushrooms.

Although no hunting is permitted in the park, hunters can pursue elk, deer, cougar, bobcat, and grouse in the surrounding forest.

This park lies in the foothills of the Olympic Mountains, conveniently close to other recreational areas. The Olympic National Forest is just five miles from Bogachiel, while Olympic National Park is only seven miles. You can also enjoy the ocean at Ruby Beach, located 20 miles south, or at La Push and Rialto beaches, 20 miles northwest.

Facilities: 41 standard campsites, each with a stove and table. The park has modern restrooms with hot showers. Although there are no hookups, trailers and motor homes up to 35 feet in length can be accommodated in some sites. The park's day-use area features seven picnic sites. Five of these are located within a community kitchen.

For further information, contact: Bogachiel State Park, Star Route 1, Box 500, Forks, WA 98331, ☎ (360) 374-6356.

Bridgeport State Park

Location: 3 miles northeast of Bridgeport, off Highway 17.

History

Bridgeport State Park is nestled on the shore of peaceful Lake Rufus Woods. Construction of this park actually began in 1960, when Ralph VanSlyke applied hard work and dedication to both build and maintain Bridgeport. Using his own garden tools, "Van" transformed the desert sagebrush country into a beautiful, green oasis. A plaque honoring VanSlyke is located in the park.

Bridgeport State Park was formally developed through the cooperative efforts of the US Army Corps of Engineers and the state of Washington. It was dedicated as a recreational park in 1968. The 825-acre reserve contains a large lawn with shade trees, natural areas, and Columbia River frontage.

Topography / Flora & Fauna

On the park side of the river, "haystack" boulders dot the land-scape. These were deposited by mile-high glaciers 20,000 to 100,000 years ago. On the far side, terraces of basalt columns bear testa-ment to the huge lava flows that spread over most of southeast Washington 10 to 25 million years ago.

Bridgeport State Park also has contrasting natural habitats that support a variety of wildlife. Among the most common animals are marmots, rabbits, mule deer, coyotes, quail, chukars, Hungarian partridges, owls, songbirds, ducks, geese, bull snakes and rattle-snakes.

Activities

There are several other attractions near the park. To the southwest is Chief Joseph Dam, named after the great Nez Percé Indian chief. The dam stands 230 feet high and 4,300 feet long, and boasts 27 electricity-producing generators.

You may also enjoy touring the visitor center at ComSat, one of three communication satellite stations on the West Coast. Here, a 10-story white disc antenna receives satellite transmissions from around the world.

Facilities: 28 non-hookup campsites, 25 picnic sites, group camp-ing area for organized groups of up to 40 people (by reservation only), restrooms (no showers), trailer dumping station. Waterfront facilities include a boat launch and swimming beach. Twenty-five acres of lawn provide open space for free play.

For further information, contact: Bridgeport State Park, Box 846, Bridgeport, WA 98813, ☎ (509) 686-7231.

Brooks Memorial State Park

Location: 13 miles north of Goldendale,
south of Satus Pass, on US Highway 97.

Dedicated to Nelson R. Brooks, a public-minded local citizen, Brooks State Park offers a wide diversity of unique recreational opportunities, ranging from star-gazing and wildlife observation to fishing and photography.

There are nine miles of designated hiking trails inside the park. Walking along these provides an introduction to the "yellow pine zone," in which the park is located. This zone is characterized by dry, warm summer days and cool evenings. The principal trees are ponderosa (yellow) pine, Douglas fir and Oregon oak. Numerous varieties of wildflowers bloom here from March until July, including lady's slipper, balsam root and lupine. Permanent residents include turkeys, deer, raccoons, porcupines, beavers, bobcats, coyotes, red-tailed hawks and owls.

Along the Klickitat River, you can watch beavers construct dams across the waterway to form ponds. The green branches stored at the bottom of these ponds insure an ice-free winter food supply for the beaver. During winter, the surrounding area offers such activities as sledding, cross-country skiing, snowshoeing, and snowmobiling. Although no hunting is allowed in the park, the surrounding country offers some of the best small and large game hunting in the state.

Fifteen miles from "Brooks" is Goldendale Observatory State Park, which boasts the country's largest public telescope. Group accommodations for observatory users may be found at Brooks Memorial's Environmental Learning Center.

Facilities: 45 campsites, 23 with full hookup capabilities, and a primitive group camp that accommodates 50 people. The Environmental Learning Center has a kitchen, dining hall, seven cabins and four tepees; it can be reserved by groups of up to 104 people for overnight or day use. The day-use area has 40 picnic sites, two covered picnic kitchens, a baseball field, a playfield and horseshoe pits. Facilities are limited from November through March; contact the park manager for availability.

For further information, contact: Brooks Memorial State Park, Route 1, Box 136, Goldendale, WA 98620, ☎ (509) 773-4611.

Camano Island State Park

Location: Camano Island, 14 miles southwest of Stanwood in Island County.

Situated in the shadow of the Olympic Mountains, this area receives much less rainfall than surrounding regions – 15 to 20 inches annually.

History

The earliest inhabitants of Camano Island were the Kikialos and Snohomish Indians. They lived in temporary dwellings during the summer, where they gathered clams, fish, berries, and game. They called the island *Kal-iut-chin,* meaning "land jutting into a bay." The island was later named after Jacinto Camano, a Spanish explorer.

The first European settlers came to this island in 1855. They began extensive logging operations, followed by farming. The park's initial development was accomplished by nearly 900 volunteers who turned out on a single day. Such community support has created a facility which has grown from the original 92 acres to a total of 134 acres. This includes 6,700 feet of waterfront on Saratoga Passage.

Flora & Fauna

There are many varied forms of wildlife in the park – including deer, possum, skunk, and migratory birds such as the bald eagle and the northwest crow. Rabbits, deer mice, squirrels, shrews, frogs and salamanders also abound.

Changes in nature are ongoing through time. They can happen quickly, as in a forest fire, or slowly, as in a glacial retreat. They can occur by step, as in forest succession, and seasonally, as in a spring bloom.

Some of these changes occur through human influence, too. Compared to white settlers, the Indians visiting Camano Island had little impact on the natural resources. Dense evergreen forest dominated the landscape. Between 1855 and 1920, however, loggers harvested most of the island's big trees. Forestland gradually gave way to farmland. This trail has features reflecting this history of change – from nature's processes to man's presence.

The *Al Emerson Nature Trail* offers an interpretive educational trip through nature. A 17-point nature path about a half-mile long, the Trail takes about 30 minutes to complete. Among the sites visible along the trail are a Douglas fir snag (cavities created by woodpeckers, which provide shelter for nesting birds), Oregon grapes, western hemlocks, fire-scarred trees, glacial erratics, (boulders transported by a glacier), and western red cedars. There are also nurse logs (fallen trees that become a nursery for young trees and shrubs), a groundcover garden (with swamp gooseberry, ocean spray, red huckleberry and salal), an exposed Douglas fir root system, Pacific yews, bigleaf maples, red alders, stinging nettles, and sword ferns. Decaying logs provide examples of nature's recycling; there is also evidence of early logging in some old-growth stumps.

Activities

Camano Island State Park is an excellent location for picnicking, beachcombing, swimming, skin diving, or fishing. It's also a great place to relax while observing boat traffic along Saratoga Passage, or while watching a spectacular sunset over the Olympic Mountains. Two major rivers, the Stillaquamish and the Skagit, are within a 20-minute drive of the park. They are ideal for duck hunting, bird watching and fishing.

Facilities: Two campgrounds, with a total of 87 non-hookup campsites; an overnight group camp area (also without hookups) can accommodate about 150 people. Contact the park for group camp accommodations. A boat launch at Point Lowell makes saltwater recreation easily accessible. A small grocery store and gas station are located two miles east of the park. Groceries, service stations and restaurants are located in Stanwood, about 15 miles northeast of the park.

For further information, contact: Camano Island State Park, 2269 South Park Road, Stanwood, WA 98292, ☎ (360) 387-3031.

Central Ferry State Park

Location: From Pomeroy, take Highway 12 west to Route 127, then head north on Route 127 across the Snake River.

Amid the rolling wheat fields of southeastern Washington's Whitman County lies Central Ferry State Park, a 185-acre reserve. The still waters of the Snake River – surrounded by high bluffs – border the park on one side, providing an outstanding view. This section of the river is called Lake Bryan; it is a 10,000-acre, freshwater body formed by Little Goose Dam.

Lake Bryan offers many recreational opportunities. Fishing, boating, water-skiing, swimming and beachcombing are all popular. So are hiking, picnicking, birdwatching and hunting in nearby Snake River Canyon (no hunting is allowed in the park).

Bird life is abundant in Central Ferry State Park. There are meadowlarks, robins, bluebirds, and killdeers, as well as mallard ducks, coots, Chinese pheasants, Canada geese, swans and seagulls. Among the other wildlife here: field mice, rabbits, raccoons and deer. Be warned that rattlesnakes and other reptiles lurk in the brush beyond the park; you may also encounter black widow spiders and some toxic plants.

Facilities: 60 full utility sites for overnight camping, with tables and stoves at each campsite; modern restrooms with hot showers. Swimming, boating and fishing are popular here; moorage and boat launching facilities are available. Groceries, beverages and fishing gear may be purchased at the park's concession or at the Central Ferry Store, two miles south of the park. Gasoline is also sold at the store.

For further information, contact: Central Ferry State Park, Route 3, Box 99, Pomeroy, WA 99347, ☎ (509) 549-3551.

Chief Timothy State Park

Location: 8 miles west of Clarkston on Highway 12.

This area was once a large valley crated by the Snake River, but Lower Granite Dam's completion in 1975 flooded the valley, leaving only a small island. It was here, in 1979, that the Corps of Engineers constructed Chief Timothy State Park.

History

The park is named after one of the leaders of the Nez Percé nation. A friend of the white settlers here, Chief Timothy died in 1891 at the age of 91. Nestled in the Lewis and Clark Valley, Chief Timothy State Park has a rich heritage. This site was inhabited for thousands of years prior to the Lewis and Clark expedition. These people lived primarily by hunting and gathering their food.

Within 50 years of the expedition, the Nez Percé, led by Chiefs Timothy and Red Wolf, began to change to a more agrarian way of life. The site of the former Indian village was eventually replaced by the white farming community of Silcott. However, the town was short-lived. The settlement had just established roots in the late 1880s, only to deteriorate in the 1920s and eventually disappear.

The Alpowai Interpretive Center, located within the park, includes displays and audio-visual programs depicting the geologic and human history of this area.

In 1802, President Jefferson was granted money to send an overland expedition to the Pacific Ocean in hopes of increasing fur trade, strengthening a hold on the Oregon territory and finding a short passage to the Orient for trade. The expedition was sent secretly to avoid alerting the French government. (The latter controlled the Louisiana territory, which the expedition would have to cross to reach Oregon.) Secrecy was no longer needed when the French sold the territory to the US to cover expenses for their battle with England. The expedition was deemed a complete success, even though the "short passage" to the Orient was not found. As more and more explorers trekked through their native land, the Nez Percé began to see the demise of their traditional lifestyle. The two Nez Percé chiefs promoted the acceptance of white ways by accepting Christianity and making a treaty with the US government in 1863. The latter drastically reduced the size of their reservation, placing the Alpowai on the outside of the new US boundary. As white settlers moved into the main village, the Alpowai was taken over and became the aforementioned town of Silcott.

Some of the wildlife seen in this park are deer, Canada geese, ducks, chukars, and pheasants.

Facilities: 33 hookup campsites, 17 pull-through sites and 16 tent sites. The day-use area provides a boat launch, playground equipment, eight picnic shelters, grills, swimming beach, fishing, bathhouse, and concession stand.

For further information, contact: Chief Timothy State Park, Highway 12, Clarkston, WA 99403, ☎ (509) 758-9580.

Conconully State Park

*Location: The eastern foothills of the North Cascades,
20 miles northwest of Omak, off Highway 97.*

Conconully State Park includes 5,400 feet of freshwater shoreline on the Conconully reservoir.

History

The park's name is derived from the Indian word *Konekol'p*, which means "money hole." This was appropriate, because the creek was full of beaver and their pelts were used as money at the local trading post. Established in 1910, the park is the oldest Bureau of Reclamation irrigation project in the United States. It provided the town of Conconully with picnicking facilities, a baseball field and place for a school. The historic mining town of Conconully, the original seat of Okanogan County, was washed away by a flood. In 1945, the area became part of the Washington State Park system.

A log cabin and bell are located in the day-use area. The cabin, reconstructed in 1978, is a replica of the first Okanogan County Courthouse. The bell was used on the Old Coconully Schoolhouse, which was originally located in the park.

Activities

Area activities include picnicking, camping, swimming, boating, freshwater fishing, hiking, cross-country skiing and snowmobiling. Conconully tends to be cooler in the summer than nearby areas, due both to its many shade trees and its elevation (2,300 feet).

Facilities: 65 standard campsites, six primitive sites and 10 water hookup sites; each site has a table and stove. Some sites can accommodate up to a 32-foot trailer/car combination or motorhome. Hot showers, a boat launch and a trailer dump station are available. The town of Conconully has two general stores, as well as gas stations, restaurants and resorts.

For further information, contact: Conconully State Park, PO Box 95, Conconully, WA 98819, ☎ (509) 826-7408.

Crawford State Park

Location: 11 miles north of Metaline,
in the extreme northeast corner of Washington.

History

The story of Crawford State Park centers around that of Gardner Cave. With a slope of 1,055 feet, this cave is the longest limestone cave in Washington state.

About 500 million years ago, much of North America was covered by ocean. As sea creatures died, their shells settled to the bottom, forming a limestone ooze that eventually turned into a rock called the Metaline Limestone. As mountains were forming about 70 million years ago, this rock was folded and faulted. The acid that formed when rainwater absorbs carbon dioxide eventually created a cave passage, complete with stalactites, stalagmites, and columns. Rimstone pools and flowstone were created by calcite deposits as water flows over walls and other surfaces. The result – Gardner Cave – was named for Ed Gardner, a local bootlegger who discovered the cave around 1899.

In 1921, a Metaline merchant named William Crawford acquired the land around the cave. Later that year, he deeded 40 acres of it to the Washington State Parks system. For this reason, the park carries his name.

From the parking lot, a paved trail leads up a small hill about 200 yards to the cave entrance. Lights, stairways, and walkways have been installed to provide safety for visitors and protection for this natural resource. To access the cave, you must participate in a walk conducted by park staff. Crawford State Park is open 9a.m.-6 p.m. in the summer months. Call the park for specific tour hours or special group arrangements.

Facilities: Picnic tables and a comfort station are located near the parking lot.

For further information, contact: Crawford State Park, General Delivery, Metaline Falls, WA 99153, ☎ (509) 446-4065 or Mount Spokane State Park at ☎ (509) 456-4169.

Crow Butte State Park

Location: 14 miles west of Paterson, on an island in Lake Umatilla; accessible by State Highway 14.

Crow Butte State Park is located on an island created in the Columbia River by the construction of the John Day Dam. This tract was first opened for homesteading in 1850. One of the first local settlers was the Crow family. The site of their home, as well as the site of the adjacent community of Carley, is now underwater as a result of the dam's construction. The butte was named by the Corps of Engineers who surveyed the site in 1941.

The island offers many recreational activities. Boating, swimming, picnicking, hiking and fishing are all available within park boundaries. The Umatilla Wildlife Refuge occupies the remainder of the island, providing an opportunity for visitors to observe and enjoy a natural setting. A panoramic view of the surrounding area is visible from the butte; on a clear day, this may include a view of Oregon's Mt. Hood. The south side of the island, with its undeveloped shoreline, has several small bays and sandy beaches at the base of its sand dunes.

Approximately 30 miles east of the park is McNary Lock and Dam, which is open to the public. Tours of the powerhouse are available, and there is a fish viewing room. McNary Wildlife Park is adjacent to the dam. It features a self-guided, ¾-mile nature trail. Photoblinds are scattered throughout the park, affording an excellent spot to view waterfowl and other wildlife in their natural habitat.

Facilities: 50 campsites with full hookups, picnic tables and stoves. The day-use area has complete bathhouse facilities, picnic tables, and stoves. There are also three gazebos and a large lawn leading to a buoy-protected swimming beach. Additional picnic tables, a boat basin and two boat launch ramps are included in the marina. A sanitary dump station is located between the administrative complex and the marina. Hermiston, Oregon, a full-service community 37 miles from the park, offers restaurants, shopping centers and medical facilities.

For further information, contact: Crow Butte State Park, Box 277, Paterson, WA 99345, ☎ (509) 875-2644.

Curlew Lake State Park

Location: 10 miles north of Republic on Highway 21.

Curlew Lake State Park covers over 128 acres in one of Washington state's most expansive and unspoiled recreation areas. Close by are the Kettle River to the north and the Sanpoil River to the south. Surrounding the park on three sides are the peaks and rolling hills of the Colville National Forest.

History

The Curlew Lake area was home to an early Indian settlement. Stone tools, Indian relics and flint chips have all been uncovered in archaeological digs here. Homesteaders later laid claim to the land; remains of their old homesteads and log cabins can be seen in the general area. You can also see evidence of old mining shafts, since gold mining was a popular activity here around the turn of the century.

The grave of Ranald MacDonald is located near Toroda, eight miles west of Curlew. Born in 1824 at Fort Astoria to a Scottish fur trader and a Chinook Indian princess, Ranald MacDonald learned Japanese from sailors and later traveled to that country, which had been closed to outsiders for centuries. MacDonald is remembered as an adventurer who helped open up world trade with Japan.

Flora & Fauna

Curlew Lake is a habitat for many different animals, including chipmunks, squirrels, deer and a wide variety of bird life. The forest is composed mainly of pine and fir trees, although a number of other varieties are found in the park.

Activities

In the summer, fishing, swimming, boating, water-skiing and picnicking are popular here. In the winter, snowmobiling is the activity of choice. The weather here is characterized by mild summers and cold winters.

Facilities: 82 campsites, 18 of which have full trailer hookups. All have access to restrooms and showers. The park also has a boat launch and trailer dumping facility. Airplane tie-downs are available for those visitors who fly in. Along the lake are four privately owned resorts that offer additional camping, boat rentals, showers, gas, groceries, fishing tackle and licenses.

For further information, contact: Curlew Lake State Park, 974 Curlew State Park Road, Republic, WA 99166, ☎ (509) 775-3592.

Dash Point State Park

Location: Puget Sound, 6 miles north of Tacoma and 20 miles south of Seattle.

Dash Point State Park consists of 400 acres acquired by the state in four separate purchases, beginning in 1958. This tract offers one of the few sandy beaches on Puget Sound south of Seattle. Adding to its allure is a 1% slope extending 2,200 feet into the water. Because the water here is warmer than that of the adjacent sound, this is an ideal spot for swimming.

Activities

Nearby attractions are numerous. For those hoping to escape the urban rat-race, Dash Point offers peace and solitude among towering fir trees. Lush ferns and laurels grow out of stumps left from the days when loggers harvested the mighty timbers. Madrone trees with their distinctive peeling bark join flowering dogwoods, elderberry, and trilliums near pungent skunk cabbage.

Favorite activities in this park include hiking, picnicking, beach-combing, swimming, and fishing. Visitors who prefer less active pursuits will enjoy watching the boat traffic on the sound, or the sun setting over the Olympic Mountains and Vashon Island.

Towns near this park offer additional opportunities for recreation. Tacoma's Point Defiance Park has an aquarium and a zoo, not to mention flowering gardens and the restored Hudson's Bay Company's Fort Nisqually.

To the north is Seattle, and a variety of unusual experiences. Visit the Kingdome, home of professional sports, or spend a day at the Seattle Center, the site of the 1962 World's Fair. Here, visitors can travel to the top of the Space Needle for a breathtaking view of Puget Sound and the city below. Historic Pioneer Square, located on the waterfront, offers unique shops and interesting restaurants that recall the city's bygone days. Across the Narrows Bridge is Bremerton, which is home to both a US Naval shipyard and the *USS Missouri,* the craft which hosted the signing of the armistice that ended World War II. Nearby are smaller towns like Gig Harbor and Port Orchard; here you will find interesting shops and restaurants within a short drive of the park.

Facilities: 138 campsites (28 with full hookup capabilities), hot showers, modern restrooms. A trailer dumping station is located near the park entrance. A primitive group camp is available within the day-use portion of the park. Over six miles of hiking trails, plus picnic tables, stoves, a play area and swimming beach are also located here.

For further information, contact: Dash Point State Park, 5700 SW Dash Point Road, Federal Way, WA 98003, ☎ (206) 593-2206.

Deception Pass State Park

Location: 9 miles north of Oak Harbor on Highway 20.

The first inhabitants of this area were the coastal Indians. Known for their peaceful ways, they fished and hunted the nearby waters and forests. However, their way of life was often interrupted by raids from the Haida Indians farther north. The Haida Bear monument, located on the north end of the West Beach, displays the clan totem of the Haidas. Another unusual landmark is the "Maiden of Deception Pass," a Samish Indian story pole on the trail to Rosario Head.

History

Captain George Vancouver originally named the local waterway Port Gardner in 1792. When he later discovered that the inlet was actually a narrow passage between two islands, he renamed the waterway Deception Pass. The island to the south of the pass was named Whidbey, in honor of one of Vancouver's officers, Master Joseph Whidbey. This man was credited with discovering the western entrance to the passage. The island to the north was named "Fidalgo" for the Spanish explorer, Lieutenant Salvador Fidalgo.

While preserving this history, Deception Pass State Park has a unique history of its own. The park's natural beauty was enhanced largely through the efforts of the Civilian Conservation Corps (CCC) in 1934 and 1935. It was this organization that built the park's rustic picnic shelters, restrooms, residences and hiking trails.

Activities

Recreational activities here include fishing, boating, swimming, hiking, scuba diving, photography and bird watching. Freshwater fishing is allowed in Cranberry Lake and Pass Lake. Only boats using electric motors are permitted. A fishing license is required, and the season is year-round in both lakes.

In addition to freshwater launches at Cranberry, Heart and Pass Lakes, saltwater launches are available at nearby Cornet Bay and Sharpe's Cove in Bowman Bay.

Cornet Bay Environmental Learning Center Camp

An interesting facet of this park is the Cornet Bay Environmental Learning Center camp. Located in Deception Pass State Park, nine miles south of Anacortes on Highway 20, this camp is nestled among deep evergreen forests. Many trails are available for hikes to other parts of the park and along the beach.

Cornet Bay is located on a saltwater inlet, with several freshwater lakes nearby. This is a good place to study the diversity of nature. Each member of the delicately balanced eco-system is unique in its particular life, sounds and smells, yet each is dependent on a neighboring system for survival. Individual life zones are referred to as "ecological encounter environments," which can be experienced and explored as an introduction to natural systems. Goose Rock is a dry, windswept habitat rising 500 feet above the camp. It supports evidence of glacial activity, including striations, glacial yardsticks, and characteristic soil types. Traces of early Indian cultures add an historic note to this site.

Also in this park is Deception Pass Nature Trail, which showcases an altogether different kind of plant community. This trail's rocky surface provides insufficient moisture for root growth, thus restricting plant life. Mosses, lichens and other micro-organisms are slowly converting this rock into usable soil. There are 17 points along this trail that are worth seeing, including a grand fir struggling to exist with little sunlight and space, a native, bark-shedding madrone tree (whose presence indicates that the ground is dry or rocky), juniper (whose berries are used to flavor gin), kinnickinick (a crawling evergreen shrub with edible berries, and whose leaves Indians used for tobacco), Pacific yew (whose tough, springy wood is used for archery bows), salal (a shrub which forms an impenetrable thicket), western red cedar (which grows best in damp woods; its soft, decay-resistant wood was used by Indians for canoes, carvings, clothing and housing), and many other interesting plants and exhibits.

The Environmental Learning Center's facilities include: dining hall/kitchen, two restrooms, 16 sleeping cabins, a cook's cabin, first-aid cabin, administration building, recreation hall, a campfire circle, and playing fields. A heated swimming pool is open from June 1 through Labor Day. The buildings are fully winterized, enabling groups to take advantage of this beautiful setting year-round. The camp accommodates 142 for overnight use and 250 for day use. For reservations and information, contact: ELC Reservation Center, Washington State Parks and Recreation Commission, 7150 Cleanwater Lane, KY-11, Olympia, WA 98504, ☎ (206) 586-6022.

Facilities: 251 non-hookup campsites, four of which are walk-in sites for bicyclists or backpackers. Tables and stoves are located at each site, with kitchens and shelters nearby. Restrooms, hot showers and a trailer dump station are also available. Over 18 miles of trails run throughout the park. Maps are available at the park office. Cranberry Lake has a swimming beach and bathhouse, as well as a seasonal concession stand. For information on facilities at the Environmental Learning Center, see above.

For further information, contact: Deception Pass State Park, 5175 NSH 20, Oak Harbor, WA 98277, ☎ (360) 675-2417.

Dosewallips State Park

Location: 1 mile south of Brinnon and 40 miles north of Shelton, on Highway 101.

Situated on 514 acres at the foot of the Olympic Mountains, the park offers spectacular views of Mt. Walker and Mt. Constance. Because the park is located at the confluence of the Dosewallips River and Hood Canal, both saltwater and freshwater recreation are available. Pleasant Harbor Marine State Park and Toandos Peninsula Tidelands are satellite areas.

The name "Dosewallips" is derived from *Dos-wail-opsh,* the name of a legendary Twana Indian who was turned into a mountain, forming the source of the Dosewallips River. For years the area was called "Dose Meadows," and served as the site of several homesteads. Old railroad beds can still be found on the southeast side of the park. These were used to ship logs from the high country to the water, where they were rafted to nearby lumber mills.

Year-round fishing makes for a lot of activity here. The river harbors numerous steelhead, while salmon and a large variety of bottom fish may be found in the warm saltwater of Hood Canal. Visitors can also enjoy clamming, crabbing, and oyster picking on the shores of the canal. More information about native shellfish is available at the Point Whitney Shellfish Laboratory, six miles northeast of the park on Quilcene Bay. Wildlife which may be seen in the park include deer, elk, raccoons, beavers, skunks, seals, eagles, and waterfowl may be glimpsed.

Interested tourists can travel 40 miles north to historic Point Townsend. Spectacularly situated at the entrance to Puget Sound, with more than its share of quaint shops and historic homes, this community is representative of a late 19th-century seaport. Restaurants and a general store (as well as a service station, post office, ambulance and church) are all located a half-mile north of the park on Highway 101. Medical services are available in both Shelton and Port Townsend.

Facilities: 128 campsites, including 40 sites with full hookup capabilities. Modern restrooms, hot showers, and a trailer dumping station are also available. The day-use area east of Highway 101 offers picnic sites and a large parking area for day visitors. There is a public boat launch at Point Whitney and a private launch located three miles to the north. Moorage is available at Pleasant Harbor Marine State Park, two miles south of Dosewallips.

For further information, contact: Dosewallips State Park, PO Box K, Brinnon, WA 98320, ☎ (360) 796-4415.

Fay-Bainbridge State Park

Location: The northeast tip of Bainbridge Island, 3 miles off Highway 305; 6 miles west of north Seattle, for those traveling by boat.

Situated in Kitsay County, this park boasts 17 acres and 1,420 feet of waterfront on Puget Sound. The state purchased the land for this park in 1944, from the estate of a University of Washington professor named Dr. Fay. After his death, Fay's children honored his wishes by making this area a park for all to enjoy.

At the park entrance is a display featuring a bell. Originally purchased by the citizens of Port Madison, it was brought from San Francisco by Captain Jeremiah Farnham in about 1883. It was to have been placed in the school belfry and used as a "town crier." However, when a courthouse was needed on short notice, the almost-completed schoolhouse was converted and the bell placed in the community hall. It was later moved to A.R. Lintner's home, Bellvista. Lintner, in turn, gave it to the Kitsay Historical Association, who presented it to the park in 1953.

Activities

Activities at Fay-Bainbridge are numerous. Overnight camping, picnicking, beachcombing, boating, fishing, scuba diving, and even a chilly dip in Puget Sound are favorite pastimes here. Hiking among maple, alder, fir and hemlock trees is also fun. Among the wildlife are squirrels, raccoons, and a variety of birds.

In nearby Suquamish is Old Man House, site of the home of Chief Seatlh, for whom Seattle was named. Although none of the original building remains, a reconstructed section of the house is used as a historical display.

The nearby communities of Poulsbo and Winslow offer quaint shops and intriguing restaurants, as well as interesting summer festivals. The city of Seattle, accessible via the Winslow ferry, offers unlimited activities, including the annual Seafair festival each summer.

Facilities: 36 overnight campsites, each with a table and stove. The day-use area includes picnic tables, two covered kitchen shelters, playground equipment, a swimming beach and a modern restroom/bathhouse with hot showers. Two mooring buoys, a boat launching area and a trailer dumping station complete the park's facilities.

For further information, contact: c/o Lake Easton State Park, PO Box 26, Easton, WA 98925, ☎ (509) 656-2230.

Federation Forest State Park

Location: 17 miles east of Enumclaw on State Route 410, the Chinook Pass Highway.

This park consists of 612 acres of virgin timber, acquired largely through the efforts of the Washington State Federation of Women's Clubs.

The original Federation Forest was a 63-acre tract just west of Snoqualmie Pass. During the 1930s, various misfortunes befell the park – including wind, fire and the lumberjack's axe. This led to the decision to seek a new location with a virgin stand of timber. Through the continued interest of the Washington State Federation of Women's Clubs and the cooperation of the Washington state legislature, the present park was dedicated in 1949.

Catherine Montgomery Interpretive Center

In 1958, Catherine Montgomery, a pioneer educator deeply interested in conservation, willed funds to the Washington State Federation of Women's Clubs for improvements to Federation Forest State Park. This money was used to construct the present interpretive center. The primary purpose of the center is to demonstrate the natural contrasts found throughout the state. In this developed portion of the park, the center's exhibits illustrate the character and diverse beauty of the native flora.

Wide climatic variances occur across this state. Because of this, the flora varies from area to area. Found here are no less than seven general biotic or life zones. (Of the 10 zones present in the entire nation, few states can claim more than three.)

Through use of words and pictures, the interpretive center illustrates the following seven life zones:

Coast Forest Zone. Extends from the beaches of the Pacific Ocean inland through the Puget Sound Basin, and upward into the lower hills of the Olympic Mountains. This zone is characterized by dense stands of Douglas fir and western hemlock (the state tree).

Mountain Forest Zone. Occupies the mountainous areas of both eastern and western Washington, to an upper elevation limit of about 5,000 feet.

Sub-Alpine Zone. The highest zone with trees; elevations range between 5,000 and 7,000 feet.

Alpine Zone. Most terrain lying above the timberline is included in this zone, which exists largely near the summits of the Cascade and Olympic Mountains.

Yellow Pine Forest Zone. This zone, found in eastern Washington, covers nearly one-quarter of the state at elevations of 1,800-3,200 feet.

Bunchgrass Zone. Found in those areas of eastern Washington that are slightly more arid than the Yellow Pine Zone. Trees are found only on streambanks, and in draws sheltered from the hot summer sun.

Sagebrush Zone. The driest desert country in the state. Stunted trees grow adjacent to the few springs and scattered watercourses located here.

The interpretive center also features living displays that contain representative samples of the plant life found in five of the seven zones. For physiological reasons, the two dry, inland biotic zones – the Bunchgrass and the Sagebrush – are not maintained as living displays. Instead, they are shown pictorially, completing the study in natural contrasts.

Trails

Fred Cleator Interpretive Trails. The nature trails within the park were developed as a memorial to conservationist and forester Fred W. Cleator. Working with the Washington State Federation of Women's Clubs, Mr. Cleator was instrumental in the acquisition and preservation of this natural wilderness site. Two separate trails have been established. The 2.7-mile *East Trail* winds past at least three distinctly different forest communities. These occupy an ancient river terrace several feet above the present channel of White River. The .9-mile *West Trail* affords glimpses of at least five different forest communities; it, too, follows the ancient river terrace. These paths have been carefully projected through the forest, in a way that disturbs only the surface layer directly beneath them. The areas to either side are almost entirely as nature has dictated. Human influences are confined largely to marks left by early pioneers around the middle of the last century. Federation Forest is located in a transition area between the Coast Forest Zone and the Mountain Forest Zone. Nature trail guidebooks are available at the interpretive center.

Naches Trail. One of the first pioneer trails between eastern Washington and the Puget Sound country, this passes through Federation Forest State Park. Westward migration prompted the establishment of this route between Fort Walla Walla and Fort Steilacoom. Work on the trail began in 1853; the first wagon train to reach Fort Steilacoom was the famous Longmire party, arriving in October of that year. The Naches Trail fell into disuse after 1884, with the opening of lower and easier passes across the Cascade Range. Part of the West Trail follows this pioneer road, whose existence is still visible today.

For information, contact: Ranger, Federation Forest State Park, Star Route, Enumclaw, WA 98022, ☎ (360) 902-8563.

Flaming Geyser Recreation Area

Location: Green River Gorge State Park Conservation Area, 6 miles south of Black Diamond and 12 miles north of Enumclaw on State Highway 169.

The two "geysers" that give this park its unusual name are actually old test holes. The lower, or Flaming Geyser, was a test hole for coal; it burns at a height of about six inches. The upper, or Bubbling Geyser, was for gas exploration, and is located in a spring. It produces methane gas and various minerals that cause the grey coloration of the creek bed.

Activities popular at Flaming Geyser include picnicking, cavorting in a specially designated play area, swimming, kayaking, canoeing, rafting, inner tubing and fishing.

The conservation area protects a unique 12-mile corridor of the Green River. The unspoiled, wild environment that prevails throughout the park is its principal attraction.

Nolte State Recreation Area, the third park in the Green River Gorge, is open April 15-October 15. Nolte is located in Deep Lake; it has a guarded swimming beach. Other activities here include fishing, a 1.4-mile walking/jogging trail around the lake, and a quarter-mile interpretive trail.

Facilities: Flaming Geyser Recreation Area is a day-use facility for picnicking and water activities. Groups up to 200 may reserve picnic areas. For reservations, contact the park manager at ☎ (206) 931-3930. Campers can stay at Kanaskat-Palmer Recreation Area, also a part of the Green River Gorge State Park. This site is located 11 miles northeast of Enumclaw and Highway 410, via Farman Road. There are 50 sites, 19 of which have electrical hookups.

For further information, contact: Flaming Geyser Recreation Area, 23700 SE Flaming Geyser Road, Auburn, WA 98002, or call the statewide information number, ☎ (800) 233-0321.

Fort Canby State Park

*Location: 2 miles southeast of Ilwaco off Highway 101,
where the Columbia River meets the Pacific Ocean.*

History

Although dedicated as a state park in 1957, this area's recorded history begins years earlier. In 1788, English explorer Captain John Meares, busy looking for the Columbia River, recorded missing the passage over the bar. In his discouragement, he named the nearby headland Cape Disappointment. In 1792, American Captain Robert Gray successfully crossed the river bar. He named the river after his ship, the *Columbia Rediviva*.

Next came the Lewis and Clark Expedition. Hoping to secure America's claim to the area and find overland trade routes, they arrived at Cape Disappointment in November, 1805. Clark wrote in his journal, "Men appear much satisfied with their trip, beholding with astonishment the high waves dashing against the rock and this emence Ocean."

This area's high waves and treacherous river bar prompted seamen to brand this the "Graveyard of the Pacific." Hundreds of ships (and many more lives) have been lost here. The Cape Disappointment Lighthouse began operating in 1856, and is now the oldest lighthouse still in use on the west coast. (The lighthouse at North Head was built in 1898.) Today, buoys, jetties and constant dredging make the bar less dangerous than it was during the last century.

To protect the mouth of the river from enemies, the cape was armed in 1862 with smooth-bore cannons. It was named Fort Canby in 1875, to honor General Edward Canby, who was killed in the Modoc Indian War. The fort was continually expanded and improved until the end of World War II.

At that time, the fort was deactivated; it was not used again until it became a state park. Today, you can explore the sites of these historic events and enjoy the spectacular beauty where the river meets the ocean.

Activities

Four trails of varying lengths offer ample opportunities to explore this 1,700-acre park's forests and headlands. The jetty road follows the north jetty to a parking area near Benson Beach. A gentle path leads to a platform on top of the jetty; this offers views of the lighthouse, the river and sea. The Long Beach Peninsula stretches north from the park. Here, you may collect driftwood or glass balls, fish in the surf, dig for clams, or simply enjoy the beauty of the beach.

Summer is the busiest season at Fort Canby. The weather is mild, with cool ocean breezes. Excellent salmon fishing attracts numerous visitors to the area. Various interpretive programs are offered by the park staff during the summer season. The fall weather is often beautiful here, with warm, dry days and cool nights. During this season, nighttime clam tides begin.

Winter is a special time at Fort Canby. The weather is cool, but temperatures seldom get below freezing. Storms bring waves crashing against the rocks. Afterwards, glass "floats" are occasionally found on the beaches. Spring brings low daytime tides, which are ideal for digging clams. Many migrating birds may be spotted overhead during this time.

Lewis and Clark Interpretive Center

All the excitement and adventure of the Lewis and Clark Expedition is here, as well as portrayals of its many scientific and social contributions. But there is something more. The presentations in this center are designed to make the members of the expedition seem more real, more approachable.

Some exhibits outline medical treatments, food, entertainment, and means of discipline. Others give brief sketches of the expedition's primary members. Still others focus on the important contributions made by many Indian tribes to the expedition. A multi-media center presents brief programs highlighting various aspects of the journey. Additional displays depict events on Cape Disappointment after Lewis and Clark, ranging from shipwrecks and the advent of lighthouses to the importance of the lifesaving station and the development of Fort Canby.

The center is open seven days a week during the summer. During the winter it is open on weekends only, by appointment.

Flora & Fauna

Coastal Forest Trail. This trail was conceived to give you the "experience" of a virgin forest. With the exception of the steep ascent at the beginning, this trail is a relatively easy hike. The short loop is is a half-mile; the long loop is 1½ miles.

The Sitka spruce-western hemlock forest represents the "climax," or final evolutionary stage, of this coastal landscape. Some of the larger spruce trees are 300-500 years old. This forest has remained basically unchanged by man, and many of these trees were actually in their prime during Lewis and Clark's 1805 visit.

Facilities: 250 campsites, all with stove and table; 60 of the sites have water, sewer, and electrical hookups. Restrooms have hot showers and are handicapped-accessible. Fifty picnic sites are located in the park, and a trailer dumping station is located near the campground entrance. Baker Bay has a two-ramp boat launch and ample parking. A concession store near the park entrance sells fishing and camping supplies, groceries, and souvenirs.

For further information, contact: Fort Canby State Park, PO Box 488, Ilwaco, WA 98624, ☎ (360) 642-3078.

Fort Casey State Park

Location: Whidbey Island, 3 miles south of Coupeville next to the Keystone Ferry terminal.

History

Fort Casey is one of the coast artillery posts established during the late 1890s for the defense of Puget Sound. Together with the heavy batteries of Fort Worden and Fort Flagler, its guns guarded the entrance to Admiralty Inlet (the only route to Puget Sound navigable by warships at that time). Together, the three forts formed a "triangle of fire," a key part of the fortification system designed to prevent a hostile fleet from reaching such prime targets as the Bremerton Navy Yard and the cities of Seattle, Tacoma, Olympia and Everett. Mounting of the guns in the batteries was completed by January 26, 1900. The first test firing was performed on September 11, 1901.

During World War I, Fort Casey was used for training activities. After the war, the army entered a period of austerity and the fort was placed in caretaker status. A salvage program was started to make ends meet. All arms were scrapped and melted down between 1922 and 1945.

World War II brought the reactivation of Fort Casey as a training center. In 1950, the fort was placed in caretaker status yet again, with the General Services Administration offering it for sale six years later. It was at that time that the Washington State Parks system acquired Fort Casey.

Admiralty Head was recommended early on as a suitable site for a lighthouse. In 1858, the United States purchased this spot (plus 10 acres) from Mr. and Mrs. John C. Kellogg for the princely sum of $400. The lighthouse was fortified in 1890; however, its active life ended in 1920. The lantern was removed in 1927 and reinstalled atop the New Dungeness Lighthouse. When the Washington State Parks acquired the land, it converted the lighthouse into an interpretive center. It now contains displays related to Fort Casey's history.

Fort Casey State Park — Heritage Area

This area features a self-guided walking tour with the following special attractions:

Battery Worth. A building with oil storage rooms, a tool room and shell and powder rooms, as well as displays of 10" guns on disappearing carriages.

Battery Moore. The 2" pipes in the walls here were "speaking tubes," used by crew members to communicate with each other.

Battery Commander's Station. These towers provided a secure station for the battery commander, who oversaw the operation of his guns and insured the proper target was engaged.

Battery Kingsbury. A battery building for the 10" guns, this was later modified to hold the dual anti-aircraft guns.

Battery Valleau. This structure contained four 6" rifles on disappearing carriages. A bulge on the top of the wall housed a deflecting shield for muzzle blasts.

Battery Trevor. This building housed 3" guns designed for close-range defense.

Switchboard Room. This underground structure was built as a bomb-proof communications center.

Primary Observing Stations. These were located on the hill behind the main line of batteries. Sightings were phoned from here to the plotting room; adjustments for weather, temperature, tide, etc. were also deter mined here and sent to the plotting room. In addition, range setting was plotted here and then sent to the guns. The highest structure is the Fire Commander's Station. The fire commander would identify the targets and then direct the fire of batteries Kingsbury, Valleau and Trevor.

Fort Columbia – a Washington State Parks Heritage Site

The reservation at Chinook Point where Fort Columbia is now located was purchased in 1867, but it wasn't until 1895 that the War Department decided to install defensive weapons. The plans called for mining the river entrance and for the erection of long-contemplated gun batteries. An intensive construction program was carried out during the period 1896-1904. This program included Forts Canby and Stevens. The post was first occupied by a regular garrison in June of 1904; these were troops of the 33rd Company, Coast Artillery Corps. During the years that Fort Columbia served as a coastal defense unit – including the period during the two world wars – it never fired a shot in anger. A half-mile historical walk here takes you to some of the fort's more interesting installations. Set aside 40 minutes to complete the route.

The former *Enlisted Men's Barracks* is now used to tell the "Coast Artillery Story." Much of the building has been restored to its original 1902 appearance. Interpretive displays depicting how the men lived and worked are arranged throughout the building.

The former *Commandant's Quarters* now houses a museum sponsored by the local chapter of the Daughters of the American Revolution. The furnishings here reflect a period when the fort was an active military post.

Through an agreement with the Washington State Parks and Recreation Commission, the Art Center Corporation operates an art gallery in the former Administration Building. The work of local artists is featured.

The former *Coast Artillery Hospital* is now operated as an AYH-approved youth hostel. For a nominal fee, traveling members are given a place to wash, cook, sleep, and make friends. Hosteling promotes education through travel, physical fitness by doing, and self-reliance through "under your own steam" trips.

There is an interesting trail on Scarboro Hill. It is fairly steep for the first 800 feet. You will see the site of the Post Surgeon's Quarters, the observation stations, several searchlight buildings, and barbed wire – all of which were part of the fort's defenses. Pick up a map in the park.

Facilities: 35 basic campsites, modern restrooms and hot showers, two miles of beach, a scuba diver's restroom with hot showers, a saltwater boat launch, picnic area and an interpretive center.

For further information, contact: Fort Casey State Park, 1280 South Fort Casey Road, Coupeville, WA 98239, ☎ (360) 678-4519.

Fort Ebey State Park

Location: Whidbey Island, 8 miles south of Oak Harbor off Highway 20 on Valley Drive.

Visitors can reach Whidbey Island by state ferry from either Port Townsend or Mukilteo, or by highway from Mt. Vernon. Situated on 226 acres in the rain shadow of the Olympic Mountains, the park receives an unusually light amount of rainfall.

Fort Ebey was originally established as a coast artillery fort in 1942, to supplement the coastal artillery at Forts Casey, Flagler and Wordon – all of which are currently Washington state parks. The military declared the fort surplus property soon after World War II, and donated the property to the state in 1968. Fort Ebey was developed in 1980, and the park opened to the public in February, 1981.

The park features a variety of habitats. Old-growth fir trees hundreds of years old stand next to second-growth regenerated areas, while a marine environment thrives in Admiralty Inlet. In addition, because of the rain shadow effect, Fort Ebey in one of the few places in western Washington where several varieties of cactus can be found. A wide variety of wildlife can be seen here, including bald eagles, deer, geese, ducks, raccoons, rabbits, pheasants and grouse.

Activities popular here include hiking, beachcombing and fishing in Lake Pondilla, where the bass are reportedly exceptional. Nearby attractions include historic Port Townsend, which is accessible by the Keystone ferry south of the park. This town is famous for its Victorian homes and quaint shops. By traveling north, tourists can ride the Anacortes ferry through the scenic San Juan Islands to Canada's Vancouver Island.

Two miles of hiking trails and three miles of Puget Sound beach are available to hikers. The park is open from 6:30 a.m.-10 p.m., April 1 through October 15; and from 8 a.m.-5 p.m., October 16 through March 31.

Facilities: 50 non-hookup campsites with tables and stoves, 35 picnic sites, and modern restrooms with hot showers.

For further information, contact: Fort Ebey State Park, 395 North Fort Ebey Road, Coupeville, WA 98239, ☎ (360) 678-4636.

Fort Flagler State Park

Location: North end of Marrowstone Island, across the bay from Port Townsend.

This 783-acre park is on the National Register of Historical Places. Nestled in the "rain shadow" of the Olympic Mountains, Fort Flagler is also surrounded on three sides by saltwater. The park enjoys beautiful weather most of the year, with an annual rainfall of less than 17 inches.

History

Fort Flagler – together with the heavy batteries of Fort Wordon and Fort Casey – guarded the entrance to Puget Sound. These posts were established in the late 1890s; as mentioned earlier, they later became the first line of a fortification system designed to protect the Bremerton Navy Yard and the cities of Seattle, Tacoma, Olympia and Everett.

Construction of the fort began in 1897. By 1900, the initial armament installation had been completed, along with barracks for the Third Artillery Unit. Final construction was completed in 1907.

Fort Flagler was placed on caretaker status in 1937, after which many of the original buildings were removed. In 1940, 24 new buildings were constructed here. Men from the Harbor Defense of the Puget Sound – including the 14th and 248th Coast Artillery Regiments – moved in until 1943. Between 1945-1954, the fort was used for training engineers and amphibious military units. It was closed in 1953, and purchased as a state park in 1955.

Fort Flagler Environmental Learning Center

Given its historical significance, its forested areas and its saltwater beaches, Fort Flagler boasts a multitude of venues just waiting to be explored. The fort features one of the 10 environmental learning centers within the Washington Park System. It is located approximately 20 miles southeast of Port Townsend on Marrowstone Island.

Here, the military theme carries over into barracks-style living units. Facilities included in the main camp are a dining hall/kitchen, three barracks with restrooms and showers, and an administration building with campfire circles. There is also a BOQ (Bachelor Officer Quarters) with a kitchen-dining area, sleeping facilities and restrooms. In addition, two recently renovated buildings have been opened; Buildings 101 and 102 come complete with small kitchens, restroom facilities, and bunks. The maximum capacities are: BOQ, 54; 101 and 102, 25; Main Camp, 180. Additional staff quarters may be available upon request.

The possibilities for natural history studies here are endless, and extremely varied. Besides the usual opportunities for plant and animal study, there are sandy beaches to explore.

The tidepools – with their many marine species – provide a new learning experience for most students. Another attraction near the fort is Marrowstone Field Station, a research facility of the Bureau of Sport Fisheries and Wildlife that is located on Marrowstone Point. Tours of the facility are available upon request.

Visitors to this park enjoy camping, picnicking, boating, beachcombing, hiking, scuba diving, bottom and salmon fishing, clamming and crabbing. They might see deer, foxes, coyotes, rabbits, squirrels, raccoons, crows, bald eagles or migratory waterfowl.

Facilities: 116 non-hookup standard campsites, 40 picnic sites with stoves and tables, modern restrooms with hot showers, trailer dumping station. The day-use area has two boat launches, dock and moorage facilities, and food and grocery concessions. Other facilities include a kitchen shelter and a group area for 30 people, a wagonwheel-type campsite for 30 units, and an environmental learning center that can accommodate 270 people. These are all available on a reservation basis only.

For more information, contact: Fort Flagler, c/o Dept. of Parks & Recreation, PO Box 42650, Olympia, WA 98504-2650, ☎ (360) 385-1259. For ferry information, ☎ (800) 542-0810. Group rates are available for 10 or more individuals.

Fort Simcoe Historical State Park

Location: Western end of State Highway 220, west of Toppenish.

Comprised of 200 acres, Fort Simcoe Historical State Park was established in 1953 with the assistance of the Fort Simcoe At Mool-Mool Restoration Society. The park is administered by the Washington State Parks and Recreation Commission under a 99-year lease from the Yakima Indian Nation. A brick museum contains displays of Indian craftwork and other exhibits depicting the history of Fort Simcoe and vicinity.

History

Fort Simcoe served as the advance post of the Ninth Regiment, United States Infantry from 1856-59. After that, it became an Indian agency and school.

It is important to note that the fort occupies an ancient tribal gathering place on the Yakima Indian Reservation. This pleasant site, a spring-fed natural oak grove at the head of Simcoe Valley (where the Toppenish plain meets the foothills of the Cascade Range) was known widely as Mool-Mool (Bubbling Water) for its especially active spring. Its strategic location at the intersection of the main trails is what dictated its selection by the military.

Of the military structures that framed the 420-foot parade ground, five remain: the commanding officer's handsome house, three trim dwellings that were captain's quarters, and a squared-log block-house on a slight elevation at the southwest approach.

Most of the buildings erected for agency and school use (including children's dormitories, employee dwellings and workshops, lieu-tenants' and servants' quarters, a storehouse, hospital, and saw-mill) have been razed either by accident or design.

Some of those associated with the history of the fort are: Chief Kamiakin, Yakima war chieftain; Louis School, the architect; Rev-erend James H. Wilbur, local missionary; and Colonel George Wright, who chose the location for Fort Simcoe. These are just a few of the people profiled at the Fort Simcoe State Parks Heritage Site.

The park is open daily, year-round.

Facilities: picnicking facilities with piped water, stoves, tables, and benches are available in a grassy portion of the park's extensive oak grove. There is a spacious parking area.

For further information, contact: Park Office, ☎ (509) 874-2372, or Washington State Department of Parks and Recreation, 7150 Cleanwater Lane, PO Box 42650, Olympia, WA 98504-2650, ☎ (800) 233-0321 (nationwide).

Fort Ward State Park

Location: Bainbridge Island, along Rich Passage,
6 miles southwest of Highway 305 on Pleasant Beach Road.

Covering 137 acres of dense forest and underbrush, Fort Ward State Park is an area full of natural beauty. Impressive views of Rich Passage, the Olympic Mountains, and varied marine wildlife can be seen at the park. Common activities here include: boating, fishing, picnicking, jogging and bicycling. Clam digging, bird watching, and scuba diving are other favorite pursuits.

Fort Ward, originally known as Bean Point from 1890-1903, was named in honor of Colonel George H. Ward, 15th Massachusetts Volunteer Infantry. Colonel Ward died of wounds during the battle of Gettysburg on July 2, 1863. Fort Ward was formally designated a seacoast fort in 1903, and was staffed by the 150th Coast Artillery Corps. As a coastal fortification, its primary objective was to protect the Bremerton Naval Shipyard. After a short time, Fort Ward was placed on inactive status and essentially abandoned.

The fort remained deserted until 1935, when the state used it as a children's camp. During World War II, a submarine net was installed across Rich Passage, as were a radio station and training school for naval communication personnel. Radio towers capable of breaking enemy codes were built within the fort. In 1958, the US Army deactivated the site. The Washington State Parks and Recreation Commission purchased Fort Ward in 1960.

Fort Ward is a satellite of Fay-Bainbridge State Park, located approximately 12 miles northeast. Visitor services are available in Winslow or Poulsbo. Both towns have various community events throughout the summer months.

Facilities: Fort Ward State Park has two boat ramps, a parking lot with 25 spaces for cars and boat trailers, two vault toilets, and two mooring buoys. There are two picnic areas in the park. The lower area is situated along the beach. Accessible by foot only, it has eight picnic sites. The upper picnic area is accessible by automobile and has eight picnic sites. Each venue has vault toilets as well as potable water. The upper and lower picnic areas are open from April 15 to September 15.

For further information, contact: Fort Ward State Park – Satellite to Fay-Bainbridge State Park, 15446 Sunrise Drive NE, Bainbridge Island, WA 98110, ☎ (206) 842-3931.

Fort Worden State Park

Location: Near Port Townsend on Point Wilson, a part of the Olympic Peninsula about 50 miles from both Seattle and Tacoma.

Relax on a ferry or drive along beautiful Hood Canal. Only 50 miles from downtown Seattle, a jewel beckons on the Olympic Peninsula. The Fort Worden experience will make you glad you left the city. Don't worry about the weather – with an annual rainfall of only 19 inches, you have an excellent chance of leaving the Pacific Northwest clouds behind you.

Fort Worden State Park is accessible either by auto or ferry. In the park is a collection of Victorian houses and barracks, as well as a theater, a school, and a balloon hangar. There are also parade grounds and elaborate hidden bunkers from which no shots were ever fired in combat.

History

Fort Worden is located on Point Wilson, an area which was discovered in 1792 by Captain George Vancouver. The first fort here, Fort Wilson, was built in 1855 to protect the settlement of Port Townsend from the Indians. It was abandoned in 1856 when the hostilities with the Indians ended. Fort Wilson was renamed Fort Worden in 1900 to honor Admiral John L. Worden. The admiral commanded the ironclad battleship *Monitor* in the famous civil war battle with the Confederate ship *Merrimac*. He later became superintendent of the US Naval Academy. As an interesting aside, Fort Worden is the only army fort to be named after a navy man.

Fort Casey, Fort Flagler, and Fort Worden were built between 1897 and 1911; together, they formed the first line of defense guarding the Puget Sound cities and the naval shipyard at Bremerton. At the time they were built, these forts featured the most modern weapons ever designed; Fort Worden's giant cannons became obsolete with the advent of more sophisticated weapons. After the army left in 1953, the fort was used as a juvenile treatment center.

Fort Worden became a state park in 1972. Since that time, the Washington State Parks and Recreation Commission has made the fort's buildings available as conference facilities and vacation housing.

Historic Buildings and Sites

Commanding Officer's House. The Commanding Officer's House, Building #1, was completed in 1904. Thirty-three different families resided here. The 2½-story house is one of Fort Worden's finest structures. Special features include the house's cross-gabled slate roof, as well as its fancy chimneys and decorated boxed cornices. It also features fireplaces in the living room, dining room and study; and built-in dining room cabinets with leaded glass doors. The dwelling also has 10-foot pressed ceilings and a brass chandelier in the dining room. The east portion of the veranda opens onto an excellent view of Admiralty Inlet.

Each room is furnished in a different style; all of them are representative of the Victorian period. The front hall features a portrait of John L. Worden, the fort's namesake, while the living room sports coal fireplaces decorated with Belgian tiles, and furnishings dating 1889-1891. The dining room showcases handcarved black oak furniture and Maddock English China; in the study, visitors are treated to a portrait of the house's first occupant, Colonel Grimes, as well as an oak roll-top desk. There's a 1915 Montgomery Ward washing machine in the kitchen, while the simple servants' quarters feature a quilt started in 1912 and never finished. A child's room is home to a c. 1900 French china-head doll; Italian marble sinks dominate the bathrooms. In the guest room, you will see a very old "moss" rug made from scraps of silk underwear. The Master Bedroom boasts a black walnut carved headboard and dresser, both of which date to 1875. In the hall and the airing closet are examples of clothing that include a French nightgown, an eighth grade graduation dress, and a silk christening dress.

Rothschild House. Built in 1868 for D.C.H. Rothschild, a prominent Port Townsend merchant, the Rothschild House has been restored through the efforts of local citizens, the Jefferson County Historical Society and the Washington State Parks and Recreation Commission. The most noticeable alteration has been the removal of two dormer windows on the roof. The parlor and hall still have the original wall and ceiling paper, while the original carpeting still graces the guest bedroom and both the upstairs and downstairs halls. The herb garden, a source of many seasonings for the kitchen, has also been restored. The flower garden features many old varieties of peonies, roses and lilacs acquired throughout the United States.

Fort Worden Historic Walk ·

This self-guided walk offers an introduction to the history of Fort Worden and some of its more important buildings. It is a one-mile loop trail that takes approximately 30 minutes to walk. Coast Artillery insignias painted on the sidewalks indicate where the trail goes, and when to read the numbered paragraphs in the official trail pamphlet.

You will encounter the following buildings on your tour: #200 Headquarters Building (1908), #225 Headquarters Battery Barracks (1908), #223 Original Post Headquarters (1904), Alexander's Castle (1880s), #298 Hospital (1904), #313 Workshop (1905), #315 Power House (1907), #310 Post Exchange and Gymnasium (1908), #205 Band Barracks (1904), #305 Quartermaster's Office and Warehouse (1905), #204 Barracks (1904), #300 Guard House (1904), #25 Theater

(1932), #26 Balloon Hanger (1921), #24 Chapel (1941), Officer's Row (1904-1905), Grounds Maintenance, and Parade Grounds.

Marine Science Center

Housed in an historic building on the dock at Fort Worden, this center has large, open "wet tables" where local sea creatures can be viewed at close range and even handled. Meet starfish, sea cucumbers, tube worms, anemones, sand dollars, snails, nudibranchs, and many more. Glass tanks housing live octopus, fish and crabs complete the peek into the fascinating underwater world of Puget Sound. The Marine Center is bordered by both sandy and rocky beaches at the intersection of the Straits of Juan de Fuca and Puget Sound. The combination of strong currents and clean cold water results in an area rich with marine life.

Marine Center activities include beach walks; classes in marine ecology for children and adults; fish printing sessions; seaweed workshops; evening slide shows, films and lectures; a resource center for teachers; and marine programs in the schools.

Accommodations

Fort Worden has facilities that serve a variety of interests. Lodging for families or small groups is available in stately Victorian houses once used as officers' quarters. Group accommodations in spacious dormitories often include meals, prepared and served cafeteria style in the dining hall. Meeting rooms for groups of 10-300 are located in the park grounds. A full hookup camping area with 50 sites is situated near the beach. A canteen in the dining hall serves snacks during the day, and a PX across from the wharf provides groceries, snacks and fishing gear, along with other recreational items.

Advance reservations are necessary for any of Fort Worden's accommodations, including the campground. The park office in building 200 furnishes more specific information about housing and programs. Mail may also be posted there.

Conference Center

Fort Worden State Park is an ideal setting for business seminars, professional conferences, corporate or agency planning sessions, church retreats, and family reunions. The park's location is free from urban distractions and interruptions. Elegant Victorian parlors, spacious, carpeted dormitories, and 50 full hookup campsites can meet the needs of just about any size conference group. A wide selection of meeting rooms can accommodate groups as small as 10 or as large as 300. The fort's dining facilities are open year-round.

Conferences at Fort Worden can be held in a wide variety of settings, ranging from classrooms to firesides. All facilities are well lit and well ventilated. Seating is comfortable, and conducive to good concentration. Most of the facilities can accommodate state-of-the-art visual presentations. There is also a 350-seat auditorium that hosts jazz sessions, theater, and a variety of evening entertainment during the summer.

When a conference is scheduled, facilities are selected with the group's particular needs in mind. The Fort Worden staff is committed to insuring that each group's individual requirements are satisfied.

Many types of accommodations are offered. These include Victorian homes with three to six bedrooms and fully equipped kitchens, as well as fireplaces in the living rooms, dining rooms and some bedrooms. (However, there are no televisions, and telephone service is limited.)

For individuals who prefer a simpler style, the original barracks have been remodeled to resemble a college dormitory. The dining facilities seat up to 400 in cafeteria style, although private banquet rooms are available and box lunches may be requested. The fort also offers a Pacific Northwest beach barbecue. Alcoholic beverages are available by previous arrangement for banquets and dinners. Coffee and tea are served throughout the day, and coffee breaks can include refreshments from the bakery. A seafood bar supplies snacks on the beach; there is also a store that offers groceries, fishing gear and sundries.

Activities & Facilities

Visitors to this park may indulge in a number of recreational activities, including beachcombing, boating, swimming, skin/scuba diving, water-skiing, tennis, hiking, fishing and photography. There are many trails in the park, including a 30-minute, self-guided historic walk. Tennis courts and outdoor playfields are located within the grounds. Guests should bring their own equipment to use these facilities. The park has a boat launch, dock and mooring buoys. Use of these is free, although moorage is limited to 36 hours. The waters off Point Wilson are legendary among Northwest fishermen. Visitors can embark on many water activities from the Fort Worden pier; boat-launch facilities and mooring are provided free of charge. Several excellent golf courses are located near the grounds, and the Olympic Mountains 30 miles away offer additional opportunities. Port Townsend is only a 10-minute walk from the park. This town features quaint shops and galleries perfect for browsing. Historic Port Townsend is a popular spot for boating, antique hunting and touring Victorian architecture.

Many cultural programs are presented by the Centrum Foundation. Evenings can be filled with musical/drama events and several varieties of musical presentations. The summer session includes more than 70 major performing events. They are held in the newly refurbished Fort Worden Theater, as well as under the "big top" at the historic mule barn complex. Artists of all types gather at Worden to share their talents in activities sponsored by the Washington State Arts Commission. Besides visitors seeking recreation, there are people studying art, poetry, music, dance, crafts and more. Thus, the fort has been transformed from a center of destructive power into a place that nurtures creative energies.

For further information, contact: Fort Worden State Park, PO Box 574, Port Townsend, WA 98368, ☎ (360) 385-5582.

Goldendale Observatory State Park

Location: 1 mile north of Goldendale, Washington.

Goldendale Observatory State Park Interpretive Center houses the nation's largest public telescope. Situated on a wooded hilltop, the park offers majestic views of Oregon's Mt. Hood and Washington's Mt. Adams and Mt. St. Helens. However, the most outstanding views are those of the moon, the planets, the stars and galaxies, as seen through the park's main attraction – a 24½" reflecting telescope. This telescope is enjoyed by casual visitors interested in learning more about celestial bodies as well as amateur astronomers conducting special projects.

Individual visitors and groups up to 50 are welcome, although group tours should be arranged in advance. Slide shows, exhibits, films, and telescope use are offered. There are also lectures on various celestial phenomena and related scientific demonstrations.

Observatory staff are available for speaking engagements by request.

Not surprisingly, this observatory is a gathering place for amateur astronomers throughout the Pacific Northwest. After 11 p.m., amateur star-gazers may reserve the facility for their own special programs. (There is a small fee charged for those staying overnight.) Accommodations consist of an all-purpose room, restrooms, and a small kitchenette with a stove and refrigerator. Additional overnight accommodations are available at the Brooks Memorial Environmental Learning Center.

The Goldendale Observatory is the result of the dreams and efforts of four Vancouver, Washington men – M.W. McConnell, O.W. VanderVelden, John Marshall and Don Connor. The four began constructing the reflecting Cassegrain telescope for Clark College in Vancouver. However, they later agreed to erect it on a hilltop above the town of Goldendale, where city lights and cloudy skies would not interfere with viewing.

Funds for the modern building and the dome housing the telescope were provided both by a federal grant and the city of Goldendale. The facility was dedicated and opened on October 13, 1973. From 1973 through 1980, a volunteer, non-profit organization – The Goldendale Observatory Corporation – successfully operated the facility. The observatory was acquired by the Washington State Parks and Recreation Commission in 1980.

Goldendale Observatory was a major focal point during the 1979 eclipse. Designated the National Astronomical League's official headquarters for eclipse observation, the observatory was swamped by thousands of scientists, students, tour groups, and other individuals interested in glimpsing this important astronomical event.

The best time to view celestial objects is when the moon is least bright. This is usually the period around a new moon, or when the moon sets early or rises late. The sky is darkest during these times, making viewing easier.

Facilities: 24½" reflecting telescope (the nation's largest public telescope); an eight-inch, dome-mounted Celestron telescope; six portable telescopes, including two Richfield telescopes; special camera accessories; science library. Overnight accommodations are available at Brooks Memorial State Park.

For further information, contact: Goldendale Observatory State Park, Route 3, Box 68, Goldendale, WA 98620, ☎ (360) 902-8563.

Grayland Beach State Park

Location: 28 miles southwest of Aberdeen and south of the towns of Grayland and Westport, on State Route 105.

Grayland Beach State Park was acquired in five separate parcels, beginning in 1959. Today, the park consists of 200 acres, including almost 4,000 feet of Pacific Ocean frontage.

Grayland received its name from Captain Robert Gray, an American fur trader who first discovered nearby Grays Harbor and the Columbia River in 1792. He originally named the harbor "Bullfinch," in honor of his ship's owner. However, Lieutenant Joseph Whidbey renamed the area Gray's Harbor soon afterwards. Whidbey's charts were subsequently published and thus, the new name became official.

Activities in this area are numerous. Fishing from the jetty near Westhaven State Park (north of Grayland) often yields salmon, rockfish, surf perch, ling and crab. Surf fishing along the entire stretch of beach is also popular. Charter salmon fishing is available in nearby Westport, "Salmon Capitol of the World." Trips leave daily from the dock area. Clam digging is seasonal here and a license is required. History buffs are invited to tour the 1898 lighthouse at Westport Light Beach Approach. Appointments may be made through the Coast Guard station in Westport.

The park features a self-guided nature trail that describes local flora and fauna. Among the plants found here are evergreens, huckleberries, Sitka spruce, lodgepole (shore) pines, and kinnikinnick. Wildlife here includes rabbits, raccoons, deer, blue herons, ducks, pheasants and even an occasional bear.

Facilities: 60 full hookup campsites, modern restrooms and hot showers.

For further information, contact: Grayland Beach State Park, c/o Twin Harbors State Park, Westport, WA 98595, ☎ (360) 268-9717.

Horsethief Lake State Park

Location: 2 miles east of US 197 on State Road 14, 33 miles west of Goldendale.

Horsethief Lake State Park encompasses nearly 340 acres and boasts 7,500 feet of freshwater shoreline on the Columbia River. The park was built by the Army Corps of Engineers after the completion of the Dalles Dam in 1964. It is a satellite of Maryhill State Park, located 21 miles east on US 97 at Sam Hill Bridge. The park was included in the National Historical Register in 1972.

This area, formerly known as Colewash Bottom and Spedis Valley, was inhabited by Indians for centuries. The tribes who lived here fished with coastal and plains Indians. During their 1805 expedition, Lewis and Clark came upon the Wishram Indian village of Nixluidix. This consisted of 21 large wooden houses that had formed a permanent village for over a thousand years. Today, backwaters of the Dalles Dam cover most of this village's historical remains. (Colewash Bottom is now a 90-acre lake.) Yet Indian rock art can still be seen when walking west from the park entrance.

Fishing, hiking, rock climbing, swimming and picnicking are among the many recreational opportunities available here today.

Facilities: 12 standard campsites, each with table and stove. The day-use area consists of six acres of lawn with picnic tables. Also available are a swimming beach, comfort station, trailer dumping station, hiking trails and boat launches to both the river and lake.

For further information, contact: Horsethief Lake State Park, Route 677, Box 27-A, Goldendale, WA 98620, ☎ (509) 767-1159.

Ike Kinswa State Park

Location: Southeast of Chehalis, 20 miles east of the junction of I-5 and US Highway 12, on the north side of Mayfield Lake.

Located on Mayfield Lake, Ike Kinswa State Park boasts 46,000 feet of freshwater shoreline. The majority of this 454-acre tract was acquired by the Washington State Parks and Recreation Commission through a use permit granted by Tacoma City Light in 1973. (Its holdings were purchased from six individuals between 1963 and 1967.)

Cowlitz Indians originally resided here; they used an area above the bridge as their burial grounds. Indian remains were removed before the Mayfield Dam flooded the area; however, two graves were spared and marked for historic preservation.

This park was originally called Mayfield Lake State Park. The state legislature changed the name to "Ike Kinswa" in 1961 as an acknowledgement of the early resident and representative of the Cowlitz Indians.

The state of Washington maintains two fish hatcheries on the Cowlitz, in close proximity to the park. A salmon hatchery located near Salkum offers regular tours. There is also a trout hatchery, just outside of Mossyrock. Mossyrock Dam, situated five miles east of Mossyrock, is open for guided tours during the summer months. Among the notable features here is a hydro-vista overlooking the dam.

A number of fir snags lie within park boundaries. Eagles make these snags their homes during the winter, while ospreys move in and use the same nests in the summer. Other wildlife found in the park include deer, beaver, otter, skunk and blue heron.

Facilities: two camping areas, one with 41 full hookup sites, the other with 60 non-hookup sites for either tents or recreation vehicles. The park has modern restrooms with hot showers and a trailer dumping station. There is a play area for children, swimming beach, bathhouse, horseshoe pits, picnic area, snack bar and souvenir concession, a boat launch, and six miles of hiking trails.

For further information, contact: Ike Kinswa State Park, 873 Harmony Road, Silver Creek, WA 98585, ☎ (360) 983-3402.

Illahee State Park

Location: Kitsap County, 3 miles northeast of Bremerton, on Highway 306.

This 75-acre park, acquired by the state in seven parcels beginning in 1934, includes 1,785 feet of saltwater frontage on Port Orchard Bay. *Illahee* is an Indian word meaning "earth" or "country." A portion of the park was developed under the Civilian Conservation Corps (CCC) in the 1930s; some of this organization's structures still remain.

This area is rich in history. Bremerton was first platted in 1891. The land had been logged and was a field of stumps when William Bremer arrived from Seattle in 1888. Looking about, Bremer saw the rich timber resources of the Kitsap Peninsula and decided to settle here. Noting the bay's strategic location, he recognized its suitability as a naval station. It was due in part to this man's efforts that Bremerton was chosen as the site of a drydock – the beginning of the Puget Sound Naval Shipyard.

Two naval guns here are dedicated to the young men from Bremerton who gave their lives in World War I. The five-inch, 51-caliber mounts were taken from the *USS West Virginia* prior to World War II. (This ship later sank at Pearl Harbor.)

The Port Orchard Bay portion of the park is ideal for fishing, boating, water-skiing, swimming, clamming and crabbing. Wildlife in Illahee includes squirrels, chipmunks, raccoons and several kinds of birds, while Puget Sound marine life is visible from either the dock or the beach.

Facilities: 25 standard campsites, each with table and stove, and modern restrooms with hot showers. Two covered shelters with electrical hookups may be reserved for group picnics. Other amenities include play equipment, horseshoe pits and a ballfield. The park also features a boat launch, mooring buoys, a 354-foot dock, and a trailer dumping facility.

For further information, contact: Illahee State Park, 3540 Bahia Vista, Bremerton, WA 98310, ☎ (360) 478-6460.

Iron Horse State Park

*Location: Northern Kittitas County, along the I-90 corridor;
starting from the town of Easton and continuing 25 miles east
to Tunnel 47, about 5 miles west of Thorp.*

In 1981, the state acquired 213 miles of the Chicago, Milwaukee, St. Paul and Pacific Railroad right-of-way from Easton to the Idaho border. The westernmost 25 miles was transferred to the Washington State Parks and Recreation Commission; in 1984, the area was set aside as a year-round, non-motorized recreational trail and state park. The remaining 188 miles is managed by the Department of Natural Resources (DNR), and is open for public use by permit only. Call the DNR at (509) 925-6131 for additional information.

The John Wayne Pioneer Trail is the major attraction at Iron Horse State Park. The 25-mile trail begins in Easton, in a Douglas fir and pine forest at an elevation of 2,200 feet. It then descends 500 feet, winding through the rolling farmlands and canyons of the Upper Yakima River. The entire route is a gentle, scenic journey that takes visitors through several of the state's varied ecological zones.

The Chicago, Milwaukee, St. Paul and Pacific Railroad was constructed between 1908 and 1911, when the railroad was the fastest and most economical means of transportation. However, the company was plagued with financial problems. For a short period in the 1950s, the Union Pacific and Great Northern Railroads operated the Milwaukee line until the company could solve its financial problems. In 1980, the Milwaukee Railroad declared bankruptcy, and most of the 213 miles of right-of-way were acquired by the state of Washington.

Park visitors can access the John Wayne Pioneer Trail at both Easton and south Cle Elum. At Easton, take Exit 71 off I-90. Travel south through Easton for a quarter-mile to Iron Horse State Park; turn left on the trail and park at the Trail Head Gate. From south Cle Elum, John Wayne Pioneer Trail can be accessed east of the old depot, at a temporary parking area at the end of 7th Street. Both trailhead access areas are signed, but not developed.

Facilities: Horseback riding, wagon train and stage coach travel, trail or mountain bicycling, walking, fishing and, in the winter, cross-country skiing and sleigh riding. Picnicking is also very popular, especially when the berries, apples and pears are ripe. Overnight camping is allowed only by written permission from the ranger at Lake Easton State Park. Future development plans include public access and parking areas, picnic facilities, restrooms, ramps for loading and unloading horses, overnight facilities for horses, and upgrading of bridges and trestles.

For further information, contact: Iron Horse State Park and the John Wayne Pioneer Trail, PO Box 26, Easton, WA 98925, ☎ (360) 902-8563.

Jones Island Marine State Park

Location: Southwest of Orcas Island, with access by private boat only.

A valley between two hills on 179-acre Jones Island connects North Cove with South Cove. Most of this island is heavily wooded, rocky ground. Open bluffs rise above the surrounding sea, with a large meadow between the old orchard and the sea on the south side.

Along the two miles of hiking trails, visitors may encounter deer, raccoons and many birds. In addition, mink are often observed running across the rocky beaches.

Like many of Washington's other state parks, Jones Island is an area of high fire hazard. Visitors are urged to be especially careful during the summer months; Jones Island has been known to become so dry in August that even drinking water is depleted.

Facilities: Campsites at both the North and South coves have tables and stoves with nearby water faucets, garbage cans and toilets. Recreational attractions on this private-access island include boating, fishing, clamming, scuba diving, hiking, picnicking and camping. There is a dock and 275 feet of mooring float space in North Cove, as well as several mooring buoys in each harbor. Both coves have excellent anchorage areas.

For further information, contact: Jones Island Marine State Park, c/o Park Headquarters, PO Box 42650, Olympia, WA 98504-2650, ☎ (360) 755-9231.

Kanaskat-Palmer Recreation Area

Location: 11 miles northeast of Enumclaw and Highway 410, via Farman Road.

The Kanaskat-Palmer Recreation Area is part of the Green River Gorge State Park, which opened in July, 1982. The area is comprised of 296 acres, with one mile of the Green River flowing through it.

In addition to camping and picnicking, Kanaskat-Palmer Recreation Area is popular among rafters and kayakers who float the

Green River. There are points within the area that are specially designated for putting in or taking out boats.

Because the Green River fluctuates in depth, it is important that all boaters check with the park ranger before entering the river. A safety brochure outlining some of the dangers is available at several locations. There are also signs posted along the river bank.

When the river is high – generally in late September – boaters can begin at Kanaskat-Palmer and run the river 12 miles to Flaming Geyser, also part of the Green River Gorge State Park. This trip is for experienced boaters only.

The Green River is also popular for steelhead fishing, particularly in the winter and summer. Nature lovers will find a wide variety of plant life here.

In addition, there are lots of deer, raccoons, rabbits, chipmunks, squirrels, coyotes and an occasional elk roaming the park. Hikers will delight in several trails winding through the area.

Tips on boating and rafting on the Green River at Kanaskat-Palmer State Park:

⋄ Safety is a primary concern on any section of the river. If you are unfamiliar with whitewater techniques, you should not be boating in any of the waters of the Green River Gorge Conservation Area.

⋄ A map available at the park indicates recommended sites for launching and taking out your boat. These sites are well-marked within the park. The map also indicates the class of water in particular areas of the river. Note that the river below the middle take-out and launch site is Class IV water, and therefore unsuitable for open boats or canoes. Only expert boaters should attempt these waters.

⋄ Hazards vary with the water level. The Corps of Engineers regulates the flow of the Green River for flood control and fish enhancement purposes. As a result, the stream flows are subject to significant fluctuations. To determine current conditions, check with park staff.

The following equipment is considered minimal, whether you are kayaking, canoeing, or rafting:

⋄ Life jacket and helmet
⋄ Boat Flotation Devices
⋄ Wet suit/dry suit
⋄ Spare paddle/oars
⋄ Boat repair kit

Safety Precautions:

⋄ Boating alone or during flood conditions is very dangerous.
⋄ Use sturdy, shallow-draft boats.
⋄ Pack equipment in watertight bags and tie to boat.
⋄ Keep weight low in the boat.
⋄ Overloaded boats are dangerous.
⋄ Steer clear of overhanging branches and partially submerged obstacles.
⋄ Never get broadside to the current in fast water.
⋄ Always wear your personal flotation device while on the river.

If you tip over in turbulent water, do not fight the current. Lie on your back, feet pointed up, knees slightly bent and flow with the current. When you reach quiet water, swim ashore. Stay on the upstream side of the boat; if your boat has flotation, stay with it.

Facilities: 50 wooded campsites, 19 with electrical hookups, each with table and stove. Some of the sites can accommodate trailers and motorhomes up to 35 feet in length. Modern restrooms with hot showers are available. The group camping area includes eight campsites and two Adirondack shelters. The day-use area features 50 picnic sites, three small shelters, one large shelter, barbecue pits, fire rings and two horseshoe pits.

For further information, contact the Park Ranger, Kanaskat-Palmer State Park, 23101 Kanaskat-Cumberland Road, Palmer, WA 98051, ☎ (360) 886-0148.

Kitsap Memorial State Park

Location: Kitsap County, 6 miles north of Poulsbo, off Highway 3.

The *Kitsap* is one of the ferries that made the Lofall-South Point run from the 1950s until the opening of the Hood Canal Floating Bridge on August 12, 1961. The Washington State Ferry system again provided temporary cross-canal service after the storm of 1979, which sank the western half of the bridge.

Members of the Vinland Community Club selected this site in 1935 for the location of a community recreation area. With donations from private citizens, local clubs and businesses, they purchased the property in 1936 and began making necessary improvements. When the project became too costly, the site was deeded to Kitsap County in 1937. Further improvements – including a log hall and kitchen shelters – were the result of the Works Progress Administration's funds and labor.

The park was deeded to the state in 1949; it became Kitsap Memorial State Park. The name reflects the wishes and efforts of the original members who sought to establish the park. The 57-acre park includes 1,797 feet of saltwater frontage on Hood Canal.

Visitors are invited to walk the beach and investigate marine life exposed at low tide. Everything from starfish, crabs, barnacles and chitons to limpets, oysters and clams may be found in this fragile tidal zone. Birds such as goldfinch, flicker, crow, kingfish, great blue heron and seagull can also be spotted. Activities popular in this park include fishing, boating, hiking, clamming, scuba diving and photography.

Facilities: 43 standard (non-hookup) sites, each with table and stove; five primitive walk-in campsites; a group camping area that will accommodate 30 (available by reservation); hot showers; and a trailer dumping station. The day-use area features 66 picnic tables, barbecue braziers, two kitchen shelters, a baseball field, volleyball court, horseshoe pits and swings. The park has two mooring buoys, and there is a public boat launch four miles away at Salsbury Point.

For further information, contact: Kitsap Memorial State Park, 202 NE Park Street, Poulsbo, WA 98370, ☎ (360) 779-3205.

Kopachuck State Park

Location: Pierce County, 5 miles west of Gig Harbor off Highway 16.

The name "Kopachuck" originated from *Chinook Jargon,* the trade language of the Pacific Coastal Indians. It is actually the combination of two words, *Kopa,* meaning "at" and *Chuck,* meaning "water."

Visitors can participate in a number of activities in this park, including camping, picnicking, swimming, fishing, hiking and scuba diving.

Cutts Island, 5½ acres in size, is located a half-mile offshore of the park in Carr Inlet. Known as "Deadman's Island," this favorite landing spot for boaters is believed to have been an Indian burial ground. Many saltwater tribes buried their dead by resting them in canoes placed in the forks of trees. The island has a pit toilet and boat moorage buoys. However, there are no overnight campsites here, and the building of outdoor fires is prohibited.

Gig Harbor was discovered in 1841 by a survey party trying to find shelter during a heavy rainstorm. The harbor derives its name from the fact that this party used the captain's gig (a long boat with oars) to ride out the storm's fury. Much of the present-day activity in Gig Harbor centers around boating. A large fishing fleet, first organized in the 1880s, is still based in the harbor. The atmosphere of the town is peaceful and friendly, with over 40 inviting shops.

Kopachuck State Park is dominated by towering second-growth stands of Douglas fir. The understory is lush with sword ferns and salal. Wildlife in the park includes deer, bears, foxes, raccoons, squirrels, harbor seals and many varieties of birds, including shorebirds.

Facilities: 41 non-hookup campsites, restrooms with hot showers, a group camp area, an underwater scuba park and a day-use picnic area with picnic shelters. Some sites can accommodate recreational vehicles up to a total length of 35 feet. Moorage facilities are available and there is a public boat launch three miles from the park, near Arletta. Presto-fuel is available at the park office. No wood is to be removed from the grounds.

For further information, contact: Kopachuck State Park, 11101 56th Street NW, Gig Harbor, WA 98335, ☎ (206) 265-3606.

Lake Chelan State Park

Location: 35 miles northwest of Wenatchee, about 7 miles off Highway 97 on Lake Chelan's South Shore Drive, 9 miles from the town of Chelan.

Lake Chelan State Park consists of 127 acres, with 6,454 feet of waterfront on Lake Chelan and 1,640 feet of stream frontage on First Creek. The land was acquired in three separate parcels, with the last purchase occurring in 1968.

Formed by glaciation, Lake Chelan is 55 miles long and nearly 1,500 feet deep. It varies in width from a quarter mile to just over two miles. Although only four miles long, the Chelan River has cut a magnificent gorge through the rock cliffs on its 405-foot drop to the Columbia River. The best place to view the river is from the Old Chelan River Bridge.

You can enjoy a wide range of recreational pursuits here, including swimming, water-skiing, sunbathing, camping, fishing, hiking and scuba diving. To help visitors enjoy these activities, the park has a guarded swimming beach and boat launch facility.

Road access to this lake is limited. The ferry *Lady of the Lake* travels daily between Stehekin, at the head of the lake, and Chelan. The excursion takes a full day.

Public tours are available at Rocky Reach Dam, located on Highway 97, south of Chelan. You can tour two interpretive museums, watch salmon climb the fish ladders from a special viewing room, or picnic on the landscaped lawns. The Department of Game's fish hatchery is located four miles from Chelan. Open year-round, it affords a chance to learn about the life cycle of many area game fish.

Facilities: 144 campsites, 17 with full hookups. Hot showers are available in the five restrooms located throughout the park. The day-use area offers a playground for children, guarded swimming beach, 52 picnic sites, store, horseshoe pits and a small softball diamond. A boat launch with parking space for 28 cars and trailers – plus limited extra vehicle parking – complete the park's facilities.

For further information, contact: Lake Chelan State Park, Route 1, Box 90, Chelan, WA 98816, ☎ (509) 687-3710.

Lake Cushman State Park

Location: 7 miles northwest of Hoodsport,
between the lower foothills of the Olympic Mountains.

History

Lake Cushman was discovered in 1852 by explorer B.F. Shaw. He named it in honor of his friend Orrington Cushman, a logger better known as "Devil Cush." The area remained undeveloped until the 1880s, when iron and copper deposits were discovered in the vicinity. Although mining activity never lived up to expectations, the area was visited by miners until after World War I.

At the turn of the century, tourism was the prevalent industry here. The lake was a popular spot for fishing, hiking and hunting; in addition, two resorts were built here. By 1920, both resorts had closed, and the city of Tacoma was granted a lease to construct a dam on Lake Cushman.

When the dam was completed, it was the second-largest in the west and had increased the size of the lake tenfold (from 400 acres to 4,000).

Activities

Fishing is the traditional and favorite sport at Lake Cushman. Varieties of fish here include kokanee, sea-run cutthroat, Dolly Varden (char family), and rainbow. There are even unconfirmed reports of an occasional bass. The lake is unique in that it has the only known king salmon to reproduce in a totally freshwater environment.

Hiking is also popular in this park, and at such places as Staircase (Olympic National Park) and Mt. Ellinor. In 1978, Lake Cushman State Park made major additions to its trail system. The network now extends over four miles, offering scenery ranging from the lake's edge to deep woods. Mushroom picking has become a prevalent off-season activity here. Other activities of choice include cross-country skiing, snowshoeing and rock climbing, as well as swimming, hiking, fishing or just plain relaxing.

Park hours are 6:30 a.m.-10 p.m., April 1-October 15; and 8 a.m.-5 p.m., October 16-March 31.

Facilities: 50 non-hookup sites, 30 hookup facilities, picnic area with a kitchen shelter, boat launch and swimming beach. The park's modern restrooms are equipped with hot showers.

For further information, contact: Lake Cushman State Park, PO Box 128, Hoodsport, WA 98548, ☎ (360) 877-5491.

Lake Easton State Park

Location: Off of I-90, 16 miles east of Snoqualmie Pass summit, 1 mile west of Easton, and 15 miles west of Cle Elum.

Situated on the west and north sides of Lake Easton, this glacial valley park features 196 acres of forested land. At an elevation of 2,190 feet, it consists of fairly flat terrain. However, the nearby Washington Cascade Range – with mountains exceeding 4,000 feet – offers plenty of challenges for hikers.

Lake Easton State Park affords numerous opportunities for camping, picnicking, swimming, freshwater fishing, boating, water-skiing, hiking, snowshoeing, cross-country skiing and mushroom hunting.

Areas adjacent to the park offer additional recreational activities. These include downhill skiing at Snoqualmie Pass, snowmobiling, dog sled racing, ATV trail riding, golfing and rock hunting. Hiking, backpacking and high lake fishing are available in the surrounding Cascade Range.

Lake Easton is a 247-acre reservoir owned by the US Bureau of Reclamation. It is approximately a half-mile wide and one mile long. The average depth is between 35 and 45 feet, with a maximum depth of 85 feet at the base of the dam.

Lake Keechelus and Lake Kachess are stack-up reservoirs for maintaining and stabilizing Lake Easton. Lake Easton Reservoir is used for irrigation purposes; its canals serve the central portion of eastern Washington. Lake Keechelus, Lake Kachess and Lake Cle Elum are nearby bodies of water that are popular for both fishing and boating.

Wildlife is abundant here. Resident animals include foxes, raccoons, chipmunks, squirrels and a variety of birds, including ducks and geese. Deer and elk are occasional visitors. A pair of ospreys nest in a large snag on the west side of the lake. Fish in Lake Easton and nearby streams include rainbow trout, Dolly Varden trout, silver trout, cutthroat trout and whitefish.

Facilities: two camping areas with a total of 145 campsites, each with picnic table and stove; 45 of these are full hookup sites located in the trailer campground. Each campground has a modern restroom with hot showers. The day-use area features a bathhouse with hot showers, a play area for the children, a non-guarded swimming beach, adjacent boat launch, 30 picnic tables and 18 barbecue grills. A trailer dumping station is located near the park entrance.

For further information, contact: Lake Easton State Park, PO Box 26, Easton, WA 98925, ☎ (509) 656-2230.

Lake Sammamish State Park

Location: 1½ miles northwest of Issaquah,
and 17 miles east of Seattle, off of I-90.

Lake Sammamish State Park is comprised of 431 acres, including more than 6,800 feet of waterfront. Much of this acreage was donated by Hans Jensen, a Danish-born immigrant who came to this country in 1904. He gave his farm to the park in remembrance of the children he had enjoyed watching as they played on his beach.

This area was once a gathering place for local Indian tribes. They celebrated their *potlatch*, or winter festival, with games, berry-gathering, hunting, and fishing in preparation for the coming season. Perhaps this is why the area is called Sammanish, which comes from the Indian word *samena*, meaning "hunter." In more recent years, this area was known for its coal mining. Local coal was transported by train to Seattle.

Today, Lake Sammamish State Park is primarily a day-use facility. Two satellite areas maintained by Lake Sammamish State Park are Ollalie Recreation Area and Squak Mountain. Neither is open yet to the public.

Activities / Flora & Fauna

Activities include swimming, rafting, sunbathing, picnicking, hiking, fishing, bird watching, boating, jogging and soccer. The lake is open year-round for fishing. Issaquah Creek, which runs through the entire park, is also used for fishing (as well as canoeing and rafting). Varieties of fish common here include trout, salmon, bass, perch, crappie and steelhead.

There are many forms of wildlife in Lake Sammamish State Park. Coyote, fox, raccoon, opossum, deer, weasel, beaver, mink, muskrat, and porcupine are all native to the region. In addition, the Audubon Society has identified 125 species of birds in the area.

Many different trees grow in this park. Among them are Douglas firs, grand firs, cedars, pines, poplars, willows, maples and birch. The underbrush is often dense with blackberries, salmonberries, pasture grass and thistle.

Facilities: Nine-ramp boat launch, two activity areas, ballfields, a large picnic area, and 1,800 feet of guarded swimming beach. No overnight camping is permitted here, except in the Hans Jensen Youth Group Area. This area can accommodate 100 overnight tent campers and a maximum of 40 cars. Two group day-use areas are available by reservation; one can accommodate 300 people, while the other will handle 100. The nearest state park camping is at Saltwater State Park, 25 miles southwest of this facility.

For further information, contact: Lake Sammamish State Park, 20606 Southeast 56th Street, Issaquah, WA 98027, ☎ (360) 902-8563.

Lake Sylvia State Park

Location: 1 mile north of Montesano, off State Highway 12.

This small, forested park is comprised of 234 acres, including 30-acre Lake Sylvia.

History

This area has a rich history of logging. The first lumber mill in Grays Harbor County was constructed here in the late 1860s; it operated until 1930, when the equipment became obsolete. When the sawmill was no longer profitable, the land was donated to the city of Montesano. The city donated the land to the state parks system in 1936.

The mill owners made a dam of logs to provide a backwater pond for log flotation. Today, when the lake is lowered, this old log superstructure is still evident; it serves as a debris screen for the existing dam. The new concrete dam was built by Puget Power and Light Company.

Log rolling was once a popular activity at the sawmill. One of the workers carved a spruce log into a near-perfect ball almost four feet in diameter. The ball was used for several years before it became waterlogged and sank. In 1974, the lake was lowered and the log ball was discovered. It is now on display in the park.

Flora & Fauna

Many forms of wildlife find sanctuary in Lake Sylvia State Park. White-tailed deer, raccoons, bears, mountain beavers, otters, chipmunks and squirrels are dwellers in these forested hills. In addition, the lake is populated with bass, and stocked each year with rainbow or cutthroat trout.

This park offers many recreational opportunities. Besides camping, picnicking and fishing, there are hiking trails and a guarded swimming beach. During the summer, a private concessionaire rents boats and sells food, beverages and fishing equipment here.

Facilities: 35 standard (non-hookup) camping sites and two walk-in sites for hikers or bikers. Some sites can accommodate recreational vehicles up to 35 feet long. There are also 137 picnic sites and an enclosed picnic shelter with fireplace and tables. A group camp area can accommodate 120 people; it is available by reservation.

For further information, contact: Lake Sylvia State Park, PO Box 701, Montesano, WA 98563, ☎ (360) 249-3621.

Lake Wenatchee State Park

Location: Near Highway 2, northwest of Wenatchee and Leavenworth.

Lake Wenatchee State Park is nestled in one of Washington's most unspoiled and scenic recreation areas. The 489-acre facility boasts 12,623 feet of waterfront on Lake Wenatchee. Here, park patrons can swim, boat or fish in the glacier-fed water. In addition, numerous man-made and natural trails afford closer looks at the park's abundant plant and animal life.

Different forms of wildlife seen in the park include deer, bears, coyotes, squirrels and chipmunks. Some of the more common birds in this area are bald eagles, ospreys, crows, kingfishers and Canada geese.

Snacks, beverages and firewood are available from the park's concession. Canoes can be rented there, too. The horse concessionaire offers guided, hour-long excursions through the park. Campers may attend scheduled campfire programs, nature walks, and junior ranger programs.

The area around the park offers recreational opportunities for every season. Several communities have springtime festivals, and fishing, hiking and boating are popular warm-weather activities. In the fall, many people tour the area to enjoy the changing colors of the leaves. Winter brings four feet of snow, with miles of snowmobile and cross-country ski trails to enjoy.

This park is situated in prime bear country. Please store all food in cars when you are away from your campsite; your tent is easily accessible to a bear.

Facilities: 197 campsites and a group camp, open spring through fall. The campgrounds have centrally located comfort stations with hot showers as well as trailer dumps. No trailer hookups are available at Lake Wenatchee. Several areas are plowed for winter use by snowmobilers, cross-country skiers and sledders.

For further information, contact: Lake Wenatchee State Park, 21588A Highway 207, Leavenworth, WA 98826, ☎ (509) 763-3101.

Larrabee State Park

Location: State Highway 11 (Chuckanut Drive), 7 miles south of Bellingham.

In October, 1915, the Larrabee family donated 20 acres of land to the state for a park. In 1923, the tract became Washington's first state park; it was officially named in honor of Charles Xavier Larrabee. Additional donations and purchases from the Larrabee family, Cyrus Gates, Swen Larson and others increased the size of the park to 1,886 acres, including 3,600 feet of saltwater shoreline on Samish Bay.

Larrabee State Park is situated on the seaward side of Chuckanut Mountain, part of a geologic formation extending many miles north and southeast from the park. The meeting of sea and sandstone has created many beautiful sculptures along the beaches and cliffs of Samish Bay. In turn, the crevices in the rocks provide a natural habitat for intertidal life. With each change of the tide, a visitor can explore the intricate workings of this active and lively environment.

Marine Life

Visitors are invited to sit awhile and watch the activity in one of the pools left from the receding tide. Turn over a rock and discover what lies beneath it. Several varieties of starfish, crabs, barnacles, sea cucumbers, chitons, limpets, mussels and fish may all be found. Feel free to touch and observe these creatures, but remember these animals will not survive if taken from their habitats. Edible species such as crabs and clams may be taken, providing state laws are obeyed. For shellfish regulations and tide information, contact the park manager.

Visitors can take a quarter-mile self-guided walk along the shoreline. The seven numbered stops feature panoramic views and living illustrations of native plant life, tidal pool life, erosion action, and beach regeneration.

In addition to exploring sea life, visitors can hike the park's many trails. Several mountain lookouts offer panoramic views of the San Juan Islands, as well as Mount Baker and the North Cascade Mountains. Picnicking, swimming, boating, fishing and scuba diving are other popular activities here.

Facilities: 87 campsites, 26 of them with full hookups; all sites have stove and tables. There are modern restrooms with hot showers. A group camping area with capacity for 50 campers is also available. Forty picnic sites are available, plus two covered picnic areas that may be reserved for group use. A saltwater boat launch and a trailer dumping station complete the park facilities. Grocery stores, restaurants, service stations and medical facilities may be found in nearby Bellingham.

For further information, contact: Larrabee State Park, 245 Chuckanut Drive, Bellingham, WA 98226, ☎ (360) 676-2093.

Leadbetter Point State Park

Location: 3 miles north of Oysterville, on Stackpole Road.

Leadbetter Point State Park Natural Area is a day-use park preserved by two public agencies and located at the northern tip of the Long Beach Peninsula. The State Park Natural Area and the Wilapa National Wildlife Refuge, both located to the north, are unique regions characterized by shifting dunes, grasslands, ponds, marshes and forests. These varied habitats allow for a diverse abundance of plant and animal life.

Flora & Fauna

Dynamic changes are seen at Leadbetter, as the buildup of sand influenced by ocean currents, tides and weather becomes stabilized by grasses and other plants. This stabilization triggers further changes that ultimately lead to the formation of mature coastal forest. All stages of this natural process can be seen at Leadbetter Point.

Seasonal changes here are dramatic. Spring brings new life in the form of budding leaves, needles, fronds and flowers. In April and May, visitors delight in the antics of both resident and migratory birds who undertake courtship in full plumage. Summer brings the ripening of numerous varieties of berries, including three types of blackberries, two types of huckleberries, and a plentiful supply of wild strawberries. Black bears are a common sight at this time of year; they feed on the luscious berries, which are an important part of their diet.

Fall brings further change as the colors of the forest, marshes, and dunes change to herald the coming of winter. Migratory birds reappear as they begin their trip south for the winter. Mushrooms pop up throughout the forest as the rain once again becomes part of the coastal weather pattern. Even winter – with its awesome displays of stormy weather – can be interesting at Leadbetter Point. Beachcombing on the bay or oceanfront often yields fascinating new treasures with each new wave. Razor clam digging resumes this time of year on the hard sand of the ocean beach.

Activities

Activities popular at Leadbetter Point include hiking, birdwatching, photography, nature study, surf fishing, clamming and beachcombing. As mosquitoes invade the park in spring and summer, repellent will make your visit more enjoyable.

Facilities: Day-use only; restrooms and picnic area.

For further information, contact: Leadbetter Point State Park Natural Area, c/o Fort Canby State Park, PO Box 488, Ilwaco, WA 98624, ☎ (360) 642-3078.

Lewis and Clark State Park

Location: South of Chehalis, near the junction of I-5 and US Highway 12.

Lewis and Clark State Park, the second state park established in Washington, officially opened in 1923. Since that time, the 533-acre facility has been expanded to include kitchens, restrooms, and nature trails. The tract is remarkable in that it contains the last major stand of virgin timber near the interstate between Portland and Seattle.

The park was named after Merriwether Lewis and William Clark, the quintessential American explorers. Although the Lewis and Clark expedition did not reach as far north as this site, their explorations were a major factor in the discovery and settlement of the general area.

History

During the Great Depression, the Civilian Conservation Corps (CCC) made a significant contribution to the development of this park. CCC workers consructed many rustic buildings, including the ranger's log house, the shop, the kitchens and the restrooms. The picnic area and fencing are also part of their contribution.

The devastating Typhoon Freda – part of the Columbus Day storm of 1962 – destroyed much of the towering, old-growth timber that was the pride of Lewis and Clark State Park. Over eight million board feet (of the park's 13 million board feet of timber) were lost.

Flora & Fauna

Despite the losses, Lewis and Clark State Park is enjoying a very successful comeback. The ravaged areas were replanted with two-year-old Douglas firs in 1965, and ecological redevelopment is progressing rapidly.

Some of the new growth is seen along the park's nature trails. As you travel along the Trail of the Deer, you'll pass under magnificent old-growth fir and cedar trees. This trail, which covers part of the virgin forest spared by the Columbus Day storm, is an enlightening introduction to the park's varied plant life.

The *Old-Growth Forest Interpretive Trail* is a half-mile trail that offers the opportunity to experience an old-growth forest. The trail begins at the exhibit building. It is an easy, flat walk, but plan to go slowly and take your time. Allow at least 45 minutes. The trail is characterized by four "benches," which showcase native plants and wildlife and their interdependence, and highlight how the entire old-growth ecosystem is intertwined.

Other area activities include exploring the historic Jackson House, a pioneer home built in 1845, located 1½ miles north of the park on Jackson Highway.

Facilities: 25 non-hookup campsites, comfort stations with showers, 52 picnic sites, three kitchen shelters, and a group camping area with a day-use capacity of 100. The largest kitchen can be reserved. Reservations are also taken for group camping. In addition, there are two horseshoe pits, a natural wading pool, a children's play area and areas for hiking and fishing.

For further information, contact: Lewis and Clark State Park, 4583 Jackson Highway, Winlock, WA 98596, ☎ (360) 864-2643.

Lewis and Clark Trail State Park

Location: 5 miles west of Dayton, on Highway 12.

Lewis and Clark Trail State Park is a 37-acre recreational area that provides picnic and camping facilities along the Touchet River.

History

The park is so named because of its location on the overland route taken by Merriwether Lewis and William Clark on their return to Missouri. In his journal on April 27, 1806, Lewis wrote, "The Indians informed us that there was a good road which passed from the Columbia to the entrance of the Kooskooske (now called Clearwater River); they informed us that there were plenty of deer and antelopes on the road, with good water and grass." Following Indian trails, the explorers saw a type of country they had missed when following the river bottoms. This leg of the trip was relatively peaceful.

The property in which this park is now located later belonged to the Butler family, who sold it to the state of Washington in 1933. Some Civilian Conservation Corps (CCC) work was completed within the park in 1934.

Flora & Fauna

Surrounded by cultivated land, this facility preserves a number of plants common along the river in Lewis and Clark's time. These include ponderosa pines, cottonwoods, chokecherries, blue elderberries and white clematis.

Wildlife here includes whitetail deer, gophers, beavers, raccoons, and squirrels. Over 100 species of birds have been spotted.

Activities

Swimming the Touchet River or fishing for steelhead and German brown trout are both popular activities at Lewis and Clark Trail. Campfire programs are held on summer evenings here, and interpretive programs are available upon request. Many visitors use the park as a base camp for hiking the Blue Mountains or hunting in nearby areas. There is a one-mile hiking trail and a ¾-mile interpretive trail showcasing the natural vegetation along the river.

Facilities: 30 non-hookup campsites, four primitive sites, group camp area, kitchen shelter with electrical hookups, and a trailer dumping station.

For further information, contact: Lewis and Clark Trail State Park, Route 1, Box 90, Dayton WA 99328, ☎ (509) 337-6457.

Lime Kiln Point State Park

Location: San Juan Island. Access by ferry or private boat.

Lime Kiln Point is a unique state park where visitors can experience the thrill of observing whales in their natural habitat. Both Orca and Minke whales can be spotted regularly throughout the year as they pass the west side of San Juan Island. Summer is peak observation time.

Whale Watching

The whales that cruise the waters off Lime Kiln Point are considered residents of the Greater Puget Sound area. They do not migrate great distances, but spend their entire lives in these waters – feeding, breeding and playing. Orca whales are more common in the summer because they eat the salmon traveling past Lime Kiln Point to the freshwater rivers of Puget Sound. Sightings of whales generally occur once a day, although there are sometimes two or more sightings.

The approximately 30-foot-long minke whales generally avoid traveling in large groups or "pods," and are rarely seen doing acrobatics. Observers need to watch the ocean surface and listen carefully to increase their chances of seeing a minke. The smallest members of the blue (baleen) whale family, they are fairly dark in color and have a small dorsal fin on their back.

Orca (killer) whales are easier to see as they approach the park. The large black dorsal fin – located midway down the body – is very apparent when the orca surfaces. You often hear an orca before seeing it. But when one surfaces, it is truly a breathtaking sight. Males and females are distinguished by their dorsal fins; the males' fins are six feet in height, while those of the females are only three feet. Resident orcas travel in groups or "pods," so once one orca is spotted, others are likely to follow.

Guided walks and interpretive talks are offered to park visitors between May and September. The talks are conducted between 9 a.m. and 6 p.m. on weekdays and at various times on the weekends. A series of interpretive signs outlines the anatomy of both whales and porpoises, explaining their habits and activities. Remember to stay on marked trails, as there are dangerous points along Lime Kiln.

The Whale Museum on San Juan Island features fascinating exhibits on local research. Videos of the whales are displayed throughout the day, and there is a playroom for children. The museum is located in Friday Harbor, just a few blocks from the ferry terminal on the top of First Street Hill.

Other Activities

Other popular activities here include picnicking, exploring intriguing tidal pools or a treasure-filled beach, or touring the historic lime kilns just outside the park.

Another of the park's attractions is the Lime Kiln Lighthouse, with its automated light and foghorn. Currently leased by the Whale Museum, it is used primarily as a whale research center. The building and the surrounding land are still under US Coast Guard ownership, and closed to the public. Visitors to the park are requested not to interrupt the ongoing research projects.

For further information, contact: Lime Kiln Point State Park, c/o Dept. of Parks and Recreation, PO Box 42650, Olympia, WA 98504, ☎ (360) 755-9231.

Lincoln Rock State Park

Location: 7 miles north of East Wenatchee, on Highway 2.

This park is situated on the east bank of the Columbia River, surrounded by the foothills of the Cascade Mountain range. Comprised of 150 acres, it was developed in cooperation with the Chelan County Public Utility District, and completed in 1981. The park overlooks Lake Entiat and Turtle Rock Island; the latter is accessible only by boat.

Lincoln Rock was named after a prominent geological feature, a rock outcropping that resembles the profile of Abraham Lincoln. First named in 1889 by Billy Schoft and Ed Ferguson, it gained notoriety through a photograph Schoft took of the "profile." Entered in a *Ladies' Home Journal* photography contest, it won first prize. Because of the *Journal's* nationwide appeal, the name "Lincoln Rock" stuck.

Visitors can enjoy many activities here, including swimming, hiking, camping, picnicking, fishing, boating and water-skiing. Winter activities include skiing at nearby Badger Mountain or Mission Ridge. Lincoln Rock is home to many kinds of wildlife. Rabbits, badgers, deer, beavers, nighthawks, swallows and rattlesnakes are found here.

Facilities: 27 standard campsites, with tables and stoves at each. The day-use area features a swimming beach, moorage and boat launch, kitchen shelter, bathhouse and play equipment for the children. The park also has a trailer dumping station.

For further information, contact: Lincoln Rock State Park, Route 3, Box 3137, East Wenatchee, WA 98801, ☎ (509) 884-8702.

Lyons Ferry State Park

Location: At the confluence of the Palouse and Snake Rivers,
17 miles southeast of Washtucna; both Lyons Ferry State Park and
its satellite park, Palouse Falls, are accessible by Highway 261.

This park is named for Dan Lyons, the last operator of the ferry boat that carried settlers across the Snake River for over 100 years. This ferry was an important link on the Old Mullan Road, built by John Mullan to move military troops between Fort Benton (on Montana's Missouri River) and Fort Walla Walla (on the Columbia). This historic ferry is permanently moored in the park.

Activities at Lyons Ferry include swimming, picnicking, camping and hiking. Boating and water-skiing are popular summer pursuits. Included among the wildlife here are mule deer, yellow-bellied marmot, cottontail rabbit, porcupine, coyote, skunk, and beaver.

Topography

Located in the Columbia Basin, the park is rich in geologic history. Formations remain where the Snake River carved its way through the old lava or basalt, and where the Palouse River – which originally flowed through Washtucna – was re-routed by a major flood over 10,000 years ago.

Another important part of the park is the Marmes Rockshelter, site of a 1968 archaeological dig. It was here that geologist Ronald Fryxell unearthed the "Marmes Man." Estimated to be 10-13,000 years old, these were – at the time – the oldest human remains found in the Western Hemisphere.

Two historic plaques mark the grave of "Old Bones," chief of the local Palouse Indians. Located near an overlook picnic shelter, these can be reached via a winding hiking trail.

Facilities: Lyons Ferry State Park has 50 standard campsites, each with table and stove; two primitive hiker/bicycler campsites; restrooms with hot showers. The day-use portion of the park features picnic tables and shelters, 400 feet of swimming beach, a boat launch, bathhouse and trailer dumping station. Palouse Falls has 10 primitive campsites and pit toilets; access is by non-motorized vehicle.

For further information, contact: Lyons Ferry State Park, Box 217, Starbuck, WA 99359, ☎ (509) 646-3252.

Manchester State Park

Location: 6 miles east of Port Orchard, on Puget Sound's Rich Passage.

Comprised of 111 acres – with 3,400 feet of waterfront – this area was first used by the army as part of the Coastal Artillery Defense System. Named "Fortress Mitchell," the emplacement guarded Rich Passage. Across the water on Bainbridge Island was Fort Ward, now also a state park.

A large brick building presides over the day-use area. Completed in 1905, this was originally built as a torpedo warehouse. It has since served as an officers' club, barracks, bachelor officers' quarters, and mess hall. (It is currently a picnic shelter.) The small concrete building east of the warehouse was originally used as the Mining Casement, and later, to store coal. At the tip of the point lies Battery Robert Mitchell. Two three-inch guns were scheduled to be stationed here, but were never mounted. All three of these structures are on the register of National Historic Monuments.

Manchester is home to blacktail deer, grey and red foxes, red squirrels and skunks. Bald eagles, pileated woodpeckers, mallard ducks, hummingbirds, and countless other birds also live here. The park also harbors an extensive collection of poison oak and stinging nettles, so stick to the trails and beware!

Two festivals are held in this vicinity every year. The city of Port Orchard sponsors "Fathoms of Fun" in late June and early July. This festival culminates with a Fourth of July fireworks display over Sinclair Inlet. Each August, the annual Kitsap County Fair is held at the fairgrounds near Bremerton.

Facilities: 50 standard campsites and three primitive campsites for bicyclists; 16 of these sites are pull-through, while six are "buddy sites." The restrooms have pay showers. This park also has an unguarded swimming beach and a bathhouse with showers. Boats can be rented and launched in the city of Manchester. A large brick picnic shelter is available during the summer for groups up to 150 people; contact the park staff to reserve. The park's 65 picnic sites, volleyball court, horseshoe pit and two small picnic shelters are maintained for daytime use on a first-come, first-served basis.

For further information, contact: Manchester State Park, PO Box 36, Manchester, WA 98353, ☎ (360) 871-4065.

Maryhill State Park

Location: Klickitat County, 12 miles south of Goldendale on US Highway 97.

This park consists of 98 acres, including 4,700 feet of Columbia River frontage. It is situated east of the Sam Hill Memorial Bridge, adjacent to the community of Maryhill.

Northwest of the park is the Maryhill Museum. At the time of its construction in 1914, this structure was intended as the home of noted lawyer and northwestern financier Samuel Hill. The son-in-law of James J. Hill, builder of the Great Northern Railway, Samuel Hill left a legacy of good works for the people of Washington.

Hill named Maryhill after his daughter, his wife, and his mother-in-law, all of whom were named "Mary." The structure was transformed into a museum in 1923 as a means of displaying Mr. Hill's art collection. When Romania's Queen Marie dedicated the museum in 1926, it marked the first visit to America by European royalty. It wasn't until 1940, however, that the museum was opened to the public. It is now open daily from March 15 to November 15.

Facilities: 50 campsites, each with full hookup facilities, stove and table, modern restrooms with hot showers, and a trailer dumping station. A swimming area, bathhouse, boat launch, dock, water-skiing, fishing, picnic and kitchen facilities are located in the day-use portion of the park. Nearby Biggs Junction offers restaurants and gasoline stations. Medical services are available in Goldendale.

For further information, contact: Maryhill State Park, 50 Highway 97, Goldendale, WA 98620, ☎ (509) 773-5007.

Millersylvania State Park

Location: 12 miles south of Olympia, off I-5.

Millersylvania's 841 acres were originally homesteaded by Squire Lathum in 1855. Later, the property was sold to John Miller, whose family gave it to the state in 1921, with the stipulation that it be used as a park. An engraved stone memorial honors the Miller family, and the orchard that surrounded their homestead is still in evidence. Also in the park are traces of a narrow gauge railroad and the old skid roads once used by the logging industry. The stumps of trees logged in the early 1800s still carry the notch-scars where springboards supported brawny loggers.

The park headquarters was constructed by the Civilian Conservation Corps (CCC) in 1935 and stands today among the old-growth cedar and fir trees as an example of this style of construction. Plans call for replicas of the CCC-style buildings to be constructed as replacements are required for the original structures.

Adjacent to the day-use area is Deep Lake, which is stocked annually with trout. Animal life here includes rabbits, deer, beavers, domesticated ducks and geese, squirrels and wild fowl. Many trails exist throughout the park, affording ample opportunity to observe a large variety of flora and fauna. Beaver are constantly at work creating little swamps and backwaters; there is also a stand of virgin timber, a rapidly vanishing resource. Fish abound in the lake, and swimming and boating are popular during the warm summer months.

Millersylvania Environmental Learning Center

The Millersylvania Environmental Learning Center (ELC) is located in Millersylvania State Park on the banks of Deep Lake. A few trees from an old apple orchard remind visitors that this site was once a farm. Today, new buildings have been constructed to form a well-planned camp.

Facilities consist of a dining hall/kitchen building; two restrooms with showers; 16 cabins for sleeping; three staff cabins; and a sheltered outdoor classroom. The camp will accommodate 158 people. The buildings are winterized and heated, so that the center may be operated year-round.

This and other ELCs are specialized facilities within the state park system, and are used by groups or organizations that offer camping and outdoor learning experiences. Youth organizations, schools, churches and conservation groups are typical of the organizations using these centers. User groups are responsible for their staff and any programs they wish to present.

Facilities: 164 campsites, plus 52 sites with electricity and water hookups; all campsites have tables and stoves. A primitive camp area can accommodate 20 people. There is a trailer dumping station in the park. The day-use portion of the park has two swimming areas and four kitchen shelters. A physical fitness trail and an ecology trail – plus several fire roads for hiking – complete the park's facilities.

For further information, contact: Millersylvania State Park, 12245 Tilley Road S., Olympia, WA 98502, ☎ (360) 753-1519.

Moran State Park

Location: Orcas Island, 80 miles north of Seattle;
accessible via the Washington State ferries from Anacortes.

Dominated by Mt. Constitution, Moran State Park is a blend of dense virgin forest, open fields and sparkling lakes. Visitors to the park can enjoy a number of activities, including camping, picnicking, fishing, swimming, boating and hiking.

The original park was a gift from Robert Moran, a shipbuilder and former mayor of Seattle. Today, it contains nearly 700 acres, encompassing two mountains and Mt. Constitution. The latter, a remnant of an ancient range connected to the Cascades, is the highest point in the San Juan Islands. From the top, you can look out over two mountain ranges and many of the San Juan Islands, as well as the Canadian Gulf Island, Vancouver Island, Mt. Baker and Mt. Rainier.

At the summit of the mountain stands a stone tower constructed by the Civilian Conservation Corps (CCC) in 1936. Patterned after ancient watch towers of the Caucasus Mountains in southeast Europe, it was designed by noted architect Ellsworth Storey. Wrought iron and sandstone blocks from a quarry on the north end of Orcas Island were both used in the construction.

Flora and fauna are varied and abundant on Orcas Island. Blacktail deer, river otters, muskrats and raccoons are common park visitors. Bald eagles, kingfishers, and great blue herons are year-round residents. In the winter, numerous ducks can be found on Cascade Lake.

Moran State Park's trees are primarily western hemlock and western red cedar. Several types of lilies, asters, stonecrop and grasses grow in the exposed fields of the south flank of Mount Constitution. The summit is forested by hardy stands of lodgepole pine.

Facilities: 151 campsites, all without hookups. Most comfort stations feature hot showers. The day-use area includes 44 picnic sites, five kitchens and shelters. There are over 21 miles of trails. In addition, there are bathhouses, boat rentals, a swimming beach and a boat-launch area. No outboards are allowed.

For further information, contact: Moran State Park, Star Route Box 22, Eastsound, WA 98245, ☎ (360) 376-2326.

Mount Spokane State Park

Location: North of Spokane, off of U.S. Highway 2.

In 1912, the owner of Mount Carleton's mountain top decided to rename his real estate treasure; Mount Carleton became Mount Spokane. Francis H. Cook had just completed a road to the summit, obviously hoping others would come to appreciate Mount Spokane's natural attractions.

Just three years later, the mountain and its environs were turned into a national park. In 1927, this 1,500-acre tract was transformed into a state facility, becoming Mount Spokane State Park. The park has grown quite a bit since that time; it now encompasses over 16,000 acres.

Francis Cook's original cabin was enlarged in the late 1930s by the Civilian Conservation Corps (CCC). At that time, it was used as a ski lodge. The Vista House, situated on the mountain's crest, is an unusual rock building and a favorite retreat.

Flora & Fauna / Activities

Visitors to the summit of Mount Spokane are rewarded with a spectacular view of two countries, three states, two mountain ranges and eight lakes – a scenic panorama that attracts visitors year-round. Looking outward from the top, you'll see Washington, Idaho and Montana, as well as part of Canada. Two distinct mountain ranges – the Rockies and the Selkirks – form a rugged contrast to the blue-green lakes far below.

Bobcats, coyotes, porcupines and ground squirrels can be seen at Mount Spokane State Park; other wildlife occasionally observed include Douglas squirrels, skunks, mule deer, white tail and black-tail deer, moose and black bear.

Hikers will experience dramatic differences in climatic zones as they amble along the park's trails. Switchbacking up the sunbeaten side of the mountain and descending along the cool, shaded side, these trails reveal the unique variety of plants and animals found at different elevations.

Winter recreation is a specialty at Mount Spokane. The mountain's snowy flanks – combined with two lodges and five chairlifts – attract numerous enthusiasts, who come for downhill and cross-country skiing, snowmobiling and sledding. In the summer, hiking, horseback riding, picnicking, overnight camping and huckleberry picking are popular. Whether blanketed in snow or in brightly colored flowers, Mount Spokane State Park provides its visitors with unforgettable memories.

Facilities: 12 campsites, each with table and a stove; these are available during the summer only. An overnight group camping area with a log cabin shelter can accommodate 90 campers; it is available to organized groups by reservation. There is a restroom, water and pit toilets. Eighty-five picnic sites are located throughout the park; there are also three shelters.

For further information, contact: Mount Spokane State Park, Route 1, Box 336, Mead, WA 99021, ☎ (509) 456-4169.

Ocean City State Park

Location: 2 miles north of Ocean Shores, on Highway 115.

This park is situated on North Beach, which follows the Pacific coastline from the North Jetty of Grays Harbor to Moclips. This 27 mile-stretch of sandy ocean beach attracts recreationists to area parks throughout the year.

Ocean City State Park maintains facilities at 13 beach points. Griffith-Priday Ocean State Park is located four miles north, while Pacific Beach State Park, a concession-operated park, is situated 14 miles north of Ocean City State Park. Visitors should observe the following beach regulations:

◇ Drive only on the uppermost wet, hardpacked sand area at a speed limit of 25 MPH.
◇ Observe the laws and regulations posted at each beach access road.
◇ Surf swimming is dangerous; beware of undertow on outgoing tides, and stay clear of logs in the surf.
◇ Do not ford rivers or large creeks, and do not disturb any sea mammals or birdlife.
◇ No fires or driving on the dunes or through vegetation.

Activities

The park boasts a wide variety of habitats, making it attractive to bird-watchers, mushroom hunters and visitors exploring either by canoe or kayak. Nearby activities include beachcombing, fresh and saltwater fishing, golf, and horseback riding. In addition, there are go-carts, an arcade, weekend gaming, boat and moped rentals, kite flying, nightly dining and entertainment.

Clamming is fun, and success brings delicious rewards. To protect razor clam resources, the following regulations must be followed:

◇ Daily limits, digging hours and seasons are specified on an annual basis.
◇ Every digger must have a clam license, available from local merchants.

- ❖ Vehicles and horses must not travel on clam beds; ride or drive only on the uppermost wet, hardpacked sand area.
- ❖ For information on seasons, contact the Department of Fisheries.

Facilities: 49 standard sites, three primitive sites, 29 full-utility sites, a trailer dumping facility and hot pay showers (25¢). A small picnic area with six tables and stoves is located near the beach. The overnight group camp may be reserved for tent camping.

For further information, contact: Ocean City State Park, Rt. 4, Box 2900, Hoquiam, WA 98550, ☎ (360) 289-3553.

Old Fort Townsend State Park

Location: The southeast side of the Olympic Peninsula in Jefferson County, 4 miles south of Port Townsend off Highway 20.

Comprised of 377 acres, Old Fort Townsend State Park slopes to a 150-foot cliff, commanding a scenic view of Admiralty Inlet, Port Townsend Bay and the Cascade Mountains.

The fort in the park's name was established in 1856 by the US Army. During the Indian wars of the mid-1850s, settlers on the northeast tip of the Olympic Peninsula were subject to Indian hostility.

The fort was built with timbers hewn from logs, laths cut in the forests and clam shells that were burned and ground for plaster. It was ready for occupancy by the summer of 1857.

Old Fort Townsend was destined to know only sporadic moments in the limelight. Troops were sent here in 1859 to help in a dispute referred to as the "Pig War." This was a squabble with England over the boundary of the San Juan Island. Troops were withdrawn in 1861, and the fort was placed in "caretaker" status. In 1874, the fort was reconstructed and for nearly 20 years served as a thriving military post. In January, 1895, a kerosene lamp exploded, destroying the barracks. Orders were issued to decommission the fort; it was turned over to the US Department of the Interior in 1927.

During World War II, the fort was used as an enemy munitions defusing station. The Washington State Parks and Recreation Commission purchased it for a state park in 1958.

In addition to several hiking trails winding through the park, there is a historic walk starting at the large display board. There is also a nature walk starting across the road from the display board.

Facilities: 40 standard campsites, each with table and fireplace; a trailer dump station located to the left of the main park entrance; showers in the upper campground restroom; pit toilets; and water. A large kitchen shelter and tenting camp is available for groups; reservations can be made starting January 1 by calling (206) 385-4730. Two small shelters along the cliff are available on a first-come, first-served basis.

For further information, contact: Old Fort Townsend State Park, c/o Ft. Worden State Park, Port Townsend, WA 98368, ☎ (360) 385-3595.

Olmstead Place State Park

Location: 4½ miles southeast of Ellensburg, off I-90.

Olmstead Place State Park is a heritage site that commemorates early farming methods and techniques, as well as pioneer living. The park is listed on the National Register of Historic Sites.

History

This property was settled by Sarah and Samuel Olmstead in 1875; it was one of the first homesteads in the Kittitas Valley. Like many early residents, the Olmsteads were attracted to the valley by its verdant grasslands, the rich soil, a climate conducive to farming, and a plentiful supply of water.

The Olmsteads' cabin, though simple and rugged by today's standards, was considered large and comfortable in 1875. By 1900, the farm had entered its period of greatest development. Many of the historic buildings can be toured at Olmstead Place, including the dairy barn, granary, wagon shed, Olmstead cabin and residence.

The Seaton Cabin Schoolhouse was built in the 1870s and reconstructed at Olmstead Place in 1980. In 1968, Leta May Smith and Clareta Olmstead Smith, granddaughters of Sarah and Samuel Olmstead, deeded the 217-acre farm to the Washington State Parks and Recreation Commission.

Today, Olmstead Place remains much as it was when it was founded, from the pioneer furnishings in the cabin to the agricultural equipment in the barn.

Trails

Altapes Creek Trail. This half-mile trail should take about 30 minutes to walk, one way. The Indian name *altapes* means "most beautiful creek in the valley." The creek becomes a series of beautiful waterfalls in the foothills, after which it winds across the valley, joining other mountain streams to eventually reach the Yakima River. The fish, plants and wildlife here furnished the Native Americans with an abundance of food. In the late 1870s, log cabins replaced the Indian teepees as pioneers began to settle in the area. The trail contains the following stops:

◇ Red Barn: built in 1908.
◇ Granary and Wagon Shed: built in 1892.
◇ Milk House and Dairy Barn: built in 1920.
◇ Red Oster Dogwood: used by the local Indians for many daily needs.
◇ Currants: tasty berries frequently made into jellies and pies.
◇ Fallen trees: beavers use these to make dams.
◇ Ditches and dams: farmers dammed these waters for irrigation purposes.
◇ Wild rose: this shrub was used for tea, and is an excellent source of vitamin C.
◇ Willows: these fast-growing trees are found in moist areas.
◇ Seaton Schoolhouse: reconstructed at this site in 1979.

Facilities: Olmstead Place State Park is a day-use park. Picnicking, bird watching, photography and fishing are activities that are popular with park visitors.

For further information, contact: Olmstead Place State Park Heritage Area, Route 5, Box 2580, Ellensburg, WA 98926, ☎ (360) 902-8563.

Osoyoos Lake State Veterans' Memorial Park

Location: North of Omak, off of US Highway 97, near the Canadian border.

Osoyoos Lake State Veterans' Memorial State Park is located in the scenic Okanogan River Valley. The green pastures and orchards of the valley floor form a stark contrast with the rugged cliffs and glacial features of the Okanogan country, making a beautiful setting for this recreation area.

This region is located near an early Indian gathering place. The name "osoyoos" is derived from the Kalispel Indian word *soyoos,* meaning "the narrows." A colorful local Irishman named O'Sullivan suggested that no name was complete without the Irishman's "O," so the lake became "Osoyoos." The park site was once home to the Okanogan County Fair, which featured horse racing, roping events, exhibits and a grandstand show. (The fair was later relocated to a more central location, in the town of Okanogan.)

The Okanogan River flows through Canada and into the upper end of Lake Osoyoos. The lake is 14 miles long, with four miles in the United States and 10 miles in British Columbia. The river continues at the south end of the lake, eventually emptying into the Columbia River at Chief Joseph. The park is situated at the south end of the lake, upon the glacial debris that originally dammed up the river, forming Lake Osoyoos. Other glacial features are readily visible from the park.

Fish are abundant in the lake and river. Among them are bass, trout, carp, perch, crappie, catfish and kokanee. Bird watchers will find the trees and marshlands along the river excellent for viewing gulls, ducks, blackbirds, woodpeckers and killdeer. The Greater Canada Goose has nested in these marshes for centuries. Squirrels, muskrats, and turtles are seen frequently in the park.

Facilities: 86 non-hookup campsites with tables and stoves, 60 picnic sites, 300 feet of swimming beach, a bathhouse, food and grocery concession, hot showers, trailer dumping station and boat launch ramp.

For further information, contact: Osoyoos Lake State Veterans' Memorial Park, Route 1, Box 102-A, Oroville, WA 98844, ☎ (509) 476-3321.

Paradise Point State Park

*Location: 5 miles south of Woodland and
18 miles north of Vancouver, off exit 16 from I-5.*

Paradise Point State Park borders the south shore of the east fork of the Lewis River. It probably received its name from a Portland motorboat club that traveled down the Columbia River and up the east fork of the Lewis River in the 1920s and 30s. The club members camped at a place called Kaner Rock, naming the area "Paradise Point" because of its beauty and tranquility. Kaner Rock is the outcropping on which the northbound lanes of I-5 now stand.

Visitors can enjoy many activities in this park, including camping, picnicking, hiking, fishing, boating, water-skiing, and swimming. There are miles of quiet waters that are excellent for canoeing. Paradise Point is the termination point for float trips down the river. Wildlife lovers should be on the lookout for deer, bobcat, squirrel, opossum, raccoon, fox and many types of birds.

Facilities: 70 non-hookup campsites, four drive-in primitive campsites, five walk-in tent sites, and restrooms with shower facilities. The day-use area has picnic tables, a boat launch, and an ungraded swimming beach.

For further information, contact: Paradise Point State Park, Route 1, Box 33914 NW Paradise Road, Ridgefield, WA 98642, (360) 263-2350.

Peace Arch State Park

*Location: the international boundary between the United States
and Canada, straddling I-5, 22 miles north of Bellingham.*

The Peace Arch was the first structure of its kind in the world, and was built with volunteer labor from both the US and Canada. The surrounding parks were completed with donations from school children in both Washington and British Columbia. Contributions were limited to 10¢, but some children could only give a penny. Today, the monument is surrounded by a beautifully landscaped park that is maintained jointly by Washington and Canada. Peace Arch State Park Heritage Site is a day-use park with an ideal setting for a family or group picnic.

Peace Arch was dedicated in 1921 and commemorates the lasting peace between two great nations. Samuel Hill, president of the Pacific Highway Association, proposed construction of the arch to commemorate the signing of the treaty of Ghent in 1814 and the Rush-Bagot Amendment of 1817. Both treaties resulted from the War of 1812, with the Treaty of Ghent marking the beginning of a period in which Great Britain and the United States chose to settle their disputes peacefully.

Half of the Peace Arch rests in each country. Across the face of the American side of the monument are the words, "Children of a Common Mother." The Canadian side reads, "Brethren Dwelling Together in Unity." A bronze plaque on the American side bears a replica of the pilgrim ship, the *Mayflower*. A similar plaque on the Canadian side illustrates the fur trade ship, *Beaver*.

This park is used extensively for international ceremonies, including the annual International Peace Arch celebration the second Sunday in June.

A variety of flowers – including rhododendrons, azaleas, and heather – bloom brilliantly in the spring, while 27,000 annuals brighten the months of July and August. In the fall, trees and shrubs set the park ablaze with vivid hues of red, orange, and yellow.

Facilities: Day-use only. Groups may reserve a kitchen building by phoning or writing the park.

For further information, contact: Peace Arch State Park, PO Box 87, Blaine, WA 98230, ☎ (360) 902-8563.

Pearrygin Lake State Park

Location: 5 miles northeast of Winthrop;
accessible from the North Cascades Highway.

Located in the upper Methow Valley and surrounded by the towering peaks of the North Cascades, Pearrygin Lake State Park has 578 acres of rolling, sage-covered foothills.

The Methow Valley was a hunting ground for the Indians prior to the arrival of white men in the early 1880s. Within a decade, settlers were homesteading here on the shores of the upper Skagit River.

Among the early arrivals was Benjamin Franklin Pearrygin, who settled near the lake that now bears his name.

The region's topography is the result of massive glacial movement during the latter part of the Pleistocene Age, approximately 14,000 years ago. Pearrygin Lake, a natural spring-fed lake, was probably formed by the retreat of a glacier. An ice dam was left at the lake's end, forming a large till deposit. As this melted, it blocked the previous drainage system.

Wildflowers abound in the glacial till – particularly in the spring, when the hills are gold with the blossoms of balsam root and spring sunflowers. Other commonly seen wildflowers include yellow bells, lupine, larkspur, mariposa lilies and roses.

Wildlife is abundant in this park. Most common is the yellow-bellied marmot (groundhog), which can be seen sunning itself or eating grass in the campground. Deer and other small animals may also be observed. Many varieties of birds nest here, including several species of waterfowl, game birds and songbirds.

Facilities: 30 full hookup sites, 27 with water hookup only, and 26 standard sites. The park is open for snowmobiling during the winter. Summer activities include fishing, swimming, picnicking, boating, water-skiing, hiking and sightseeing.

For further information, contact: Pearrygin Lake State Park, Route 1, Box 300, Winthrop, WA 98862, ☎ (509) 996-2370.

Penrose Point State Park

Location: 30 miles west of Tacoma, in Mayo Cove on Key Peninsula.

This park contains 145 acres of wooded property, with more than two miles of saltwater frontage.

The Key Peninsula and surrounding Puget Sound area are rich in Indian and logging history. An Indian rock carving known as a petroglyph may be found in the park. Noteworthy for the simplicity of its design, this particular petroglyph is composed of three seemingly unrelated characters.

Penrose Point State Park was named after Dr. Stephen Penrose, president of Whitman College in Walla Walla, Washington from

1884 to 1934. For more than 30 years, Dr. Penrose and his family spent their summers vacationing on what is now park property. A prominent church and educational leader in the Northwest, Dr. Penrose was a firm believer in outdoor recreation for his children.

Flora & Fauna

Penrose Point State Park is characterized by lofty, second-generation stands of Douglas fir and cedar. A magnificent example of a grand fir may be seen in the campground area. Cascara and yew trees – as well as many old maples – grow within the park grounds. Trilliums and rhododendrons sprout in abundance.

Wildlife here includes deer, raccoons, squirrels and one or two small black bears. Birds are plentiful, with many varieties visiting the park. Owls, woodpeckers, and great blue herons are spotted year-round. Geese and ducks visit the park on their migratory flights. Pheasant, grouse and quail have been released on the property.

A spacious day-use area offers 1,700 feet of beach, with excellent opportunities for clam digging, picnicking, beachcombing, and unsupervised swimming. Two and one-half miles of secluded trails are available for exploring.

Facilities: 83 non-hookup campsites, a group campground, four comfort stations, hot showers, three kitchen shelters, picnic areas, hiking. The park's natural yacht basin protects a 120-foot dock and eight moorage buoys.

For further information, contact: Penrose Point State Park, PO Box 73, Lakebay, WA 98439, ☎ (206) 884-2514.

Posey Island Marine State Park

Location: 1 mile northwest of Roche Harbor, on San Juan Island.

Comprised of approximately one acre, tiny Posey Island Marine State Park was acquired in 1969. There is no water available on Posey Island. Privacy and its proximity to San Juan Island are the main attractions.

Accessible only by private boat, it boasts only one campsite, and is used mainly by small groups in kayaks, canoes or small sailboats.

There are no docks, floats or mooring buoys at Posey Island, and the surrounding waters are shallow and rocky.

Flora & Fauna

Interesting birds and an occasional seal may be seen on the rocks around the island. It is believed that at one time an old Indian lived alone here.

Mushrooms and wildflowers abound in the lush, mossy environment of the San Juan County forest. Local flora includes Douglas firs, red cedars, madrones, oaks and broadleaf maples. Undergrowth consists mainly of salal and Oregon grape.

Blacktail deer and raccoons are often seen in this park, as are bald eagles, ravens and many other varieties of birdlife. Disturbing wildlife and vegetation is expressly prohibited.

The climate of the San Juan islands is mild and comfortable, year-round. The average high temperature is 69°, with the winter equivalent 45°.

Facilities: none.

For further information, contact Park Ranger, c/o Stuart Island State Park, 6158 Lighthouse Road, Friday Harbor, WA 98250, ☎ (360) 902-8563.

Potholes State Park

Location: South of Moses Lake, at the Potholes Reservoir, near the junction of I-90 and State Road 17.

Topography

The potholes in this park are actually geologic depressions formed in the sand dunes during the ice ages. The sand came from the basalt rock of the Columbia Basin lava flows that once covered much of eastern Washington.

During the ice ages, glaciers ground much of this basalt rock into coarse sand. This was then blown by the wind into dunes. When O'Sullivan Dam was built as part of the Columbia Basin Irrigation Project, the water table rose and filled many potholes, creating pothole "lakes." The rocky, channeled area to the southeast of the park is a different formation created by tremendous ice age floods.

Thousands are attracted to Potholes' desert area, where they enjoy fishing, bird watching, water sports and sunshine. This desert region is unique for its abundance of water. Sand dunes, rocky canyons, and hundreds of lakes offer something for nearly everyone.

Flora & Fauna

The park and its environs supports a great variety of wildlife. Migratory and resident birds include white pelicans, cranes, hawks, and eagles. Mammals such as deer, badger, beaver, and rabbit are also abundant. Species of fish common here include rainbow trout, large and small-mouth bass, perch, crappie, bluegill and walleye.

Facilities: 126 campsites, 60 with full hookups; restrooms with hot showers; boat launch area; trailer dumping station; and public telephone. The day-use area offers an expansive lawn with shade trees, tables and stoves. A trail along the Frenchman Wasteway is popular with fisherman and hikers. Additional visitor services are available at nearby resorts.

For more information, contact: Potholes State Park, 670 O'Sullivan Dam Road, Othello, WA 99344, ☎ (509) 346-2759.

Potlatch State Park

Location: Highway 101, 12 miles north of Shelton and three miles south of Hoodsport.

Potlatch State Park is situated on Annas Bay, on the Great Bend of the Hood Canal. This area once served as a gathering place for the local Indian tribes, who held their festivals, or "potlatches," here. Local tribes still have occasional get-togethers at the park. The site was also home to a logging mill and, following that, a private resort that lured many visitors to Hood Canal.

Flora & Fauna

Because of its beauty and abundant sea life, Hood Canal itself is the park's main attraction. Oyster picking and clam digging are popular activities at the park. Mussels, cockles, butter clams and little-neck clams are abundant at low tide. Shrimp, dungeness crab and red rock crab are also plentiful.

The canal attracts a variety of water birds, while the park's woodlands are home to many other species. Squirrels, skunks, rabbits, deer, and mountain beavers are among the other wildlife here.

During the spring and summer, visitors might venture to nearby Shelton for the annual Rhododendron Show, the Forest Festival and the Mason County Fair.

Facilities: 18 full hookup sites, 17 standard tent sites and two primitive sites for bicyclists and hikers; seven of the hookup sites are pull-through. All sites have a table and stove; restrooms have coin-operated hot showers. A public boat launch is located ¾-mile north of the park.

For further information, contact: Potlatch State Park, Route 4, Box 519, Shelton, WA 98584, ☎ (360) 877-5361.

Rainbow Falls State Park

Location: Ocean Beach Highway 6, 18 miles west of Chehalis.

Discover the quiet, wooded splendor of Rainbow Falls State Park, nestled in a secluded stand of virgin timber along a scenic ocean beach highway.

Land for this park was first set aside in the early 1900s by the burgeoning lumber communities of Dryad, Doty and Pe Ell. Around 1920, residents of Dryad cleared the south side of the park for picnicking and camping. Later, the Pe Ell Kiwanis Club initiated a land exchange, enabling the state to acquire most of the present 124 acres for Rainbow Falls State Park.

Activities

Favorite attractions here are the handhewn log buildings and footbridge. Built by the Civilian Conservation Corps between 1933 and 1935 from native trees and stone, the structures provide a rustic retreat for recreation-minded visitors. Popular activities here include camping, hiking, fishing, kayaking and picnicking, as well as unsupervised swimming in the Chehalis River.

Hikers can travel through cedar, fir and ancient hemlock trees along the park's half-mile interpretive trail. The south side of the park is a heavily wooded, natural area with trails, a picnic shelter and comfort station. Visitors will be treated to a typical western Washington forest on this half-hour walk.

The region surrounding the park is replete with elk, bears, deer and grouse. Although hunting is prohibited within the park, nearby areas are open to hunters during appropriate seasons. Adjacent logging roads also provide enjoyment for both motorcycles and "jeepers." These areas are generally open to the public, except during periods of high fire danger and during active logging.

History buffs are invited to explore Claquato Church, located three miles west of Chehalis. Built in 1854, this is one of the oldest buildings in the state and served as Lewis County's first courthouse. Dedicated to the determination of the early settlers, Willie Kiel's grave is located 30 miles west of the park, between Menio and Raymond. Kiel was a young boy who died during his family's journey west. His father had his body embalmed in whiskey and placed in the head wagon; there, Kiel traveled to his final home.

Facilities: North side – 50 non-hookup campsites, picnic sites, trails, playground equipment, horseshoe pits, and a baseball field with 10 additional grassy acres. South side – trails, picnic shelter and comfort station.

For further information, contact: Rainbow Falls State Park, 4008 State Highway 6, Chehalis, WA 98532, ☎ (360) 291-3767.

Riverside State Park

Location: 6 miles northwest of Spokane at the junction of State Route 291, Gun Club Road, and Aubrey L. White Parkway.

Situated east of the Cascade Mountain range, the region that contains Riverside State Park has four distinct seasons, each offering varied opportunities for recreation.

History

This scenic park was first utilized in 1810, when the Spokane House trading port was built by Canada's Northwest Fur Trading

Company. A short time later, John Jacob Astor formed the Pacific Fur Company near the Spokane House. In 1813, the American firm was purchased by the Northwest Fur Trading Company; in 1821, the two companies merged to become the Hudson's Bay Company. Five years later, the post was abandoned.

Despite its short existence, the fur trade strongly influenced development here. Traders and trappers did much of the early exploration, establishing routes of travel that were later used by settlers moving to the new frontier.

In 1933, this area became a state park through the generosity of Spokane's citizens and the Washington Water Power Company, which donated land for park purposes. Between 1933 and 1936, the park was developed primarily by the Civilian Conservation Corps (CCC). Today, Riverside State Park spans 5,808 acres and features 44,000 feet of freshwater shoreline along the Spokane River.

Activities

Park visitors can enjoy the outdoors year-round at Riverside. Summertime activities include picnicking, camping, hiking, horseback riding and fishing. While hiking up Deep Creek Canyon, visitors can explore fossil beds of a forest which existed over seven million years ago. For ATV and motorcycle riders, there is an Off-Road Vehicle (ORV) area; in winter, cross-country skiing and sledding are favorite activities.

Capturing the park's colorful seasons on film is an enjoyable challenge for photographers. In addition, there is a wide variety of wildlife, including deer, coyotes, squirrels, skunks, beavers, muskrats, chipmunks and raccoons.

Eight miles of hiking trails – including a pedestrian suspension foot-bridge – are found here; a jogging trail is located in the equestrian area.

Riverside State Park Off-Road Vehicle Area

The Riverside State Park ORV area is located west of Spokane on Inland Road. It consists of approximately 600 acres. The park's multi-use area is open to all types of ORVs, including dirt bikes, three and four-wheelers, 4x4s and others. The terrain provides hill climbs, sand areas, and trails through wooded sections; restrooms, parking and a loading/unloading ramp are also available.

Riders should be aware of and observe the following safety tips:

- Wear your helmet and other protective gear.
- Be sure your ORV is in good operating condition.
- Know your abilities and limitations.
- Be aware of other ORV users.
- Use spotters when jumping hills, for your safety and the safety of others.

Camping is located seven miles from the ORV area, at the Bowl and Pitcher. The ORV area is patrolled by park rangers; rules and regulations are enforced. ORV operating requirements are as follows:

- ORV permit tabs are required for operating any vehicle in the ORV area. (RCW 46.09.040).
- A US Forest Service-approved spark arrestor is required, and must be in working order; no modifications are permitted. (RCW 46.09.120).
- ORVs are required to have an adequate, operating muffling device that does not exceed noise standards of 105 decibels. (RCW 46.09.120).
- ORV users are required to stay within the posted boundaries.
- ORVs are not allowed on Inland Road; only street-legal vehicles are permitted there.

Park hours are 6:30 a.m. to 10 p.m., April 1 – October 15; and 8 a.m. to 5 p.m., October 16 – March 31.

Facilities: 101 non-hookup campsites in Riverside State Park, two group camping areas accommodating 250 people, picnic sites, kitchens, hot showers, and a boat launch area.

For further information, contact: Riverside State Park, c/o Dept. of Parks and Recreation, PO Box 42650, Olympia, WA 98504, ☎ (360) 755-9231.

Rockport State Park

*Location: 1 mile west of Rockport on Highway 20
(the North Cascades Highway).*

Rockport State Park features heavy vegetation in the fertile soil of its lower sections, and exposed rocky soil in its upper regions, all of which was caused by the last major glacial age.

The Skagit Indians were the area's first settlers; they lived in a village of long houses at the confluence of the Sauk and Skagit Rivers. They flourished here, given abundant salmon runs and bountiful evergreen forests.

In 1885, Leonard Graves homesteaded the land around the present town of Rockport, selling it to one Albert von Pressentin sometime in the 1890s. Within a few years, the town grew to include a hotel, a post office, a store, a school and mills. Ferries crossed the Skagit River and trains crossed between Rockport and Burlington daily.

Today, Rockport State Park protects a stand of old-growth Douglas fir trees that are over 300 years old. Five miles of foot trails wind through the park, with the Sauk Springs Trail built to accommodate wheelchairs.

Wildlife in the park include deer, bear, coyote, mountain beaver, and small forest mammals. Bald eagles, which winter on nearby Skagit River, can occasionally be seen circling high over the park.

Facilities: 62 campsites, 50 with full hookups; a walk-in campground with eight tent sites; four Adirondack shelters; modern restrooms and hot showers. The day-use area features a small picnic shelter.

For further information, contact: Rockport State Park, 5051 Highway 20, Concrete, WA 98237, ☎ (360) 853-8461.

Sacajawea State Park

Location: The confluence of the Snake and Columbia Rivers,
2 miles east of Pasco, off Highway 12.

History

For hundreds of years, the confluence of these two rivers was a popular meeting place for the Indians of southeastern Washington. Here, the Yakima, Wanapum, Walla Walla, Palouse and other tribes gathered to fish, socialize and trade goods.

The Indians first glimpsed white people here on October 16, 1805, when the Lewis and Clark Expedition traveled down the Snake River. They set up camp on this point, staying for two days and nights.

The early 19th century saw many traders, trappers and explorers pass through the area in search of the Northwest's many riches. Significant development occurred when the Northern Pacific Railroad began building the western portion of its transcontinental railroad. Ainsworth, a rollicking company town, grew to serve the railroad and its many workers. However, when the project was completed six years later, the town withered as quickly as it had been born.

In 1926, the Daughters of the Pioneers of Washington (Chapter 3, Pasco) accepted a gift of one acre from Thomas Carstens to preserve a campsite of the Lewis and Clark Expedition. They erected a monument on the site, and later planted trees and grass. In 1931, they deeded their tiny park to the state of Washington.

The park is named after Sacajawea, the 16-year-old Shoshoni Indian girl who was an important member of the Lewis and Clark Expedition. Recent research has discovered that the preferred spelling of the Indian woman's name is *Sacagawea*. Because the park and its interpretive center have long been known as Sacajawea, that spelling has been retained.

Facilities: Day-use facility with picnic tables and stoves. Some tables are sheltered and group picnic areas are available for a limited number of people. Contact the park office for more information. The park features mooring buoys and docks, as well as a boat launching facility. Fishing and other water-related activities are popular in the area.

For further information, contact: Sacajawea State Park, Road 40 East, Pasco, WA 99301, ☎ (360) 902-8563.

Saint Edward State Park

Location: Near Seattle. From I-405, travel northeast on 116th Street (20A), then west to Juanita Drive NE, and north to the park entrance; or, drive south on Juanita Drive from Highway 522 (Bothell Way).

Saint Edward State Park is nestled in a beautiful wooded setting in a rural section of the greater Seattle metropolitan area. The 316-acre park is the largest remaining undeveloped area on Lake Washington; it features 3,000 feet of low-bank shoreline accessible only by trail.

History

Saint Edward State Park is named for Edward the Confessor, founder of England's Westminister Abbey and King of the West Saxons during the 11th century.

In the late 1920s, Bishop O'Dea of Seattle's Catholic Diocese purchased the property with his own personal inheritance, donating it to the diocese for use as a seminary by the Supplican (educational) Order of Catholic priests. The cornerstone of the seminary was laid on October 13, 1930, during the Feast of Saint Edward. Construction began in March of 1931, and the building was completed and ready for occupancy by September 15.

Faced with declining enrollment and changes in the education of seminarians, the Seattle Diocese sold 316 acres surrounding and including Saint Edward Seminary to the state of Washington for recreational purposes in 1977.

In June, 1978, the grounds of Saint Edward State Park were opened to the public. The remaining facilities are being held for future use.

Flora & Fauna / Activities

The park boasts approximately five miles of hiking trails, all under a lush canopy of Douglas firs, Western hemlocks, red alders, bigleaf maples, Western red cedars and Pacific madrone. Many different species of plants, birds and animals may be observed within the park boundaries.

Recreational activities here include tennis, handball, racquetball, soccer, volleyball, fishing, hiking, photography, bird watching and picnicking.

Facilities: Picnic and athletic facilities are limited. Groups of over 20 people should contact the park manager for reservations. The grotto area can be reserved for weddings.

For further information, contact: Saint Edward State Park, PO Box 602, Kenmore, WA 98028, ☎ (360) 902-8563.

Saltwater State Park

Location: 2 miles south of Des Moines, on State Highway 509; accessible from I-5 via exit 149 West.

Situated on Puget Sound, Saltwater State Park offers scenic views of Maury and Vashon Islands, the Olympic Mountains, and some beautiful sunsets. The park's complete solitude offers a welcome relief from the surrounding urban environment.

Originally, this area was known as "McSorley's Gulch." It was a favorite spot for valley Indians bent on clam digging, and for residents of Zenigh, who held their annual Labor Day picnic here.

In the late 1920s, the Tacoma and Seattle communities waged a fundraising campaign with an eye to purchasing McSorley's Gulch for park purposes. The campaign was successful, and in 1933, the park was dedicated. During the dedication ceremony, a hatchet was buried, signifying the end of any hostilities between the people of Seattle and Tacoma. In 1935 and 1936, the Civilian Conservation Corps (CCC) constructed several buildings that are still in use today.

Activities

Saltwater State Park has a wide range of physical features that facilitate a variety of recreational activities. Visitors can enjoy clamming, scuba diving, picnicking, camping, or hiking in forested uplands and along saltwater beaches. Other pastimes include frolicking on the new play equipment donated by the "Friends of Saltwater," shore fishing, sunbathing, beachcombing, and pitching horseshoes.

A special attraction here is an artificial underwater reef that provides scuba divers with the opportunity to view marine and plant life. Night dives may be set up with a special-use permit; contact a park ranger two weeks in advance.

Park hours are 6:30 a.m. to 10 p.m., April 1-October 15; and 8 a.m. to 5 p.m, October 16-March 31.

Facilities: 52 standard camping sites, 88 acres of saltwater beach, picnic areas, camp areas and forest. There is a group camp area that can be reserved by organizations during the summer. A picnic shelter and kitchen area can also be reserved. In addition, there are mooring buoys and a trailer dumping facility.

For further information, contact: Saltwater State Park, 25205 8th Place S, Des Moines, WA 98031, ☎ (206) 764-4128.

Scenic Beach State Park

Location: On the Hood Canal, about 15 miles northwest of Bremerton.

Comprised of over 90 acres of picturesque forest land, this park's beauty is enhanced by an old homestead, a log cabin and nearly 1,600 feet of saltwater beach overlooking the canal. And who can forget the majestic Olympic Mountains in the background?

History

Loggers arrived here in the 1880s, followed by pioneer families. Joe Emel, Sr. subsequently bought 30 acres in what is now the lower portion of the park. Enlarging the existing house, he added several cabins and a boathouse, establishing a hunting and fishing resort shortly thereafter. Following Emel's death in 1962, the State Parks Commission purchased the resort, retaining its name for park purposes.

Joe Emel, Jr., built another log cabin here; although he resides in Seabeck, he often returns for a sentimental visit with park staff and campers. Emel can recall the days when the area was teeming with wildlife and the water was filled with fish. Today, only an occasional blacktail deer or grouse remain. (However, there is a large population of raccoons and squirrels here.)

Flora & Fauna

Many species of waterfowl frequent the offshore waters. A variety of non-game birds – such as pileated woodpeckers and goldfinches – have established habitats in the park's upland regions.

Scenic Beach is in the Pacific Coast Forest Zone, which is characterized by dense stands of Douglas fir and western hemlock (the state tree). The average annual rainfall is about 40 inches, making for lush rhododendron growth throughout the park.

Facilities: 50 campsites without hookups, 18 of which are pull-through sites, with four double, or "buddy," sites. Restrooms include hot water and showers. There are playgrounds in both the camping and picnic areas. The beach features horseshoe pits, fire rings, 78 picnic sites, an unguarded swimming beach, a bathhouse with showers, and facilities for boating or scuba diving. Boats can be rented and launched from nearby Seabeck Marina.

For further information, contact: Scenic Beach State Park, PO Box 7, Seabeck, WA 98380, ☎ (360) 830-5079.

Schafer State Park

Location: 12 miles north of Elma, on the East Satsop Road; the park is also accessible via the Brady exit from US Highway 12.

History

A fitting memorial to the hardy pioneer family that settled here in 1870, Schafer State Park is a colorful haven dedicated to the memory of John and Anna Schafer. Located on the east fork of the Satsop River, this tract was donated by the Schafer Brothers' Logging Company in 1924. Prior to 1922, this spot was the scene of many Schafer picnics. Playing as hard as they worked, the Schafer brothers threw many lively affairs attended en masse by the Schafer family and their employees. These events were characterized by dancing, strength and endurance sports, and log-rolling and hurling contests – all to the strains of a brass band!

Flora & Fauna

Schafer State Park features a few peaceful trails winding through woods abundant with wildlife. It is quite common to see a number of squirrels, rabbits and birds. Occasionally, deer can be seen grazing where the trees meet the meadows. Trout fishing is popular here in the summer; for those who like to stay dry, there are horseshoe pits and swing sets.

Schafer State Park is open on a seasonal basis. Limited facilities are offered from October 1 to March 31, with weekday hours between 8 a.m. and dusk. During this time, weekend hours are from noon on Fridays until noon on Mondays; the park is also open at noon the day before a holiday. Except on weekends, there is no access to the Satsop River for winter fishing from October 1 to March 31.

Facilities: 47 regular campsites, six partial hookup sites, two comfort stations, shower facilities and a dump station. One small shelter and two larger covered facilities can be reserved by contacting the park directly. One of the large facilities provides seven tables, a fireplace and accommodates a maximum of 300 people. The other offers a sink, stove and tables; the maximum here is 200 people.

For further information, contact: Schafer State Park, Route 2, Box 87, Elma, WA 98541, ☎ (360) 482-3852.

Seaquest State Park

Location: 5 miles west of Castle Rock, on State Highway 504; the park can also be reached from exit 49 off I-5.

Seaquest State Park lies on the shores of Silver Lake. It joined the Washington State Parks system in 1948, when Alfred Seaquest willed his 154-acre homestead to the state for park purposes. An additional 78 acres were purchased in 1979, along with 61 acres in 1981; this brought the total park acreage to 301.

In spring of 1980, the eruption of Mt. St. Helens brought worldwide attention to the area. Volcanic activity in the dormant mountain began in March, culminating in a violent explosion on May 18. The mountain made its presence known by spewing ash, leveling towering trees and filling the nearby Toutle River with mud. Scientists, government officials and tourists from all over the world rushed here to witness the historic event. Geologists predict that limited volcanic activity may continue for years to come.

The Mt. St. Helens National Volcanic Monument Visitor Center is located on Silver Lake, adjacent to the park entrance. Run by the US Forest Service, it offers information on Mount St. Helens' past, present and future. In addition to sightseeing, park visitors may indulge in picnicking, camping and hiking. Sports-minded people will enjoy hunting and fishing as well. Trout and spiny-ray fish inhabit Silver Lake, while salmon, steelhead and smelt are common in the Cowlitz River, five miles west of the park. There are several hiking trails.

Like the surrounding area, this park is heavily forested with maple, alder, hemlock and fir. Several old-growth Douglas fir trees grow here, with the largest measuring over seven feet in diameter. Wildlife native to this park includes deer, squirrels, owls and a variety of birds.

Facilities: 90 campsites, 16 with full hookups; additional tent camping area that can accommodate up to 50 people; modern restrooms and hot showers. The day-use area contains over 1,000 picnic sites, a kitchen shelter, volleyball area, swings and horseshoe pits.

For further information, contact: Seaquest State Park, Box 3030 Spirit Lake Highway, Castle Rock, WA 98611, ☎ (360) 274-8633.

Sequim Bay State Park

Location: 4 miles southwest of the town of Sequim on Washington's Olympic Peninsula, just off State Highway 101.

Nestled in the rain shadow of the Olympic Mountains, the area containing Sequim Bay State Park receives 16-17 inches of precipitation annually.

The word sequim (pronounced "skwim") is derived from the Clallum Indian word *such-e-kwai-ing,* which means "quiet water." It is believed that the Clallum Indians once had a village by this name near the entrance to Sequim Bay.

The Olympic Peninsula is an explorer's wonderland, with Sequim Bay State Park particularly suited to adventurers. The park offers picnicking, camping, tennis, boating, fishing, clamming, water-skiing, scuba diving, crabbing and horseshoeing. Hiking, bird watching and observation of the flora are also popular activities. Several hiking trails are available. The park is dominated by coniferous trees, including Douglas and grand firs, Western hemlocks, Western red cedars and Pacific yews. The ground cover generally consists of Pacific rhododendrons, Pacific elders, salal, Oregon grape, sword ferns and horsetail grass.

Sequim's Olympic Game Farm – famous for the successful propagation of endangered species – conducts tours here throughout the summer. Ramblewood, the park's environmental learning center, provides group camping in a rustic setting. It is available by reservation.

Park hours are 6:30 a.m. to dusk, April 1-October 15; and 8 a.m. to dusk, October 16-March 31.

Facilities: 60 non-hookup sites, 26 hookup sites and comfort stations with hot showers. The day-use portion of the park contains a picnic area with four kitchens and shelters, tennis courts, play equipment, horseshoe pits, a ballfield, and a boat launch with a loading dock, mooring floats and buoys.

For further information, contact: Sequim Bay State Park, 1872 Highway 101 E., Sequim, WA 98382, ☎ (360) 683-4235.

South Whidbey State Park

Location: Whidbey Island, on Smugglers Cove Road, about
7 miles northwest of Freeland and 15 miles southeast of Coupeville.

Land for South Whidbey State Park was acquired from the University of Washington, with the park opening in the early 1960s. Situated on a bluff, it contains 87 acres of land forested with old-growth virgin timber. The timber is predominantly Douglas fir, including some of the tallest and largest in the area (many of which can be seen from the park's hiking trails). Cedars, hemlock and alders are dispersed throughout.

Activities

Visitors to South Whidbey have a variety of experiences awaiting them. At low tide, the beach offers beachcombers many interesting shells and rocks. A half-mile trail leads down the 300-foot slope to the beach, with benches for resting on the trip back up.

Clamming and crabbing can be enjoyed when the tides permit. Fishing is especially popular in the late summer when the salmon are running in Admiralty Inlet. A public boat launch is located about two miles south of the park at Bush Point.

A loop trail takes hikers through the end of the park nearest the Sound. The half-mile long trail also goes through an area with many marsh-type plants.

Flora & Fauna

Wildlife in the park includes black-tailed deer, raccoons, rabbits, and foxes as well as the ever-popular squirrels and chipmunks. Many species of birds live here as well, including crows, pileated woodpeckers, bald eagles, ospreys and various sea gulls. Throughout the spring and summer, wildflowers and shrubs bloom to add color to the park. Salmonberries, huckleberries and black-cap raspberries are all popular when in season.

Facilities: 54 non-hookup campsites, each with a table and a stove; modern restrooms with hot showers; and a trailer dumping station. A primitive group camp area is available on a reservation basis; it has pit toilets, tables and stoves, and can accommodate 50 people. The day-use picnic area features 19 tables, with stoves and a picnic shelter.

For further information, contact: South Whidbey State Park, 4128 S. Smuggler's Cove Road, Freeland, WA 98249, ☎ (360) 331-4559.

Spencer Spit State Park

Location: Lopez Island, in the San Juan Islands; the park is accessible from Anacortes by Washington State Ferry or by private boat.

Comprised of 130 acres on beautiful Lopez Island, Spencer Spit State Park is a boater's paradise. However, enthusiasts must use the 16 mooring buoys located offshore, as the park does not have dock or float facilities.

History

This area was originally used by various Indian tribes as a seasonal stopover point. The first permanent settlement was established here following the Homestead Act of 1850, when the Troxell family set up a self-supporting farm.

The land was later owned by the Spencer family; the stone shelter at the base of the hill is a remnant of their home. The old log cabin at the end of the sandspit was built by the Spencers in the early 1900s, and used as a guest cottage as late as 1946. It was rebuilt in 1978. The Spencers sold the property to the state in 1967, after which the area became Spencer Spit State Park.

Flora & Fauna

A unique attraction here is the salt marsh lagoon, formed when two developing sandspits were joined into one. The lagoon is home to innumerable forms of aquatic life, as well as both sea and shore birds. There are seal, otter, sea lion and other sea mammals in the offshore area. In or near the park are bald eagles, hawks, great blue herons, squirrels, deer and wild rabbits.

Activities

Visitors can watch state ferries and both private and commercial vessels as they pass through the main navigation channel of the San Juans, just north of the park. They can also see other San Juan Islands from the beach area.

Favorite activities here include beachcombing, saltwater swimming at an unguarded beach, and clam digging. Visitors may also enjoy picnicking, camping, fishing and diving, as well as hiking on the park's many trails.

Facilities are available on a first-come, first-served basis. When the park is full, a notice is posted at the ferry terminal in Anacortes.

Park hours are 6:30 a.m. to dusk, April 1-October 15; and 8 a.m. to dusk, October 16-March 31.

Facilities: 45 campsites and a trailer dump station. The main campground has five walk-in sites, two of which have eight-bunk Adirondack shelters; 10 pull-through sites; and 15 back-in sites. Each back-in site will accommodate one 20-foot vehicle. There are 15 walk-in sites near the beach. The upper day-use area has a group picnic shelter with a grill, as well as additional picnic tables and grills.

For further information, contact: Spencer Spit State Park, Route 2, Box 3600, Lopez, WA 98261, ☎ (360) 468-2551.

Squaxin Island State Park

Location: Squaxin Island, in southern Puget Sound.
Access by private boat only.

Squaxin Island State Park provides a beautiful view of both Peale Passage and Harstene Island. Ideally situated near the southeast corner of Squaxin Island, its 30 acres are sheltered from the southerly winds.

The Washington State Parks and Recreation Commission acquired a portion of this tract in 1961, and the remainder in 1965. Although Washington owns the uplands, the local Squaxin Indian tribe retains ownership of the tidelands. A lease agreement is maintained, making access to the park boundary possible. All areas outside of the park boundary are off-limits, including the beaches.

The Squaxin Island Seafarm complex is located north of the state park. Much of the island's east side is used to raise shellfish for commercial and subsistence purposes. Because of the importance of these facilities, non-tribal persons found trespassing will be prosecuted.

A tribal ordinance prohibits the sale or consumption of liquor here. WAC 352-32-210 also prohibits the opening, consumption or storage of alcoholic beverages in Squaxin Island State Park.

Visitors can beachcomb and fish on the leased tidelands. However, the clams and oysters found there may be contaminated. Please do your part to control this pollution by using the designated facility for dumping portable toilets or, for larger boats with on-board facilities, using the pump station at the East Bay Marina facility in Olympia. Remember that the tidelands outside the park boundary are off limits. Signs marking each end of the park are placed above the high tide level.

This park is a satellite of Jarrell Cove State Park on Harstene Island. It offers an opportunity for boaters to picnic or camp at the unique Peale Passage setting. No water is provided in this park, and there are no streams here.

Facilities: 30 campsites with tables and stoves, two shelters for group picnics, and one mile of foot trails to explore. A dock and 10 mooring buoys are also available. A maximum of three boats can be tied to any buoy, and no boats may be anchored north of the last buoy.

For further information, contact: Squaxin Island State Park, c/o Jarrell Cove State Park, E. 391 Wingert Road, Shelton WA 98584, ☎ (206) 931-3907.

Steamboat Rock State Park

Location: 10 miles south of Grand Coulee off of State Highway 155, on the shores of Banks Lake.

Steamboat Rock is a butte rising 700 feet above Banks Lake. This basalt formation, which dominates the park, was originally an island in the ancient Columbia River bed. When the Columbia changed course after the ice age, the massive rock remained as a landmark.

A good hiking trail to the top of Steamboat Rock allows visitors a panoramic view of the surrounding area. Approximately 640 acres lie at the rock's summit, affording additional walking space.

Banks Lake is open year-round for fishing. It is also popular for water-skiing, sailing, and swimming. Winter activities here include cross-country skiing, sledding, ice skating, ice fishing and winter camping.

Grand Coulee Dam is 13 miles from the park. A visitor information center at the dam offers tours of the facility, as well as an evening light show. Campers attending the show should arrange for re-entry to the campgrounds prior to the event.

Facilities: 100 campsites with full hookup facilities; and restrooms here have hot showers. Tents are authorized in certain areas; tent campers should check with park personnel. The day-use portion of the park features picnic tables, playground equipment, a swimming beach, a bathhouse, and a boat ramp. A snack bar is located in the picnic area. The park has a boat launch and an adjunct launch area five miles northeast of the park boundaries. The satellite facility contains comfort stations and a boat ramp.

For further information, contact: Steamboat Rock State Park, PO Box 370, Electric City, WA 99123-0352, ☎ (509) 633-1304.

Sucia Island Marine State Park

Location: The Gulf of Georgia, 2½ miles north of Orcas Island. Accessible by ferry or private boat.

Sucia Island lies isolated in the Gulf of Georgia, giving this 562-acre park a unique, primitive quality. Located in the Olympic rain shadow, the area experiences an annual rainfall of 25 inches. Northwest winds bring sunny dry summers, while the southwest and southeasterly winds accompany wet winter storms.

History

Traditionally used by the Lummi Indians as a summer hunting and foraging area, Sucia was "discovered" in 1791 by the Spanish *Eliza* expedition. The island received its name – which means "dirty," or, in the nautical sense, "foul" – from first pilot Juan Pantoja, because of the many submerged rocks and reefs surrounding the island.

In the late 1950s, Erv Henry of Seattle organized a successful effort to save Sucia from commercial development, initiating a fundraising drive among Puget Sound yacht clubs to purchase 318.75 acres of the island. This led to the formation of the Interclub Association of Washington, and that portion of Sucia's eventual preservation through donation to the Washington State Parks system.

The state park system purchased additional acreage in 1974, enabling the whole 562-acre island to remain in the public domain. In 1986, the National Park Service deeded approximately two acres of federal land on nearby Echo Bay Island to the Washington State Parks system. This was intended as a wildlife preserve; human use is limited to wildlife protection.

Topography / Flora & Fauna

Sucia's unique shape is the result of sediments from nearby highlands being deposited in a shallow marine trough, forming many layers called "beds." At this time, many sea animals were buried, later to become fossils. These beds were bent and tilted by geologic forces, finally forming plunging layers of rock. Erosion by glaciers and ocean waves – plus later uplifting – has exposed the layered and folded rock. Six miles of trails and 3½ miles of rustic logging roads invite the hiker to explore Sucia, from its deep coniferous forests to its grassy exposed cliffs.

The rich water off Sucia Island supports an abundance of bottomfish and salmon; river otters and harbor seals are also a common sight. Dungeness crabs are plentiful, particularly in Fossil Bay. A wide variety of birds, including harlequin ducks, oyster catchers, great blue herons and bald eagles, may be observed. Echo Bay Island and Little Sucia Island are especially sensitive wildlife areas; please refrain from visiting them between January 1 and July 15.

Seven distinct plant communities inhabit Sucia. Gnarled junipers, Indian paintbrush, and camass lilies give way to red-barked madrone trees and false Solomon's seal. Near ridge tops, Douglas firs, ocean spray, and salal predominate, yielding to grand firs, big leaf maples, red cedars and sword ferns. May is the best month to savor the showy blossoms of wildflowers.

Facilities: 55 camp sites; picnic sites, including three picnic shelters; 48 mooring buoys; 250 feet of moorage floats in Fossil Bay. Limited fresh water can be obtained at Fossil Bay and North Shallow Bay from April through September.

For further information, contact: Sucia Island Marine State Park, Star Route Box 28, Eastsound, WA 98245, ☎ (360) 902-8563.

Sun Lakes State Park

Location: 7 miles southwest of Coulee City, on Highway 17.

This park is part of the geologic formation created by runoff from the last glaciation. Originally named "Dry Falls," it was rechristened in a manner that was more descriptive of the area. There are over 4,000 acres in Sun Lakes State Park, including several lakes.

The Lake Lenore Caves are of special interest here. They were formed by the rush of water from ice-age floods that removed basalt from the walls of the coulees. The caves were used as shelters by nomadic hunters and plant food gatherers in prehistoric times. A trail leading to some of the caves has been established near the north end of Lake Lenore. The caves are about 10 miles south of the Dry Falls Interpretive Center, just off Highway 17, and are open to the public during park hours.

Camp Delany, an environmental learning center, is located within the park. Its air-conditioned cabins will house up to 84 people. For more information, contact the park ranger.

Visitors can enjoy a variety of activities here. In addition to camping and picnicking, trout fishing, swimming, boating, horseback riding, hiking and golfing are available.

A private concessionaire operates many different facilities within the park, including cabins, a trailer park with hookups, a restaurant and fountain, and a general store. There are also a gas station, a laundry, boat and bicycle rentals, riding stables with rental horses, a nine-hole golf course and a heated swimming pool.

Facilities: 181 campsites, 18 with full hookups for trailers. Some of these sites can accommodate a recreational vehicle up to 28 feet in length. Each site has a table and stove, and the restrooms have hot showers. Group areas are available by reservation for both day-use and overnight camping. Contact the park ranger for more information.

For further information, contact: Sun Lakes State Park, Star Route 2, Box 136, Coulee City, WA 99115, ☎ (206) 754-1522.

Tolmie State Park

Location: 8 miles northeast of Olympia, and five miles from exit 111 off I-5.

Tolmie State Park has 1,800 feet of waterfront on Puget Sound, affording an excellent view of Pitts Passage, McNeil and Anderson Islands. Of the 105 acres comprising the park, 17 are developed.

History

The park derived its name from Doctor William Fraser Tolmie, a medical officer with the Hudson's Bay Company during the 1830s. Dr. Tolmie's first assignment was at Fort Nisqually, an area located on Puget Sound just east of the park.

During his stay at Fort Nisqually, Tolmie studied and recorded information about the plants and animals among the foothills of Mount Rainier, where Tolmie Park is now. In 1850, he married Jane Work, the eldest daughter of Chief Factor of Fort Nisqually. Tolmie's knowledge and association with local natives played a major role in returning peace to the area after the Indian Wars of 1855-56.

Activities

Tolmie State Park is an underwater marine park. Three wooden barges have been placed below the low-water mark to form an artificial reef. This man-made reef attracts fish and other sea life, providing recreational enjoyment for fishermen and scuba divers. The sunken barges are marked with white mooring buoys. Other activities popular here include hiking, swimming, picnicking, and clam digging.

The park features five interpretive sites; these describe the islands, the marsh and beach areas, and give a brief history of Tolmie. A map of their locations is posted at the entrance. The park has almost 3½ miles of hiking trails (see the posted maps for their locations).

Private property flanks both sides of this park's sandy beach. These boundaries are well marked with state park signs; please respect them.

Facilities: 42 picnic tables and 2 kitchen shelters, all available on a first-come, first-served basis. Drinking water and barbecue-style stoves are placed throughout the picnic area. An outside shower located next to the lower restroom is available for divers and swimmers to rinse off saltwater.

For further information, contact: Tolmie State Park, 6227 Johnson Point Road NE, Olympia, WA 98506, ☎ (360) 902-8563.

Turn Island Marine State Park

*Location: East of San Juan Island, near the entrance
of Friday Harbor; access is by private boat only.*

Turn Island Marine State Park boasts 16,000 feet of waterfront, three acres of cleared or open land, and 32 forested acres. Though primarily a day-use park, there are camping facilities available.

Facilities: 10 campsites, each with stove and picnic table, located near garbage cans and pit toilets. There is no dock, nor is water available here. Three moorage buoys and a clean, fine gravel beach complete the facilities.

For more information, contact: Washington State Department of Parks and Recreation, 7150 Cleanwater Lane, PO Box 42650, Olympia, WA 98504-2650, ☎ (800) 233-0321 (nationwide).

Twanoh State Park

*Location: Hood Canal, 12 miles east of Highway 101
on Highway 106 (in Union).*

Comprised of 180 acres, Twanoh State Park offers a variety of activities for the whole family. Some visitors enjoy swimming, water-skiing, boating, picnicking and camping in the spring and summer. Others come in fall and winter for the smelt dipping, oyster picking and clam digging. Twanoh is a satellite of Belfair State Park, located eight miles northwest.

The park derives its name from the Twana Indian tribe, better known as the Skokomish. This tribe consisted of several bands whose habitat included the entire Hood Canal region. It is believed that Indians from the surrounding area moved into the Hood Canal basin in search of game and remained when they discovered the abundance of wildlife.

The present park area was logged in the 1890s. Evidence of this early logging still remains, with spring notches still visible on the old cedar stumps. After the Navy Yard Highway (SR 106) was completed, the area became a private resort, then a state park.

In 1936, the 4728 Company of the Civilian Conservation Corps (CCC) from Medora, North Dakota, started construction on most of the park buildings. These structures were fashioned of brick, rock and wood.

Visitor services are available in both Union and Belfair. More facilities and activities can be found in Bremerton, located 27 miles northeast, and in Shelton, 27 miles southwest. Both of these towns host community events during the summer months.

Facilities: 38 standard campsites, nine hookup sites, four restrooms, and showers. There is also a group camp area that can be reserved. Twanoh has a boat dock, two boat ramps, five mooring buoys, 580 feet of guarded swimming beach, a children's wading pool and two bathhouses. The day-use area consists of a tennis court, horseshoe pits, hiking trails, 125 picnic sites, three kitchenettes, two large kitchens with wood stoves (one can be reserved) and a concession stand open between Memorial Day and Labor Day.

For further information, contact: Twanoh State Park, East 12190 Highway 206, Union, WA 98592, ☎ (360) 275-2222.

Twin Harbors State Park

*Location: 20 miles west of Aberdeen
and 2 miles south of Westport, on State Route 105.*

This park consists of 317 acres, including 17,710 feet of Pacific Ocean shoreline. Several different acquisitions were combined to create Twin Harbors, the first of which occurred in 1937.

The park and vicinity received its name from two nearby harbors, Grays Harbor and Willapa Bay Harbor. During the 1930s, this area was a US Army training ground. Local historians recall that the region was swampy at the time that the walkways were erected, posing a hazard to soldiers returning from a night on the town.

Twin Harbors offers many recreational opportunities. Jetty and surf fishing, as well as chartered salmon fishing from nearby Westport, are popular. So are beachcombing for treasures such as agates or Japanese floats.

History buffs may make arrangements with the Coast Guard to tour the lighthouse. Built in 1898, it is located at the Westport Light Beach Approach Road.

Nature lovers will enjoy walking the Shifting Sands Nature Trail. This ¾-mile trail is marked with 20 stations that interpret the dune ecology. Evergreen huckleberry, black twin-berry, Sitka spruce, kinnikinick and shore pine are all found here.

Wildlife in this park includes rabbits, raccoons, deer, beavers and even an occasional bear. A variety of birds dwell here, including mallard duck, black sea duck, snipe and seagulls.

Facilities: 332 campsites, 49 with full hookup capabilities and all with tables and stoves; modern restrooms with hot showers; kitchens, shelters, a play area, and a trailer dumping station area.

For further information, contact: Twin Harbors State Park, Westport, WA 98595, ☎ (360) 268-9717.

Wallace Falls State Park

Location: 30 miles east of Everett and 2 miles north of Gold Bar, off US Highway 2 (Stevens Pass Highway).

Nestled in the Cascade Mountain foothills, 678-acre Wallace Falls State Park is named for the thunderous, 265-foot falls on the Wallace River. It first opened as a state park in 1977. Wildlife in the park includes birds, deer, squirrels, chipmunks and raccoons.

The falls, river, and lake were all named after Sarah Wallace (native name *Kway-aylish*). A strong-spirited woman of the Skokomish Indian tribe, she homesteaded land between the towns of Gold Bar and Startup.

Hikers can enjoy a three- to four-hour hike on the park's loop trail system, which leads to scenic viewpoints of Wallace Falls and the Skykomish Valley. Woody Trail begins at the parking area, and enters a shady forest. At the quarter-mile point, just before the North Fork bridge, the railroad grade trail rejoins the river trail.

Headed upward, hikers soon reach the picnic shelter and the first distant view of the falls. The middle viewpoint at the two-mile hike offers the best and closest view of the falls. Winding higher, the trail levels out at the top of the falls, where it provides two panoramic views of the Skykomish Valley.

Visitors may return via the same route or by the old railroad grade, which is a mile longer but gentler and easier. The Woody Trail was named for the late state senator Frank Woody, an avid outdoorsman who was instrumental in sponsoring funding legislation for the Youth Development Conservation Corps (YDCC). The YDCC, Youth Conservation Corps (YCC) and Young Adult Conservation Corps (YACC) built the park's trails, bridges and picnic shelter.

Facilities: six tent campsites at the trailhead campground; no showers. Recreational vehicle camping is not permitted here. Picnic tables and barbecue stands are located in the campground area. Grocery stores, service stations and restaurants may be found in nearby Gold Bar and Monroe. Private campgrounds are located eight miles east of Gold Bar, and near Monroe.

For further information, contact: Wallace Falls State Park, PO Box 106, Gold Bar, WA 98251, ☎ (360) 793-0420.

Wenberg State Park

*Location: 12 miles north of Marysville
and 10 miles south of Stanwood; take exit 206 off I-5.*

Situated on the shores of Lake Goodwin, Wenberg State Park is part of a resort community. It is one hour's drive from metropolitan Seattle, one hour from the Canadian border, and only one hour from San Juan boat access points.

The park is named for a former state representative; it was developed as a community recreation area by a group of volunteers, and acquired by the state in 1947.

The nearby communities of Arlington, Stanwood and Silvana reflect a strong Scandinavian heritage, affording visitors an opportunity to experience Scandinavian traditions in baking, art and farming. Of particular interest is the annual Stanwood-Camano Island Community Fair, held each August.

Wenberg's proximity to the urban areas of Everett and Seattle encourages year-round use of the park. This facility can also serve as a tranquil base from which visitors may experience cultural and sporting events in the larger cities nearby.

A variety of activities are popular here. These include water sports on 545-acre Lake Goodwin, as well as camping, picnicking, and nature study. Lake Goodwin is an excellent spot for harvesting rainbow trout; it is stocked annually by the state game department. Kokanee, cutthroat, perch and even crawfish may also be found in the lake. There are a number of short hiking trails.

The list of fauna in this park is long. It includes deer, raccoons, mountain beavers, squirrels, skunks, otters, mink and a variety of birds.

Facilities: 65 standard campsites and 10 utility campsites, all with tables and stoves; picnic sites; boat launch ramp; a small kitchen shelter; and a trailer dumping station. A concession-operated snack bar located by the swimming beach is open during the summer.

For further information, contact: Wenberg State Park, 15430 E. Lake Goodwin Road, Stanwood, WA 98292, ☎ (360) 652-7417.

Yakima Sportsman State Park

Location: 3 miles east of Yakima, off I-82 (exit 34).

This park was created in 1940, when the Yakima Sportman's Association purchased the land. Members of this association felt that the citizens of Yakima needed a readily accessible park that would promote better game management and pollution abatement, as well as the preservation and protection of natural resources. Yakima Sportsman became a county park in 1946, and a state park in 1950.

The park lies in a fertile, irrigated flood plain of the Yakima River. Comprised of 211 acres, it contains 16,000 feet of water frontage, including several ponds, a small stream and the Yakima River. The park is surrounded by fruit orchards and semi-arid bunch grass prairies. Yakima Ridge is to the north, while the Rattlesnake Hills are to the south.

Frogs and tadpoles are both seen and heard in the lily pad-covered ponds. During the summer, painted turtles are seen sunning themselves or walking along the roads. Park visitors may also be treated to ducks, geese, songbirds, skunks, and an occasional jackrabbit darting through brush. Game animals in nearby areas include mule deer, elk, coyotes, weasels, beavers, mink, raccoons, and numerous varieties of game birds. According to the Audubon Society's Christmas Bird Count, over 130 species of birds have been identified in this region.

Fishing, bird-watching and hiking are popular activities here, although fishing in the park's stocked ponds is limited to youngsters 14 years old or younger. Camping, picnicking, canoeing and raft floating in the Yakima River are also favorite summer pastimes.

Facilities: 64 campsites, 36 with full trailer hookups; there are tables and stoves at each site. Kitchens, shelters, and modern restrooms with hot showers are also available.

For further information, contact: Yakima Sportsman State Park, 904 Keys Road, Yakima, WA 98901, ☎ (509) 575-2774.